AF581329

ROBERT DOWLING

Tasmanian son of Empire

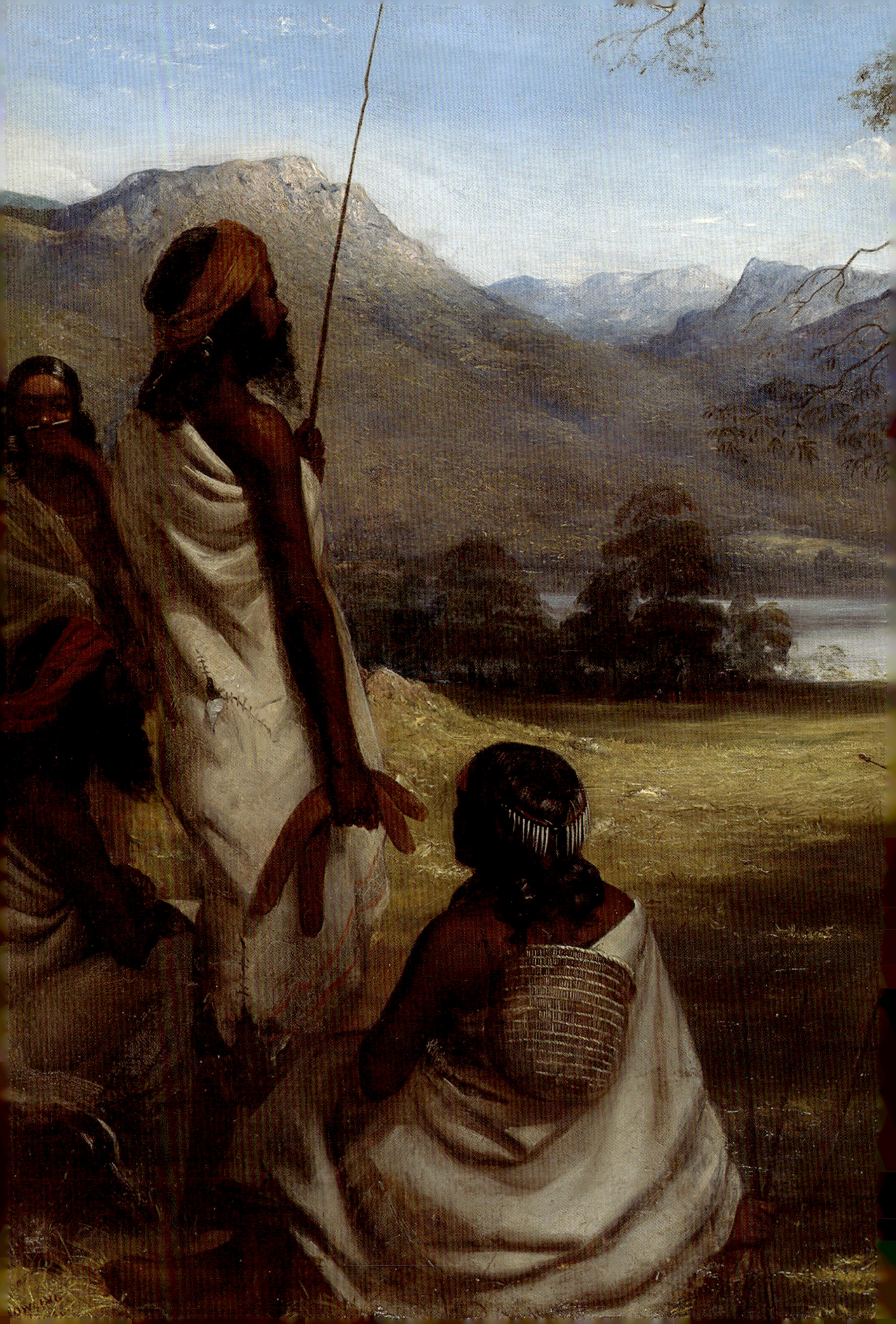

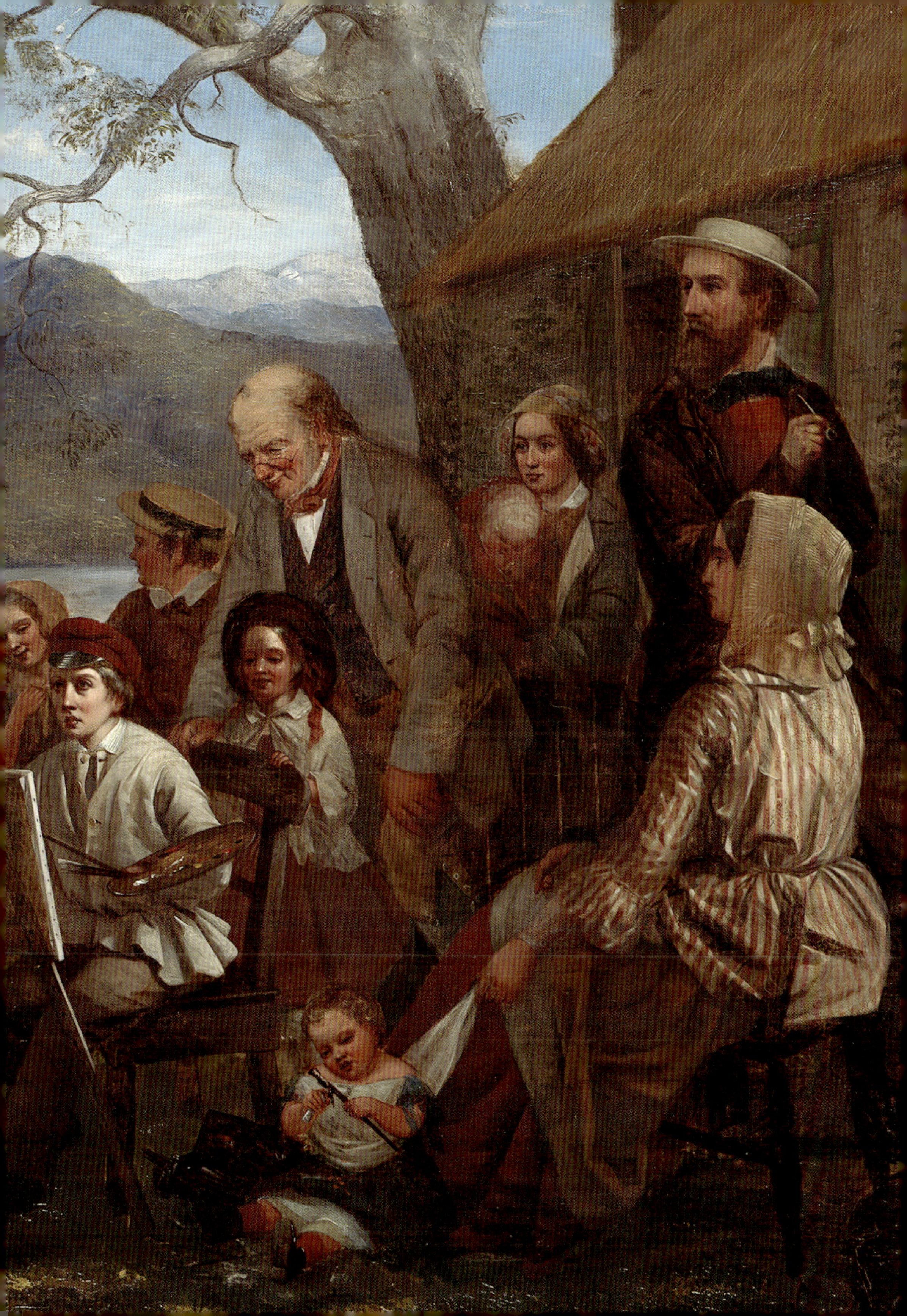

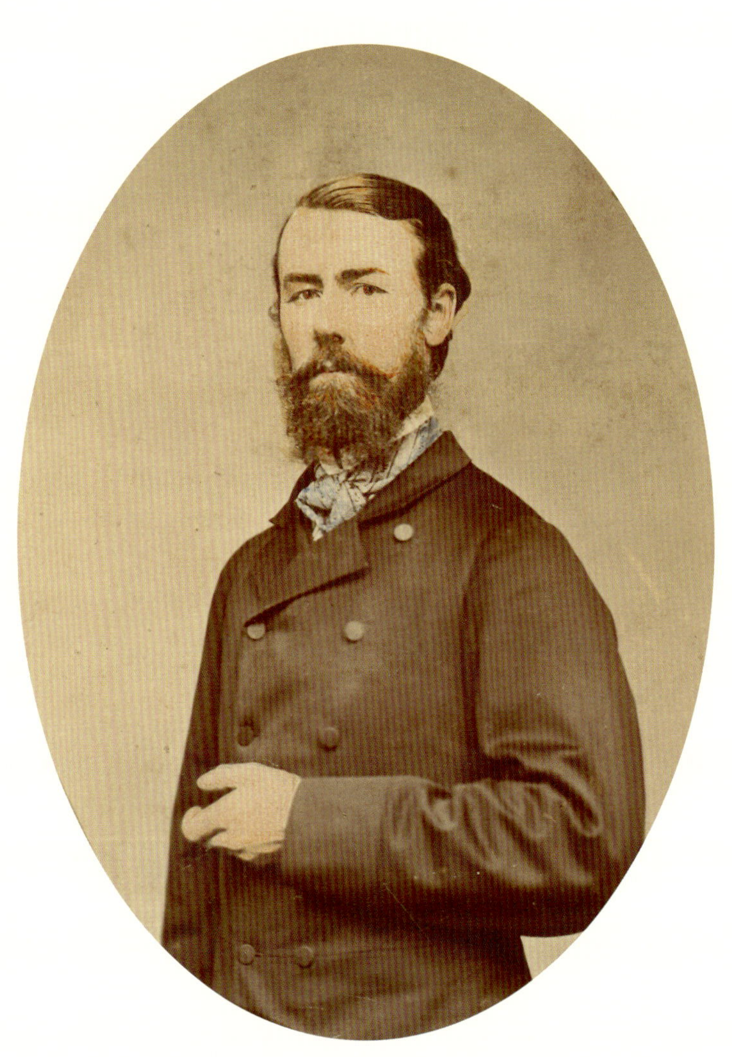

ROBERT DOWLING
Tasmanian son of Empire

John Jones

National Gallery of Australia

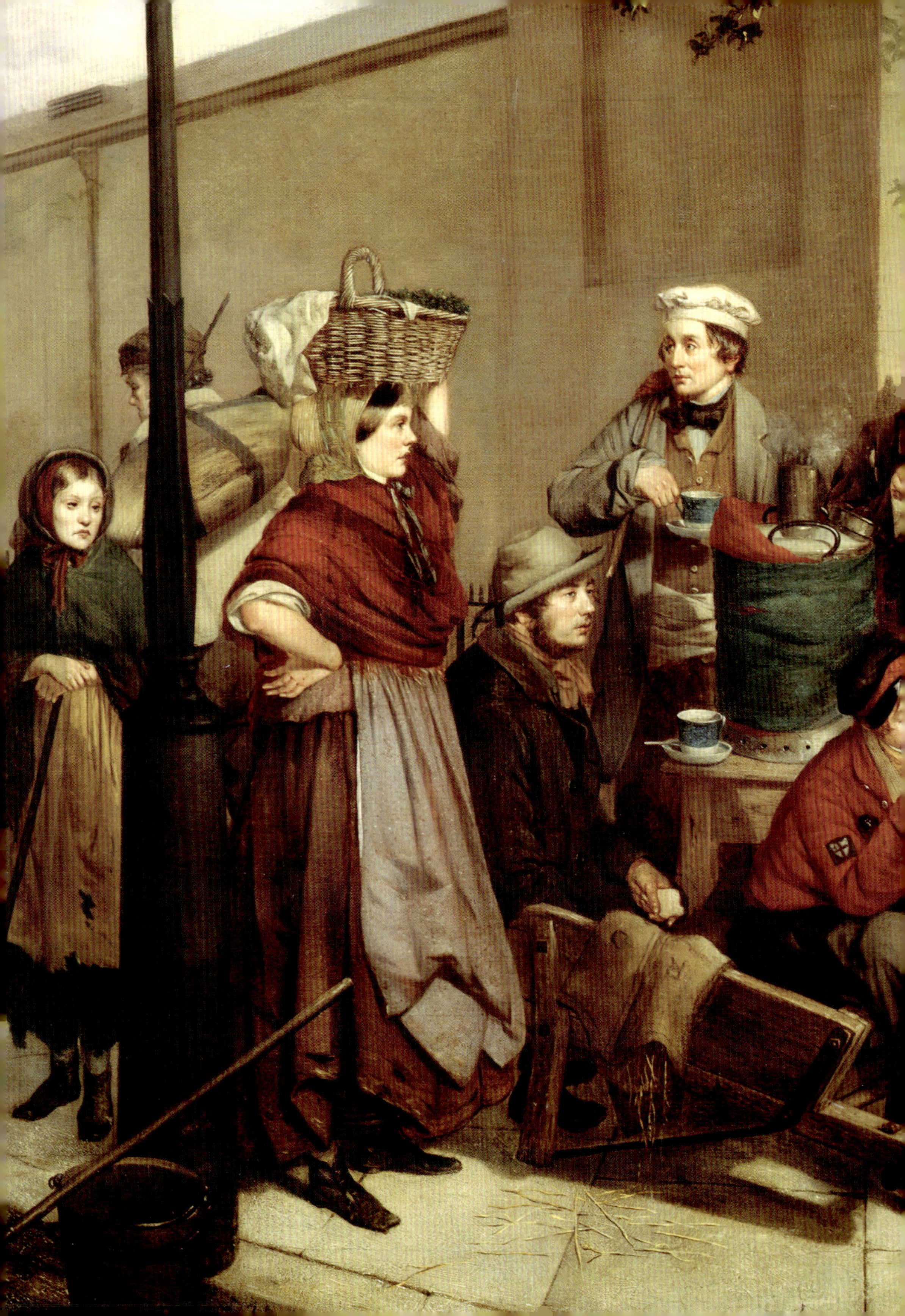

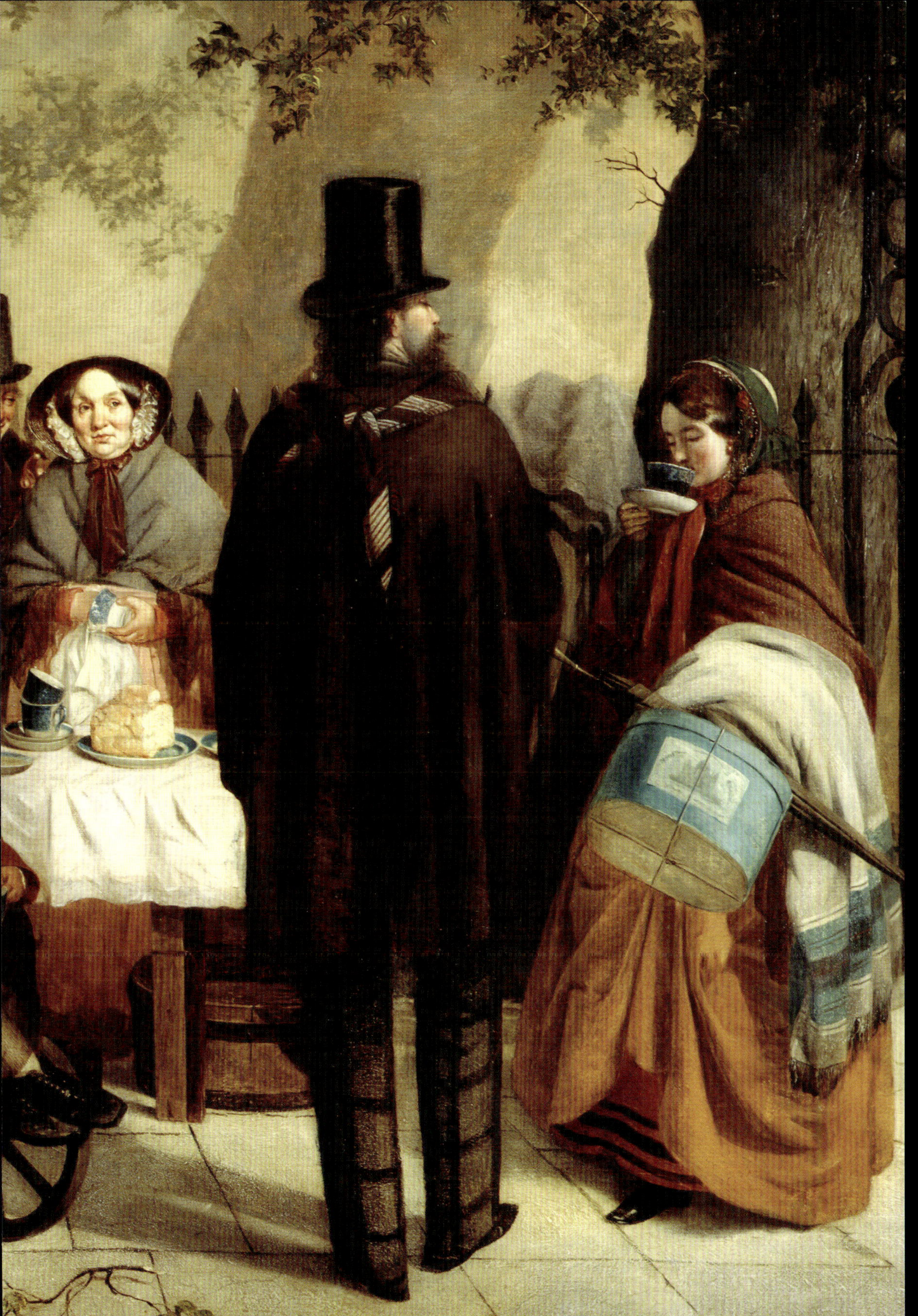

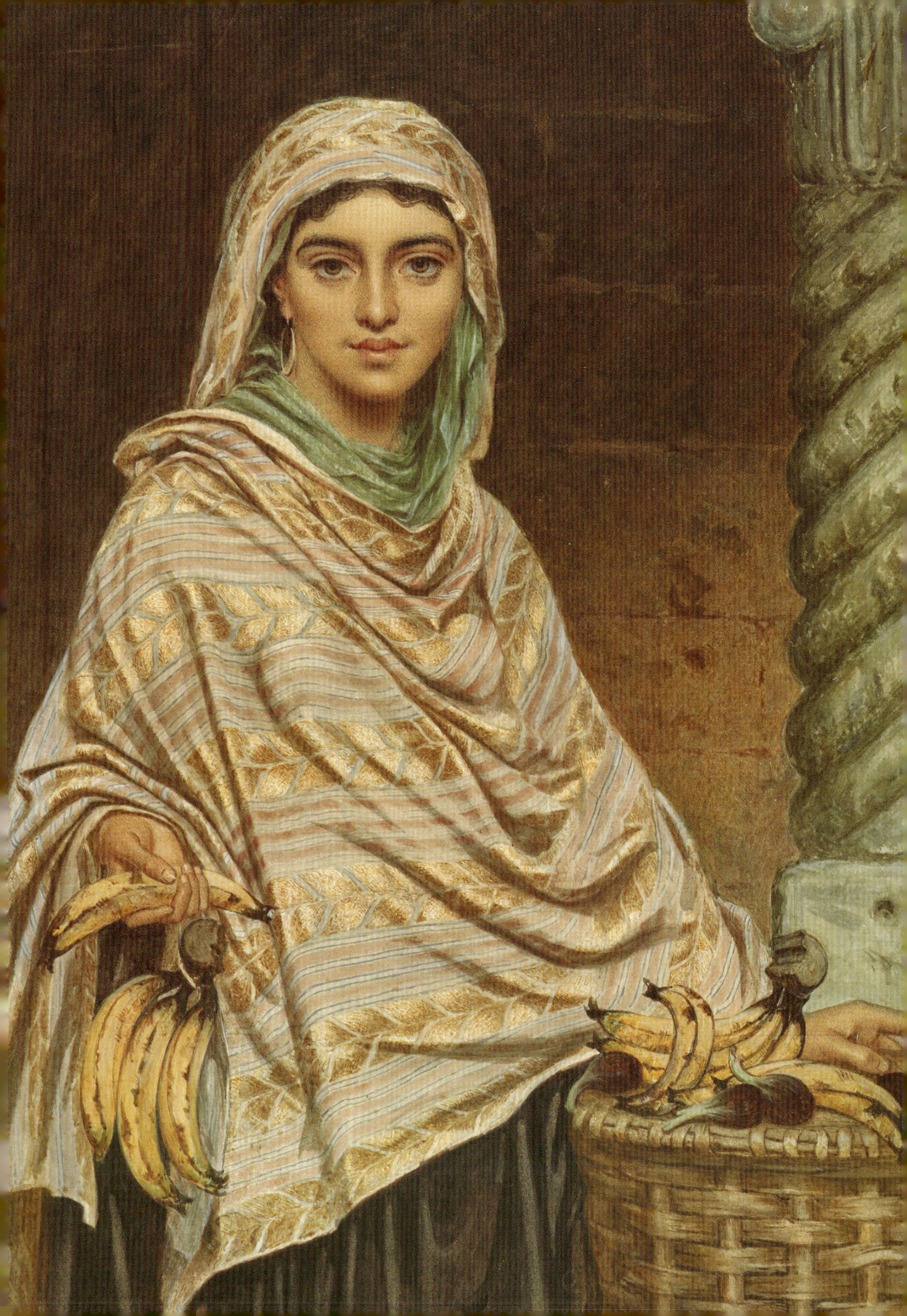

Contents

Egyptian banana seller
1878
watercolour with bodycolour over graphite on paper
private collection

(previous pages)
Breakfasting out 1859
oil on canvas
Museum of London, London

(opposite title page)
Portrait of Robert Dowling c 1855
albumen silver photograph, colour pigments
image and sheet 16.6 x 11.1 cm
private collection

(following half title page)
Early effort—art in Australia 1860
oil on canvas on board
National Gallery of Victoria, Melbourne

Author's note

Tasmanian Aborigines
1856–57 (detail)
oil on canvas
National Gallery of Victoria, Melbourne

I have identified where paintings are held by public collection or private collection. The public collections are cited in full in the first instance and thereafter abbreviated, as follows:

AGB	Art Gallery of Ballarat, Victoria
AGSA	Art Gallery of South Australia, Adelaide
BM	The British Museum, London
GGV	Geelong Gallery, Victoria
NGA	National Gallery of Australia, Canberra
NGV	National Gallery of Victoria, Melbourne
NLA	National Library of Australia, Canberra
QVMAG	Queen Victoria Museum and Art Gallery, Launceston
SLV	State Library of Victoria, Melbourne
TMAG	Tasmanian Museum and Art Gallery, Hobart
WAG	Warrnambool Art Gallery, Victoria

Dowling works which are reproduced in this book are indicated in the text by a parenthesised page number reference immediately following their first substantial mention within each chapter: (p 41), etc.

Spelling of Tasmanian Aboriginal names follows that used by N J B Plomley, 'Thomas Bock's Portraits of the Tasmanian Aborigines', in Diane Dunbar's exhibition catalogue *Thomas Bock: convict engraver, society portraitist*, QVMAG, Launceston, 1991.

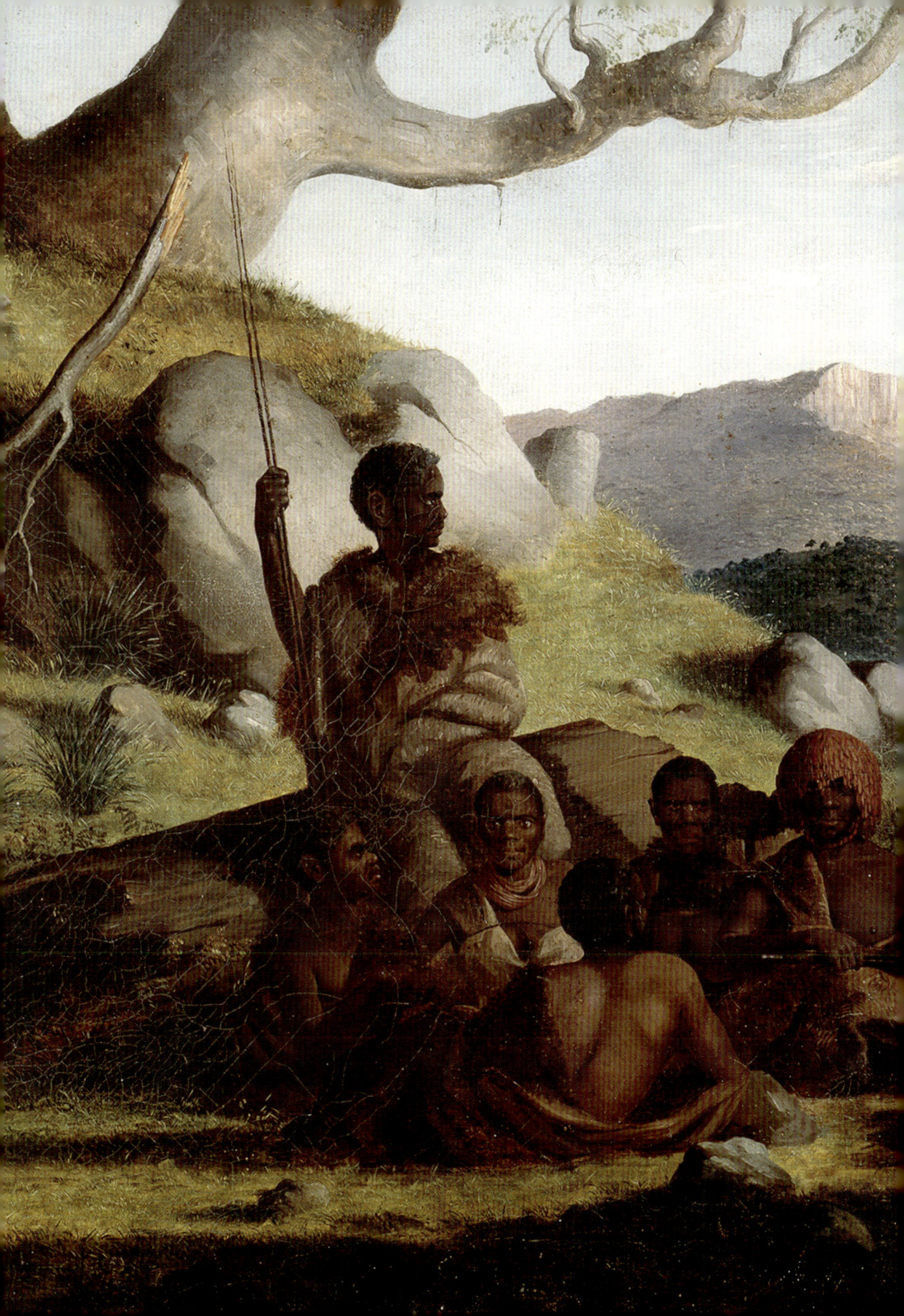

Foreword

Robert Dowling (1827–1886) was the leading figure and portrait painter of late-colonial Australian art, a period which concluded, and began to be overtaken by Australian Impressionism, in the mid-1880s, exactly at the moment when Dowling died. He is also important in the history of Australian art as the first locally trained professional artist, and the one who first forged a career in London, the centre of the Empire.

The various aspects of Dowling's career have not been fully understood before and are presented here for the first time.

The National Gallery of Australia initiated this exhibition and commissioned John Jones, a former curator of Australian Painting and Sculpture at the National Gallery of Australia, to write this accompanying publication. We congratulate him and are grateful for the work he has done. We also thank Daniel Thomas for his contribution in editing the manuscript. From the outset it was planned to open the exhibition in Robert Dowling's home town of Launceston (at the Queen Victoria Museum & Art Gallery), then show it in Geelong, where Dowling had set up practice in 1854. From the Geelong Gallery the exhibition tour concludes in Canberra at the National Gallery of Australia. We wish to especially thank the Queen Victoria Museum & Art Gallery for its enthusiastic cooperation from the first planning of the exhibition.

Both the exhibition and this supporting book have been sponsored by the National Gallery of Australia Council Exhibitions Fund, which is based upon generous personal donations from members of the Gallery Council made for the particular purpose of sponsoring special exhibitions. I also acknowledge the generous contribution of the American Friends of the National Gallery of Australia Inc, New York, with the support of Dr Lee MacCormick Edwards, toward the production of this publication.

The exhibition also has generous support from the Federal Government's Visions of Australia and the National Collecting Institutions Touring and Outreach Program. I sincerely thank these funding bodies.

I would like to extend my gratitude to all the individuals and institutions who have lent works for the exhibition, especially the institutions who have lent the most works: the British Museum, London; the Queen Victoria Museum & Art Gallery, Launceston, Tasmania; the National Gallery of Victoria, Melbourne; the Warrnambool Art Gallery, Warrnambool, Victoria; and the Art Gallery of South Australia, Adelaide. A complete list of all lenders appears on page 181.

Ron Radford AM

Director, National Gallery of Australia

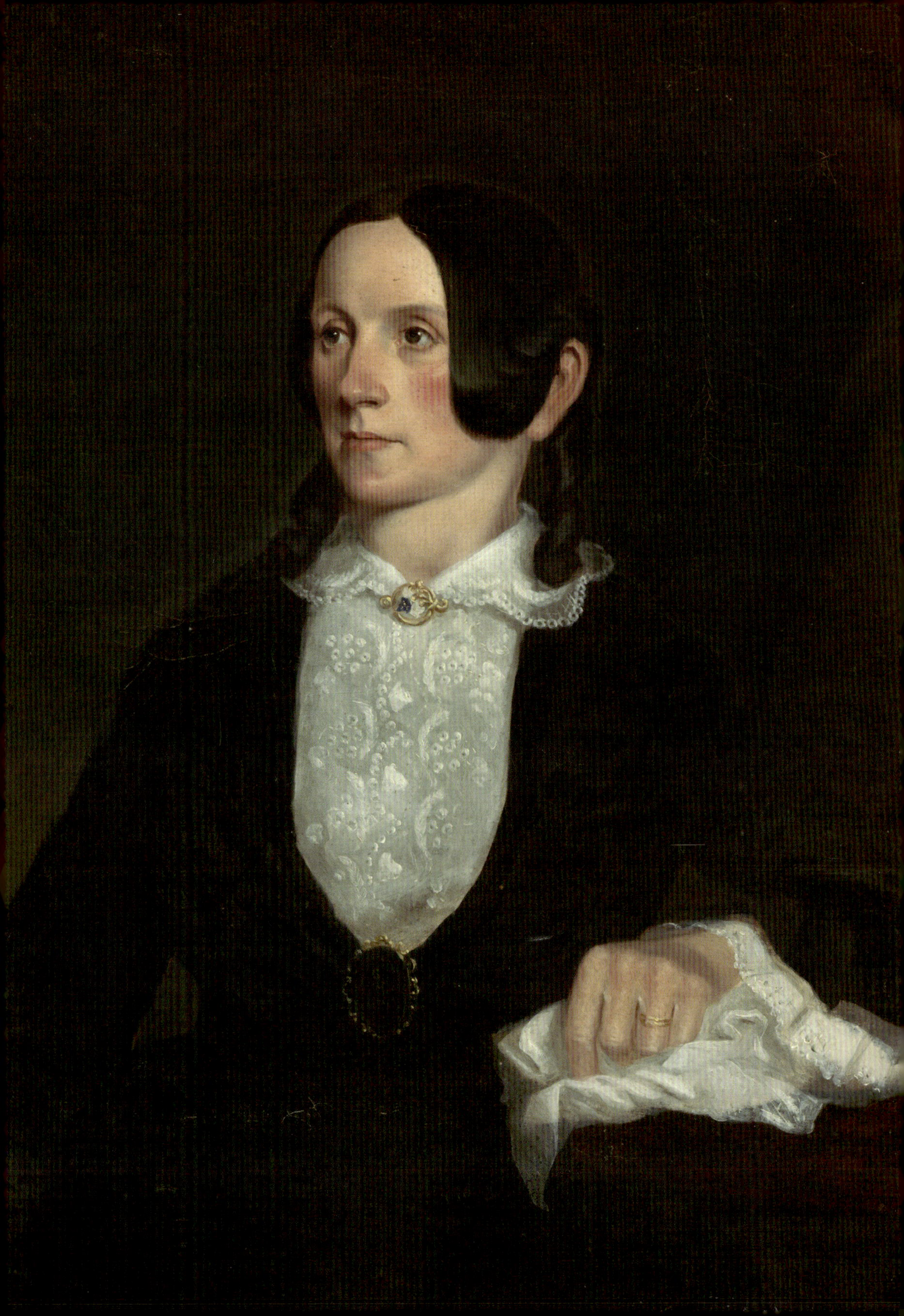

Introduction

The visual arts for more than two centuries have been central to European Australian culture, just as they have been for infinitely longer in Australian Indigenous culture. Therefore it was a momentous occasion when the colonial culture produced its first home-grown artist. Robert Dowling was that artist.

Mrs Maria Dowling
1855
oil on canvas
National Library
of Australia, Canberra

Dowling was Australia's first major colonial-trained professional artist. Aged only seven when he arrived in Australia from Britain with his family in 1834, he grew up in an educated and religious family in Launceston, the principal town in northern Tasmania. The colony of Tasmania, established in 1803, a quarter of a century later than the mother colony of New South Wales, had developed after another quarter of a century of settlement into a small society of free and ex-convict settlers that included a healthy art scene. Indeed, Tasmanian colonial art from the 1830s to the early 1850s was richer and more diverse than that of all the other Australian colonies.

In Tasmania a balanced colonial microcosm of late-Georgian British culture supported sophisticated architecture, furniture makers, silversmiths, frame makers, saddle makers and, importantly for Dowling, a surprising number of portrait painters—but also still life, marine and landscape painters. When Dowling was growing up in Launceston in the 1840s, Henry Mundy (until recently a largely forgotten artist) was the leading local portrait painter until his retirement and then suicide in 1848. Patronised by members of Dowling's family, Mundy's significant portraits would have been Dowling's main local inspiration. However, it is believed Dowling received lessons from a much less accomplished local artist, Frederick Strange. He probably also had lessons from Thomas Bock—Hobart's leading colonial portrait draughtsman and painter, and later a portrait photographer. Moreover, Dowling's father,

Tasmania's first Baptist minister, the Reverend Henry Dowling, and almost certainly young Dowling himself, knew the northern Tasmanian landscape painter John Glover, who was Australia's most experienced and accomplished—and greatest—early-colonial artist. Glover died in 1849.

In 1850 Robert Dowling, aged twenty-three, gave up his own short-lived saddlery business (he had been apprenticed for seven years), and in a newspaper advertisement in Launceston announced himself as a professional portrait painter. It was still a pre-gold-rush Australia, and our first locally formed professional painter had emerged. It is interesting that he emerged in a provincial city rather than a colonial capital.

Although Dowling grew up and was encouraged by his family in a sympathetic artistic community, there were not yet in the Australian colonies any academies of art for formal training, or any public art collections for Dowling to study. His interesting early portrait oils and miniatures executed in Tasmania appear superficially sophisticated, yet their often oversized heads and undersized hands betray the fact that he was deprived of the benefits of academic training and life drawing.

In 1854, having perhaps exhausted his opportunities for patronage in Tasmania, he migrated with his wife and infant daughter to the newer and newly gold-rich colony of Victoria. Dowling set up his art practice not in the capital Melbourne, but in Victoria's most established provincial city, the pastoral and goldfields seaport of Geelong, by then a larger and faster-growing city than Launceston. In Geelong he received commissions from pastoralists in the Western District of Victoria, including his in-laws the Ware family who, along with his brother Thomas Dowling, had settled there from Tasmania.

Most notably for today's viewers, Dowling painted group portraits of the Aboriginal people of the Western District. He also painted two groups in which colonial pastoralists and their Aboriginal servants are depicted as people of equal value. These group portraits are his most moving works and the ones we most cherish today. Painted in the mid 1850s, they also probably reflect the influence of the new art of portrait photography; in Geelong, Dowling's practice included the task of colour-tinting photographs.

Back in Launceston in 1856 (and later in London), and using Thomas Bock's earlier watercolour portraits of Tasmanian Aborigines as a basis, he began a poignant series of figure compositions depicting the Aboriginal people of Tasmania. The majority of those portrayed had died by then. Conceived as memorial pictures in honour of the first Tasmanians, these three paintings certainly achieve the intended gravitas.

In early 1857, proud of their own local artist, the citizens of Launceston helped raise money to send their Tasmanian 'son of Empire' to London, the centre of the Empire, to further his training and professional opportunities. After two years of formal art training in London, Dowling began to have his paintings accepted for exhibition at the prestigious Royal Academy. He expanded his repertory to include moralities from everyday modern life, subjects from history and literature, and undertook major biblical and Orientalist subjects, exhibiting with continued success at the Royal Academy and other associations in London. He also became a very accomplished watercolourist. Many paintings were sent back for sale in Australia. Dowling also painted portraits of Australians visiting London, and received commissions from Tasmania to paint royal portraits for public institutions in the colony.

In 1884 Robert Dowling returned to Australia and established a studio in Melbourne, where he also took commissions from other colonies besides Victoria, and for nearly two years was Australia's most successful painter. On that visit a great number of largely official portrait commissions came his way, Australia's principal city having no other competent portrait painter of similar standing; from these commissions he made a great deal of money. In 1886 he returned to London, intending to pack up and move back permanently to Australia but unfortunately died in London after only two months, aged 59. His death marks the end of late-colonial Australian art, a period in which he must be considered a central and critical figure. Australian Impressionism and a new chapter of Australian art, led by Tom Roberts, was beginning in Melbourne.

This is the first publication, and retrospective exhibition, to undertake a careful examination of Robert Dowling's art and life. The author and curator John Jones has studied this neglected subject over an extended period, and more intensely over the two years prior to this publication. In spite of the fact that no letters or diaries by Dowling have been discovered, the author's thorough research, perceptive interpretation and detailed knowledge of the period have produced a major reassessment of an important nineteenth-century Australian artist. Never before, for instance, have we known so much about a colonial artist's family or had colonial patronage of an artist so well documented. Robert Dowling, whose artistic career began over 150 years ago, at last has his proper place finally positioned within Australian cultural history.

The full range of Robert Dowling's art, executed in Australia and Britain over his thirty-five-year career, has not been fully appreciated until recently. Indeed a number of his early portraits and some later works have been misattributed to other artists in the immediate past. It is only fairly recently, too, that Dowling's work has become well represented in most Australian public collections. He has long been extremely well represented in his home town's Queen Victoria Museum & Art Gallery, Launceston, and also in the Warrnambool Art Gallery, a regional gallery established in the nineteenth century, to which his Western District relatives donated his paintings. The National Gallery of Victoria, Melbourne, acquired an important Orientalist painting in his lifetime, and a number of significant works since; in 1877, four years before his return to Melbourne, it staged a small loan exhibition of the artist's paintings. The Art Gallery of South Australia, Adelaide, and the National Gallery of Australia, Canberra, have more recently acquired diverse collections of his work. The Tasmanian Museum & Art Gallery, Hobart, the Queensland Art Gallery, Brisbane, and the regional galleries at Ballarat, Bendigo and Geelong in Victoria, hold his work, as do the National Library of Australia, Canberra, the State Library of Victoria, Melbourne and the University of Queensland Art Museum, Brisbane. However, a few important collections of Australian art still do not own any of his paintings. Ironically, the Art Gallery of New South Wales, Sydney, which lacks any works by Dowling, staged a loan exhibition of his later paintings in 1885, the year before he died.

Most unfortunate, for a colonial artist who tried to carve out a reputation in the complex and congested high-Victorian art scene in London, are the circumstances of his representation in some British and American museums. Dowling is represented in the Philadelphia Museum of Art, the Paisley Museum & Art Gallery, Paisley, Scotland (by two works) and at the Museum of London, where one of his finest works, *Breakfasting out* 1859 (his first Royal Academy exhibition success) was acquired in the 1950s with the false signature of the better-known English Victorian artist Charles Hunt (1803–1877) and the false date of 1881. Research for the present publication and exhibition helped reinstate the attribution to Dowling. Dowling's *Daniel in the lions' den* 1882, a painting he brought with him for exhibition in Melbourne in 1884, was purchased at auction in 1966 by the Philadelphia Museum of Art as being by the renowned nineteenth-century biblical painter and illustrator, Gustave Doré; the museum discovered Dowling's signature on the back of the original canvas only when conservators removed the relining canvas. Dowling's oil-sketch portrait studies of the Australian Aboriginal people, given to the British Museum in 1924, were recently reattributed to Thomas Bock but have now been given back to Dowling, again as a result of the preparation for this publication and exhibition.

These misattributions in major museums have been an unhappy fate for Australia's first artist to launch a career in the wider competitive world. Many more works by Dowling, known to have been exhibited in England in his lifetime, remain undiscovered. However his known oeuvre is still much larger than most Australian colonial artists.

Robert Dowling died a highly successful portrait painter of Australian settler society. Most importantly, he produced the largest body of mid-nineteenth-century images of the Australian Aboriginal people, images we find today extremely poignant. For all of his twenty-seven years in Britain he still remained focused on Australia. In London he was a gifted genre painter, and he is the Australian Orientalist without peer. Finally, the profound religious paintings that Dowling painted in London are not only an Australian's response to the art of the Pre-Raphaelites, but also offer a movingly personal resonance with the deep-seated faith of his Baptist childhood in Tasmania. He is here fully established as Australia's most important portrait and figure painter of the late colonial period of c 1850–c 1885.

Ron Radford AM

Director, National Gallery of Australia

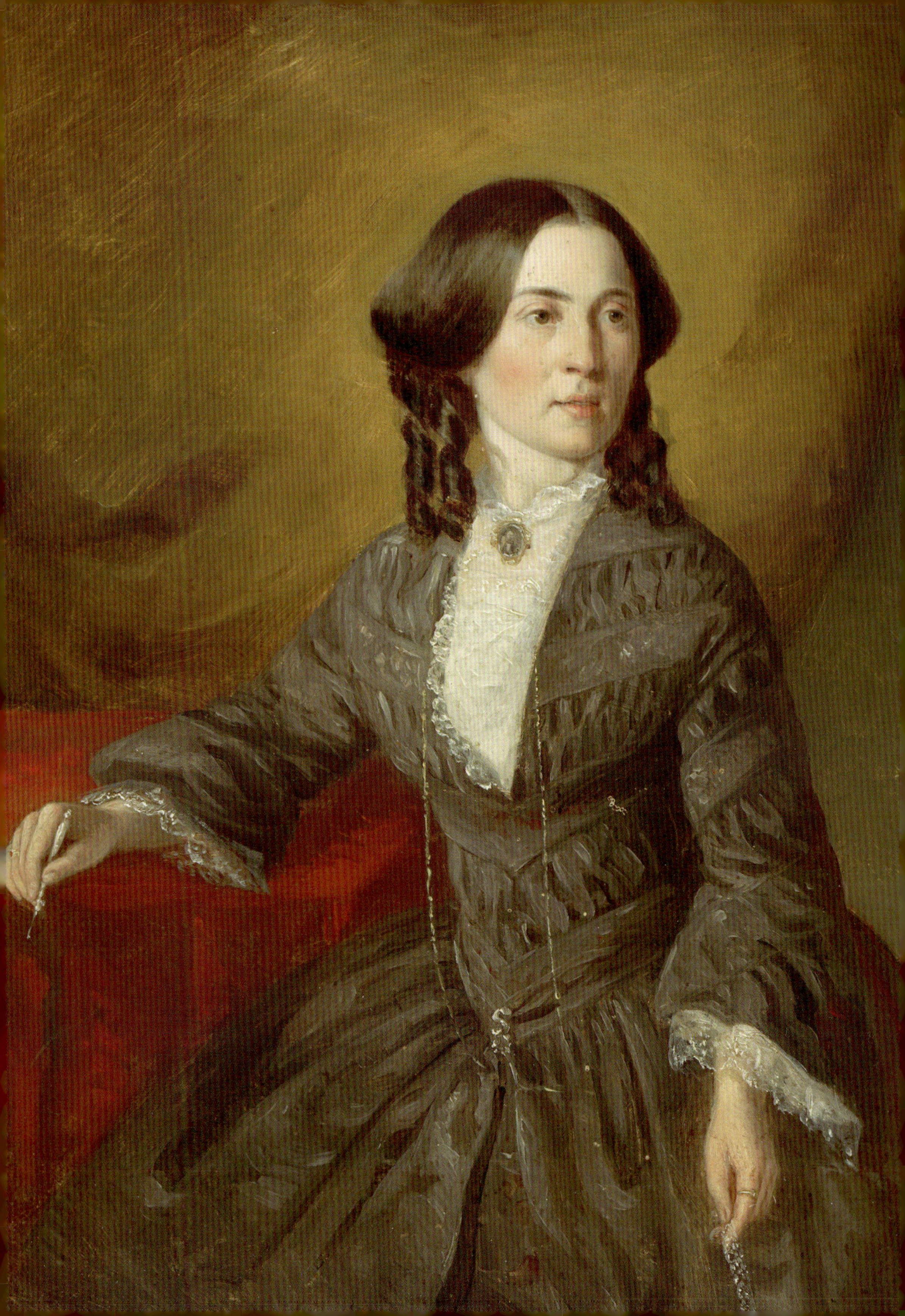

CHAPTER 1
Tasmania 1850–54: Launceston and Hobart

The Reverend Henry Dowling's sermon-like letter to his son Robert on the twenty-first birthday of the young saddler, soon to be an artist, establishes the devout environment in which Robert Dowling grew up in northern Tasmania. This is a short selection from the missive:

Mrs Arabella Dowling
c 1852
oil on board
private collection

Launceston, July 4, 1848

My beloved son,—

This day twenty-one years ago gave you birth; since that eventful moment the superintending providence of God hath kept you under the paternal roof, and you have largely shared in the maternal care of her who gave you birth.

Relationship is as lasting as life, and paternal interest can know no change; —so filial duties, my son, will know no limit, …

Under my roof you have seen no domestic strife. I trust I may say you have had no example but what may be generally considered worthy of imitation. You have bowed at the throne of Jehovah; associated in family connection in the service of God; and been directed for your moral, social, and religious guidance, to the written word of the living God; and I earnestly hope, and shall continually pray, that these features of your past life may be in the sacred chain of the future, while you aim to fill out your duty to God by living under a sense of His Divine oversight. Wait on Him in all His appointments, and seek Him for His blessing…

Your [saddlery] apprenticeship, my dear son, has terminated, and I am happy to know, honourably; and it is a matter of satisfaction to your parents that during that seven years of preparation for future life, your conduct has generally met our approval. It gives me great satisfaction also to be able to add, that you have not been inattentive to our counsels, and that when reproof has been thought needful, your subjection has been properly yielded.

From this period you will be much from the house of your father, and the scenes of your childhood, and the strong influence of such associations is seldom fully known at the time, …

Pause, my son; reflect and watch against the temptations which will lie in your future path. Danger lies where perhaps least expected. So far as human beings go in controlling, you are your own master, in the exercise of individual mind only answerable to God. This may tempt you to believe, that success in enterprise only depends upon the ability and means you possess. I may, and ought to remind you, that it is the Lord's blessing which can alone render either prosperous. Change of residence, new connections, and different habits, are now before you. Be careful of forming hasty friendships. Avoid gay and profligate companions; and even the irreligious. Keep always to truth and honour; gain by honest industry; and you will put a proper value on the reward of your efforts. Seek to possess pounds before you spend shillings. Avoid speculation and debt. Never ask for a surety in matters of business, and never become one—it generally happens that the surety smarts. Acknowledge God in all your ways; and particularly, attend to his worship. Especially respect His day of rest—never violate that command, 'keep holy the Sabbath day'…

And now, my dear son, wishing you both the full enjoyment of every needful temporal good, and looking up to the Spirit of God in earnest prayer that He may possess you with His influence to eternal life, I leave you under the Divine care and blessing.

Your affectionate, devoted parent,

Henry Dowling.[1]

Robert Hawker Dowling was born on 4 July 1827, at Colchester, the ancient Roman settlement and medieval wool town in Essex, some ninety miles (145 km) north-east of London. He was the youngest child of six sons and two daughters of the Reverend Henry Dowling (1780–1869), a Strict and Particular Baptist minister[2] and his second wife, Elizabeth, née Darke (1782–1853). Robert's mother was an adherent of the aristocratic Evangelical, Selina, Countess of Huntingdon, who had established chapels known as the

Countess of Huntingdon's Connexion. A movement within the Methodist church, its chapels gradually merged with the Congregationalists. Robert's father served for a time in one of the Connexion's chapels before becoming a Baptist. The Dowlings' youngest was named after their friend, the Reverend Robert Hawker (1753–1827), Church of England incumbent of Saint Charles the Martyr Church, Plymouth, who had died some three months before Robert's birth. Hawker was a controversial anti-slavery proponent and more famous hymn writer, who had penned, amongst others, the Baptismal hymn 'Sing to the Lord glad hymns of praise'.

The town of Colchester in 1829 had a population of 16 000. Although only 2230 of these were Protestant Dissenters, it was a known centre for their activity, with fourteen Sabbath Schools established there by 1786, and in 1824 an Anti-Slavery Society.

Difficult times fell upon Henry Dowling and his Baptist ministry in Colchester. Struggling to support himself and his growing family, in 1826 he had made application for passage to Van Diemen's Land—as Tasmania was then known—and a request for a land grant in the colony. His petition was unsuccessful. Ahead of him the first of Henry Dowling's children to emigrate was his second son, John, in February 1830, followed in September of that year by the eldest son, Henry junior with his twelve-year-old sister Hannah Maria. In 1833 the third son, Thomas, arrived in Van Diemen's Land. These four were followed the next year by their youngest sibling, the seven-year-old Robert Dowling, two other brothers, Joseph and Benjamin, and their parents, on the *Janet*, which berthed in Hobart on 2 December 1834. (The married daughter Mary remained in England but eventually came to Tasmania with her husband.)

Prospective resolution of financial problems aside, Henry senior still felt the call to preach the gospel in Van Diemen's Land. With Hobart Town in sight, after the perils of the long voyage, he wrote, 'I am reminded of making my final port in heaven! …—a safe anchorage—the deep waters of Jehovah's love to sail in—the eternal faithfulness of the Holy Trinity to cast Anchor in forever'.[3] A safe anchorage Tasmania proved to be. Aged fifty-four years, the Reverend Henry Dowling was the first Baptist minister in the colony, and served out his vocation there for another thirty-three years before his death in Launceston in 1869, 'revered and greatly loved by all'.[4]

The Dowling family had been preceded in 1823 by other members of the Baptist community, notably their London friends Jeremiah and Mary Ware. With the help of the newly arrived minister, the first Baptist church in Tasmania was constituted at the Wares' house in Elizabeth Street, Hobart, in June 1835.[5]

The Reverend Henry Dowling moved almost immediately to Launceston, where his entrepreneurial son Henry junior was established in business as a stationer (later a publisher and banker and politician) and in 1831 had founded a Sabbath School. From Launceston, for five or so more years, Henry senior exercised an itinerant ministry, by horseback up and down the island, dependent on flock and friends for a bed. He eventually established a permanent place of worship, the Baptist Chapel in York Street, Launceston,[6] on Sunday 27 December 1840. Fittingly for this somewhat variable Baptist, the first sermon was preached by his friend, the Congregationalist minister John West.[7]

It was in the modest manse beside this modest chapel (still extant) that Robert Dowling grew up. As gathered, it was a pious household. His father had stamina and physical and moral strength; so did his mother. The Reverend Henry ministered to all: the convicts, the ticket-of-leave men awaiting pardon, and the poor, as well as members of Tasmania's small Baptist community. He converted the condemned bushranger Riley Jeffs before his execution in 1843. His sermons and addresses could be graphic, forceful and highly interesting. He saw convict labour as a moral evil and espoused the cause of anti-transportation. He was a keen supporter of the Temperance and Total-Abstinence movements, of the Bible Society, the infant school and all causes of civil and religious liberty. In this moral and high-minded ambience, young Robert was raised.[8]

The second son, John, the first to emigrate, was employed at George Carr Clark's Ellinthorp Hall, near Ross in the Tasmanian Midlands, where Mrs Clark ran the colony's most fashionable school for young ladies; John eventually became a farm manager. Son Henry, some seventeen years older than Robert, was already a successful businessman in Launceston when Robert Dowling, aged fourteen, was apprenticed in 1841 to a Launceston saddlery, Tevelein & Stubbs of Charles Street. That apprenticeship lasted seven years, terminating in 1848. In late 1849, the twenty-two-year-old Dowling established a short-lived business of his own in York Street opposite the Temperance Hall. His mentor, John Tevelein, was known to Henry Dowling junior, as both were involved in the Launceston Benevolent Society.[9] The devout Tevelein was also Superintendent of the Church of England Holy Trinity Sunday School, and the subject of one of the artist's very early portraits. From his saddlery-apprenticeship years, probably in the mid 1840s, comes the first reference to Dowling's artistic aspirations. Samuel Girle, in a letter of February 1893, recalls his brother, Thomas Girle, and a fellow apprentice, James Ferguson, at Tevelein & Stubbs's Saddlery, posing as models, wigs and all, for their workmate Robert Dowling. The budding artist was attempting, prophetically, to paint a Baptism of Christ.[10] In August 1850 Dowling terminated his business as a saddle and harness maker[11] to take up the profession of an artist.

Despite claiming to be self-taught as an artist, Dowling may have taken lessons in Launceston from the artist Frederick Strange (c 1807–1873), a Dissenter and convict ticket-of-leave artist, with connections to Colchester, Dowling's birthplace. In Launceston from 1841, Strange created watercolour views of the town and distinctive portraits in oils. He also gave lessons in painting and drawing from his house in York Street. The journalist and author Henry Button (1829–1914), who married artist John Glover's granddaughter, studied drawing under Strange in 1848, and Dowling, a near neighbour, could have sought Strange out as well.[12]

Frederick Strange's portraits are rather naive. He was no competitor for the highly gifted and tragic portrait painter Henry Mundy (c 1798–1848), drawing-master at the Ellinthorp Hall school and active in Launceston as a portrait and landscape painter in the late 1830s and early 1840s. A young Dowling may have had occasional lessons from Mundy, who, after the school's closure in 1840, moved briefly to Hobart, then Launceston, and in 1841 to Seaford, an estate at Little Swanport on the East Coast, some one hundred miles (160 km) from Launceston.[13] Mundy became an alcoholic and, in a depressed mental state, took his own life in Hobart in 1848.

Henry Mundy is one of the major portrait painters of colonial Tasmania. He rivals Thomas Bock, and was the most elegant exponent of a late-Georgian grand-manner style. As a young man Robert Dowling, whose brother John had, as noted, worked at Ellinthorp Hall, would certainly have been well aware of Mundy's impressive work. Robert's stationery-businessman brother, Henry junior, sold some of Mundy's London-published musical compositions at the end of the 1830s. Robert's sister, Hannah Maria, was a student teacher at Ellinthorp Hall in the 1830s.

More significantly, Henry Mundy was connected to the Dowlings by marriage: Robert's brother John married Cecilia Lord, a former pupil at Ellinthorp, and her sister, Lavinia Lord, had married Henry Mundy in 1834. Mundy painted John and Cecilia Dowling's portraits as a wedding gift in February 1841. These portraits, held by the Queen Victoria Museum & Art Gallery but on long-term loan to the historic house Clarendon near Launceston, were until recently identified as Mr and Mrs Ambrose Dowling and wrongly attributed to Robert Dowling. As a further example of potentially confusing attributions, Robert Dowling later received, in the early 1850s, a commission from George Carr Clark to copy earlier portraits by Henry Mundy, three of Clark himself and two of his wife Hannah Maria, who had died in England in December 1847.[14]

The towering Tasmanian artist of the period was the landscape painter John Glover (1767–1849). As well as painting recalled British and Italian landscape subjects, Glover, from 1832, composed the earliest images of Tasmanian Aborigines in landscape settings. John Glover was a friend of the Reverend Henry Dowling and in 1838 painted *Baptism on the Ouse River by the Revd Henry Dowling* (Art Gallery of South Australia, Adelaide). The subject obviously engaged him and the work is likely to be a compliment by the artist to an admired friend. Robert Dowling, who often accompanied his father on these Baptist missions, may indeed be the young seated boy depicted in the painting.

Robert Dowling knew Glover and his paintings. In Launceston in March–April 1851, two years after Glover's death, that artist was represented by numerous works in an exhibition organised by the Reverend John West to liquidate the debt on his Independent Chapel at Prince's Square. Glover, a generous man, had previously given his painting *Netley Wood, Staffordshire* to West. So widely was Glover respected, a call was made in the local press for his paintings to be acquired by some public body 'to form the nucleus of a national gallery [that] might perpetuate the name of John Glover, whose admirable works were wrought in this land'.[15] A large number of 'Old Master' works purportedly by

Joshua Reynolds, Godfrey Kneller and Anthony van Dyck were also lent to that exhibition from local collectors, principally the landholder and parliamentarian Sir Richard Dry. The only living artists represented were Frederick Strange, Frederick Frith, W R Barnes, James Smith, and Robert Dowling.

The Dowling family's association with the erudite Reverend John West—a pre-federation advocate of colonial union and one of the most important figures in Australian life at the time—was close and affectionate. From his arrival in Launceston in 1839, as a fellow Dissenting minister, West was closely aligned with the Dowlings on various social issues and was a principal proponent of the Anti-Transportation Movement. In 1852 Henry Dowling junior published John West's distinguished *History of Tasmania*, the second volume of which dealt with the evils of the penal system and the harsh treatment of the Aborigines.[16]

In 1848, West had given a lecture at an earlier art exhibition, the first held in Launceston. It too was a fundraising event, for the Mechanics' Institute that West established in 1842; as elsewhere throughout the Australian colonies it was the town's first significant cultural institution. Some 300 items were lent to the exhibition, among them paintings attributed to Thomas Lawrence and William Etty, and works by local artists such as Glover and John Skinner Prout. West's 'The Fine Arts: a Lecture delivered at the Request of the Committee of the Launceston Mechanics' Institute' argued, echoing John Ruskin's view, that art was a moral force for good and had worth as an edifying agent on the lot of the common man.[17] It is likely that Robert Dowling was in the audience. West's words, 'he who increases the subsistence of mankind by the exercise of his skill, makes society his debtor', would have resonated with the young, aspiring, Christian artist who had just completed his leather-trade apprenticeship.[18]

Within two years, on the strength of this ambition and encouraged by his parents and brother Henry, Robert Dowling, aged twenty-three, began his career as a professional artist in Launceston. On 16 November 1850 he placed an advertisement in *The Examiner*:

> Portraits in Oil and Coloured Crayons—Mr Robert Dowling announces that after the 18th instant he will be prepared to execute portraits in oil and coloured crayons, as well as miniatures on ivory. He also purposes giving lessons in drawing. Specimens may be seen at his residence, York Street.[19]

The support from his family was later acknowledged by Dowling in London in 1860, with an autobiographical painting. His *Early effort—art in Australia* (National Gallery of Victoria) (p 95) portrays a young artist at his easel, surrounded by encouraging relatives and the handiwork of a saddler.

Of Dowling's new venture, George Carr Clark caustically noted:

> The old gent [the Reverend Henry Dowling] was so elated by his success that it was decided he should abandon the palm and needle and the clamp[,] shut up the saddler's shop and stick over the door R. Dowling Portrait painter[—] this is the sort of pride that the whole family of the Dowlings possess combined with that dreadful failing in my estimation[,] *Procrastination*. About this period this young blockhead fell in love with a butcher's daughter[,] a diminutive little thing with out education and a perfect bookworm. I sent for him and told him he was going to make a fool of himself and that he had as much need for a wife as a dog for side pockets and that if he would put his love in one pocket and his paint brushes in the other I would pay his expenses home and enable him to improve himself in the science of Portrait painting[;] this he declined to do and I have nothing more to do with him than to employ him as a Portrait Painter.[20]

Clark's bark was worse than his bite. He was to be a major patron and supporter of the young artist. Robert Dowling never took up Clark's generous offer of assistance with study in England, and on 13 February 1849 married 'the butcher's daughter', Arabella Dean, in his father's chapel. Their daughter, Marian Beckford Dowling, was born on 22 January 1851. The union seems to have been a happy one and was celebrated by the artist in a small pair of portraits, one of himself holding an artist's folio, the other of Arabella wearing a brooch, an oval miniature on ivory of her husband, and holding some crocheted lace and a small ivory crochet hook (private collection).[21]

The artist's premises in York Street were soon sold and Dowling moved to Charles Street. This was to be his permanent home base for the next few years. In *Wood's Tasmanian Almanack* for 1851 he advertised again, offering portraits and 'miniatures on ivory from one guinea upwards'. With a wife and child to support he was making a living, charging in 1853, for example, George Carr Clark £30 for three of the portraits previously mentioned and twelve guineas for 'frames composed of Colonial woods'.

In March 1851, at the fundraising art exhibition for John West's Independent Chapel, which was held in the Cornwall Assembly Rooms, Dowling's portraits came under critical review. *The Examiner* noted:

> Several other paintings and engravings were among the collection. The portraits by Mr R. Dowling, of which, we need only say, they are PROMISES of what his genius may effect, were favourable specimens of the apprentice, not the master's hand.[22]

Dowling was stung by this criticism, as were friends and family. In a letter of support, one judged the remarks 'calculated to wound the feelings of a youthful artist, injure him in the estimation of strangers and probably retard his progress'.[23] We do not know which portraits Dowling submitted to this exhibition but in the light of the sensitive pair of images of his father and mother (National Gallery of Australia, Canberra) (pp 36–37), which must date from around 1850, and of his own self-portrait and its pair of his wife Arabella (pp 38–39), and the competent portrait of John Bisdee (Tasmanian Museum & Art Gallery, Hobart), which is signed and dated 'August 1850', the criticism seems unjustified.

It is not possible to be certain, but Dowling may have then sought tuition from Thomas Bock, as the latter's stepson Alfred Bock later maintained.[24] Thomas Bock, a leading portrait painter in early-colonial Tasmania, would have been a judicious choice for Dowling to seek advice from. Alfred Bock also claimed that Dowling studied for a time with another Hobart artist, the Reverend James Medland (c 1817–1899), Chaplain to the Hobart Male House of Correction, and an admired copyist of Old Master paintings by Rembrandt, Correggio and Murillo. At his home Boa Vista in the Hobart suburb of New Town, Medland employed the convict artist Knut Bull (1811–1889), before that artist was granted Conditional Pardon in 1853. Bull's small cabinet-sized portraits and Dowling's small early portraits are often confused. The early 1850s, before the death of his stepfather in 1855, were within Alfred Bock's first-hand experience and although his recollections have sometimes proved inaccurate, there seems no reason to dismiss his claims about Dowling. The only query regarding Dowling's tutelage under Bock is when it took place: prior to 1850 or a little later? Thomas Bock was in Launceston in October and November 1847. He was there again in April 1848, making drawings and taking daguerreotypes of John and Henrietta Thompson. He might have met Dowling then and the 'lessons' Alfred Bock refers to could have occurred around that time. Or they may have taken place in Hobart in 1851 or 1852 at Bock's studio, 22 Campbell Street, for Dowling is recorded in Hobart during those years. Some tuition from this master would explain the sophisticated achievement of Dowling's best portraits of this period: examples include his splendid image of WP Weston (Queen Victoria Museum & Art Gallery, Launceston) (p 41), and the portraits painted in Victoria of Margaret McArthur (Geelong Gallery, Geelong) (p 61) and of Dowling's pastoralist brother Thomas and his wife Maria née Ware (National Library of Australia, Canberra) (pp 62–63). Thomas Bock, one of the earliest major Australian painters to pursue photography on a professional basis, may also be the key to Dowling's subsequent involvement in photographic art.

As we know from his dated portrait of John Bisdee, Dowling, though based in Launceston, from 1850 also worked in Hobart. The capital of the colony offered him wider employment possibilities, as did Melbourne across Bass Strait. Dowling probably visited Victoria briefly in 1849.[25] Another visit to the 'Metropolis of Victoria', advertised as imminent in *The Argus* in September 1851, did not eventuate.[26]

To work in Hobart Dowling journeyed by coach from Launceston, stayed with friends and executed commissions in his patrons' homes. In 1854 he was lodging in Hobart with the Baptist pharmacist Henry Hinsby and his wife Lucy (née Ware), who was a sister of Maria Dowling, brother Thomas's wife; the Hinsbys had been married by Dowling's father in Hobart in 1849. Robert Dowling moved frequently between the two cities: in October 1852 he advertised 'he has just returned to Hobart Town again';[27] in November 1852 'Robert Dowling portrait painter has come to Hobart for a short time';[28] in December 1852 and January 1853 he was available as a 'portrait painter and miniaturist at Mr Rolwegan's in Collins Street Hobart'. Dowling had taken on an agent, George Rolwegan, print-seller, bookbinder and publisher of *The Tasmanian Messenger: A Religious Journal for the Family*. Rolwegan belonged to the Hobart Town Congregationalist Church in Elizabeth Street, was Superintendent of the Sabbath School at Battery Point, and was well known to the Dowling family.

In both Hobart and Launceston the Irish-born artist William Paul (WP) Dowling (1827–1886) was Robert Dowling's rival and bête noire.[29] When WP Dowling established a studio in Launceston in 1851, both artists felt the need to differentiate from each other. In Hobart, Robert Dowling advertised in *The Courier*: 'as there is another artist of the same name, for the sake of distinction, the above is the son of the Rev. H. Dowling'.[30]

The statement that he was the son of the esteemed Baptist minister has some significance in regard to Robert Dowling's patronage. Tasmania in the nineteenth century was dominated by alliances of Evangelical Protestant families, some related to the Dowlings. The close relationship with the Ware family in London, re-established on the Dowlings' arrival in Hobart in 1834, continued through the 1840s and 50s. In August 1842, Robert's brother Thomas married Maria, daughter of Jeremiah and Mary Ware. Jeremiah Ware proved to be as substantial a patron as George Carr Clark, who commissioned five portraits. Ware commissioned at least six works from Dowling, including two large portraits, and two small oval pairs of himself and his wife (pp 42–43) to be taken by his sons to the Western District of Victoria. The Ware association continued in Victoria. Dowling later painted portraits of the Wares' son Jeremiah George and his wife Anne; of the Wares' daughter Maria and her husband Thomas Dowling (pp 62–63); and a group portrait of the Wares' grandchildren, George, William and Harriet (pp 68–69), offspring of their second son Joseph. It continued in London where in 1882 Dowling painted another granddaughter, Annie, daughter of John Ware. When Dowling sailed for England in 1857, it is surely no coincidence that a Mr and Mrs Ware were fellow passengers.

Most other artists also moved peripatetically between Launceston and Hobart, the two major centres of the colony, and Dowling seems to have had almost as many commissions in Hobart during the early 1850s as from his home town. Apart from the Bisdee and Propsting portraits they are difficult to date precisely, but a number of Hobart worthies sat for Dowling between 1850 and 1854. These include the amateur botanist Skelton Buckley Emmett (p 44), in a miniature and a small portrait (private collection); Mr Charles Buckland and his wife, the botanical artist Ann Eliza Buckland, and their daughter, Lady Flemming, and her son (Narryna Heritage Museum, Hobart);[31] Captain Frederick Chalmers (TMAG); the architect Francis Butler (AGSA) (p 45); and four portraits of children of Frederick Arundel Downing and his wife Harriet—Miss Emily Downing and her brothers Masters Harry, Albert and Ernest Downing (QVMAG) (pp 46–47). Before Dowling left for Victoria in September 1854, he painted the Quakers Henry and Hannah Propsting (TMAG), whose portraits are inscribed on the reverse, 'painted by R Dowling April 20 1854'.

In Launceston Dowling painted his father at least eight times. Two of these were paired: one with a portrait of his mother, Elizabeth (NGA) (pp 36–37);

the other, after Elizabeth's death, with a portrait of his step-mother Hannah (AGSA)—who was his mother's niece and hence his first cousin.[32] The large George Carr Clark commission has been mentioned. Other Launceston sitters include the Reverend John West, Mary Jane Ritchie, William Pritchard Weston, John Tevelein, and (in a pair of pastel drawings) Robert and Caroline de Little. There are four miniatures of the family of the future Tasmanian Premier, Sir Adye Douglas (QVMAG) (p 35). Many portraits known to have been painted about this time remain unlocated. These include the sitters John Swain (Henry Dowling junior's business partner), Mary Ann Swan and Dowling's initial portrait of Sir Richard Dry.

The popularity and number of portraits produced in colonial Tasmania throughout the 1830s, 40s and 50s is staggering. Dowling's oeuvre is considerable in the early 1850s despite competition from Thomas Bock, still active in Hobart until his death in 1855. Thomas Wainewright and Benjamin Duterrau were working in the 1840s in Hobart. Frederick Strange was working in Launceston and Hobart through the 1840s and 50s. Conway Hart was active in Hobart and Launceston from 1854 and in that year received the biggest commission of the decade, a large portrait of Sir Richard Dry, Speaker of the Tasmanian Legislative Assembly, for which he earned £300. Hart also painted a large portrait of Mary Morton Allport and, among others, the young William Robertson who, as a mature man, Robert Dowling would paint in Melbourne in 1885. Frederick Frith advertised portraits in oil, watercolour or by photography in Hobart in the early 1850s. Knut Bull was very active in Hobart from 1847 to 1855. W P Dowling, working in association with the Hobart picture-framer Robin Hood from 1850, and in Launceston from 1851,[33] was best known for his portrait drawings and photographs but he could also produce significant oil portraits—for example in 1853 that of the Catholic Bishop of Tasmania and enthusiast for Pugin's architecture, the Right Reverend Robert Willson. Like Robert Dowling in the 1860s, W P Dowling also painted religious subjects: St Joseph's Church, Hobart, has two large 1850s panels, one of Our Lady, the other of St Joseph. Like many other artists toward the middle of the 1850s, W P Dowling was attracted by and responded to the demand for the new medium of photography, by concentrating on photographs over-worked in oil, watercolour or pastel.[34]

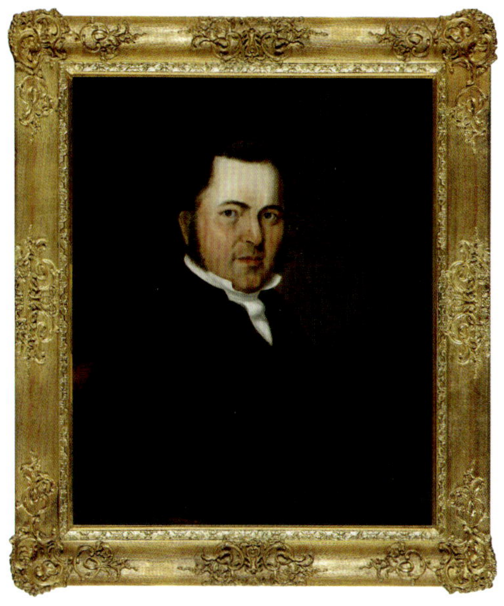

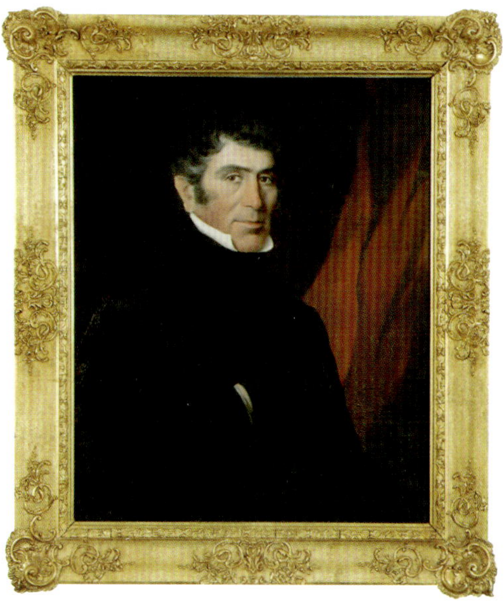

Robert Dowling
The Reverend John West c 1852
oil on canvas
76 x 64 cm
Tasmanian Museum and Art Gallery, Hobart

Mr WP Weston c 1852
oil on canvas
Queen Victoria Museum and Art Gallery, Launceston

The paintings are in their original frames. Framemaker William Wilson (1810–c 1855) Launceston

The pair of portraits of Dowling's father and mother in the collection of the National Gallery of Australia are among his best early works. There is, naturally, a warmth of feeling in these parental images. Robert's self-portrait and that of his wife Arabella (pp 38–39), of the same size and date, are similarly accomplished. These four paintings later became a group, when all were identically framed, in the 1870s in Melbourne by WJ Norman, for Robert's brother Thomas. All four display the sensitivity to colour that Dowling handled better than most of his peers, as well as a perceptive realisation of character. These qualities distinguish his portraits from the blandness of contemporary work by Knut Bull and the flashy, shallow rhetoric of Conway Hart's portrait style. Robert Dowling's very finest work from this early period is his *Mr WP Weston* c 1852 (QVMAG). The portrait is an intelligent and luminous delineation that captures the strong moral fibre of this handsome man. It comes nearest in accomplishment to Thomas Bock's c 1850 Robertson family portraits in the Art Gallery of South Australia. William Pritchard Weston, of Hythe, near Longford, was a distinguished figure. A pastoralist, politician (he was elected to the Tasmanian House of Assembly in 1856 and served two brief terms as Premier of the Colony) and competent sketcher, Weston was also a deeply religious man who helped John West establish the Congregational church in Launceston. Dowling's portrait of Weston is one of a pair; the other is his *The Revd John West* c 1852 (TMAG). In 1851, the immensely rich Congregationalist, Henry Hopkins, who had previously commissioned West's *History of Tasmania*, requested that Dowling paint these portraits of the Anti-Transportation Movement's major Tasmanian players. Though identical in size, and identically framed by William Wilson of Launceston, the Weston portrait is the stronger of the two.

Dowling created another and better realised image of West, a widely distributed colour lithograph (p 40). The background to its production was the pan-colonial abolitionist conference organised by West and held in Melbourne and Sydney in early 1851. With the help of other organisations and influential men, this resulted in the formation of the Australasian League for the Prevention of Transportation. Tasmania's last convict ship, the *St Vincent*, docked in Hobart in May 1853, and 10 August 1853 saw celebrations in Hobart and Launceston marking the fiftieth-anniversary Jubilee of European Settlement as well as the cessation of transportation. Dowling's brother Henry became the League's secretary and his contribution to the movement was honoured by a gift of a silver casket and 200 sovereigns from the citizens of Launceston. In Launceston, commemorations took place in Prince's Square where the League's flag, designed by West and first unfurled at a meeting at The Queen's Theatre, Melbourne in 1851, was flown with pride, for all 'the Australias'. Robert Dowling had been in Melbourne in August 1852 working on a commission from the League to mark this achievement.[35] There he produced the handsome, commemorative colour-lithograph of West, published by the firm Campbell & Ferguson. Below West's portrait appeared the League's motto and flag and the inscription: 'The Revd John West / To the Members and Friends of the late Australasian League this Portrait of its / Founder is respectfully inscribed by their obedient servant Robert Dowling.'

The last record of Dowling in Hobart was in August 1854. Some months earlier he had been commissioned by Dr William Crooke to paint portraits of his wife and son. Crooke was a difficult man, unprincipled and pro-transportation. Dowling had problems arranging sittings for Mrs Crooke and the portraits remained unfinished. In a last resort to gain recompense, Dowling obtained medicines from Crooke's pharmacy and left Hobart hurriedly, with the unfinished paintings delivered as a quid pro quo. An acrimonious series of letters between patron and artist ensued in the local papers.[36] Robert Dowling had other preoccupations. He was preparing to relocate in September 1854 from Tasmania to Victoria.

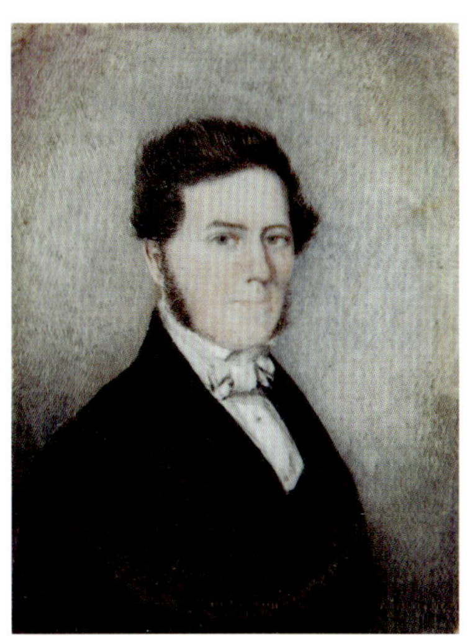

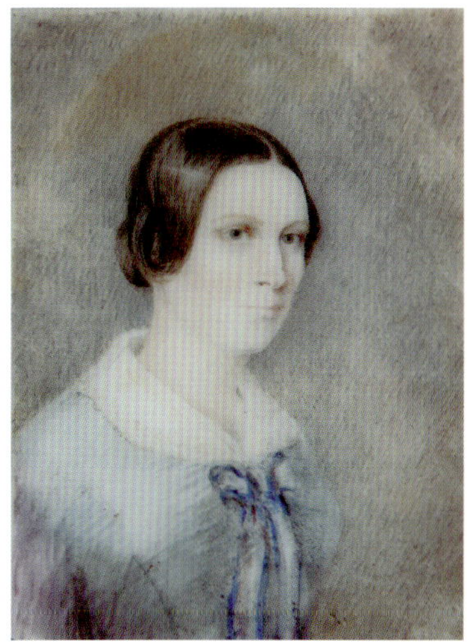

Adye Douglas c 1850
watercolour on ivory
Queen Victoria Museum and Art Gallery, Launceston

Mrs Eleanor Douglas c 1850
watercolour on glass
Queen Victoria Museum and Art Gallery, Launceston

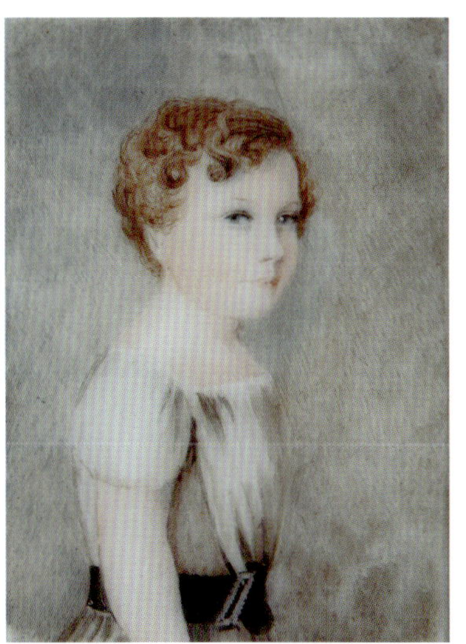

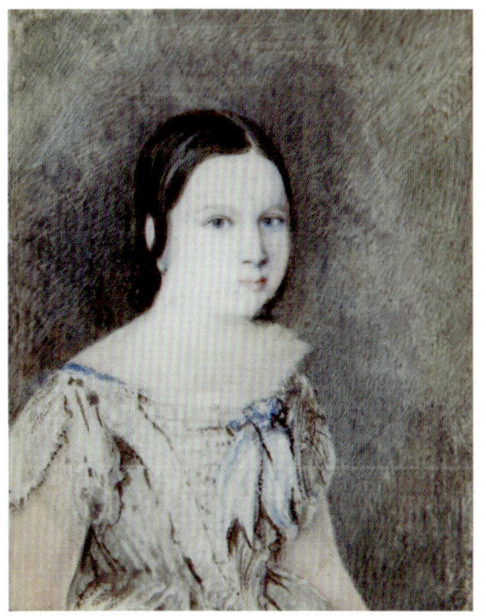

Master Archibald Douglas c 1850
watercolour on glass
Queen Victoria Museum and Art Gallery, Launceston

Miss Ada Douglas c 1850
watercolour on ivory
Queen Victoria Museum and Art Gallery, Launceston

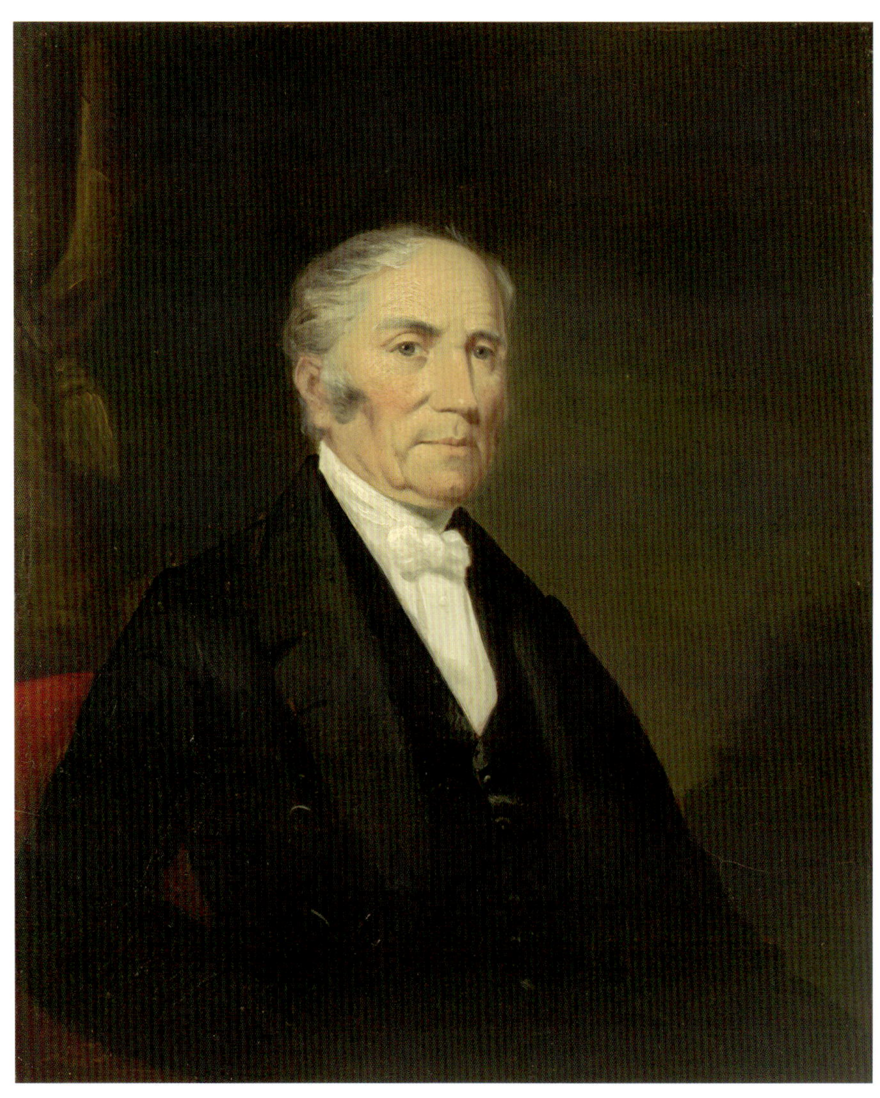

The Reverend Henry Dowling
1851–52
oil on board
National Gallery of Australia,
Canberra

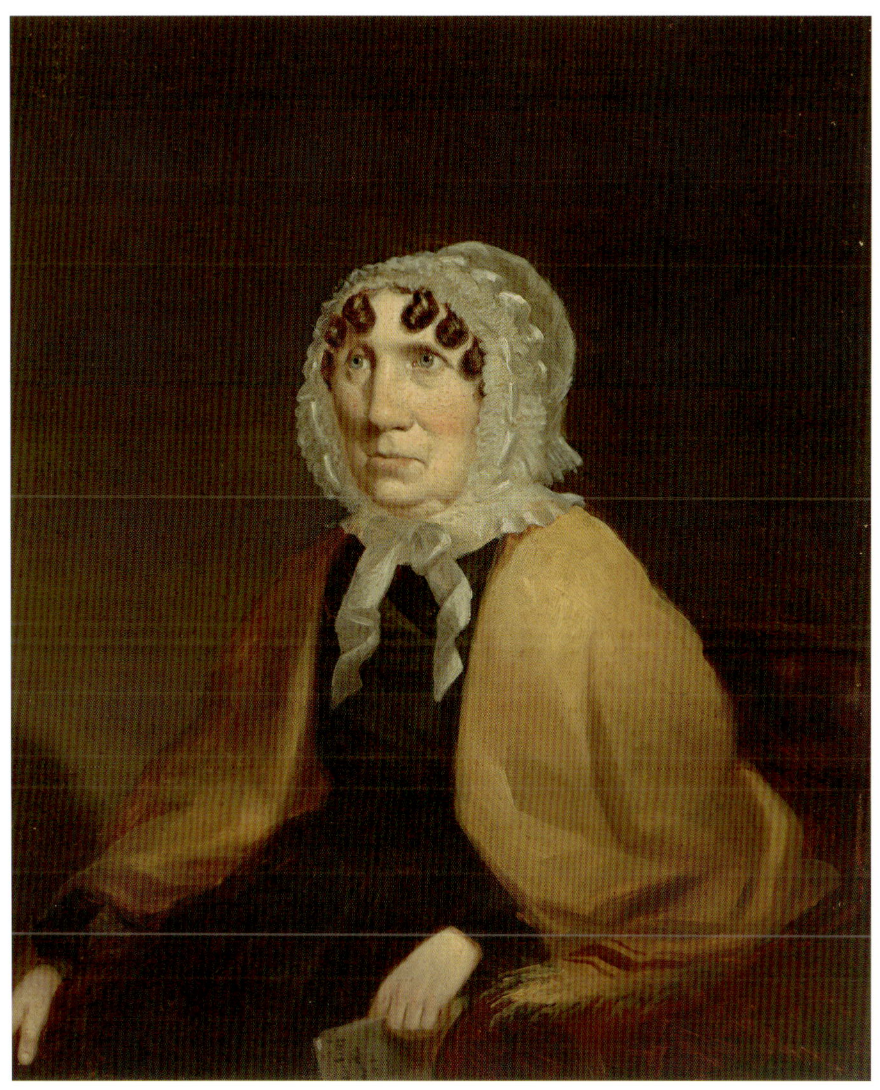

Mrs Elizabeth Dowling
1851–52
oil on board
National Gallery of Australia,
Canberra

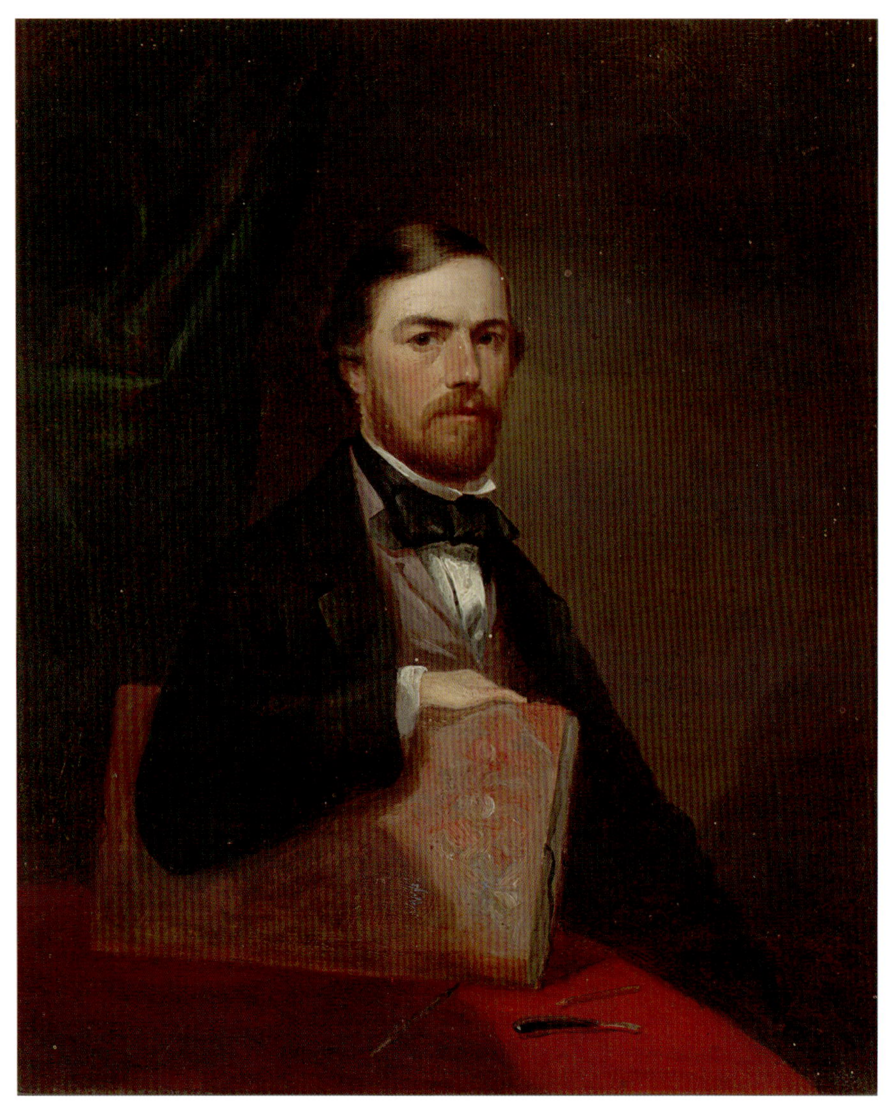

Self-portrait c 1852
oil on board
private collection

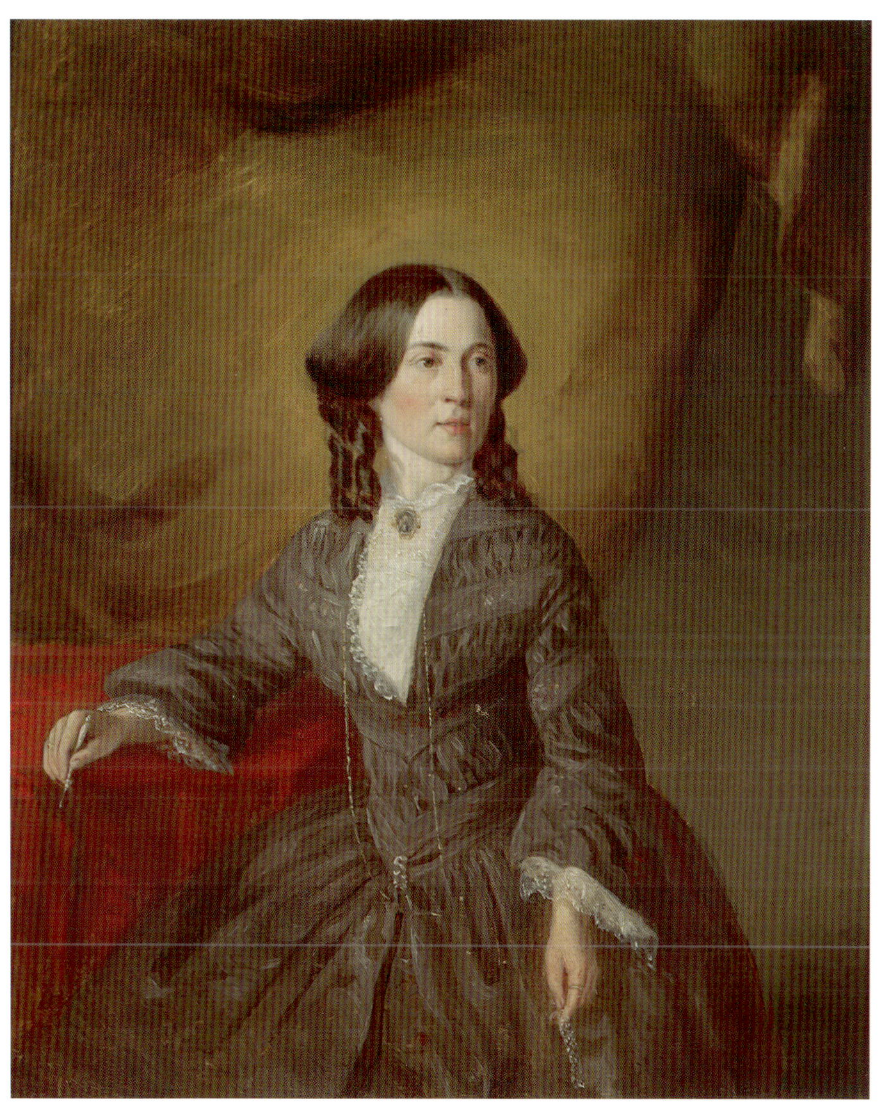

Mrs Arabella Dowling c 1852
oil on board
private collection

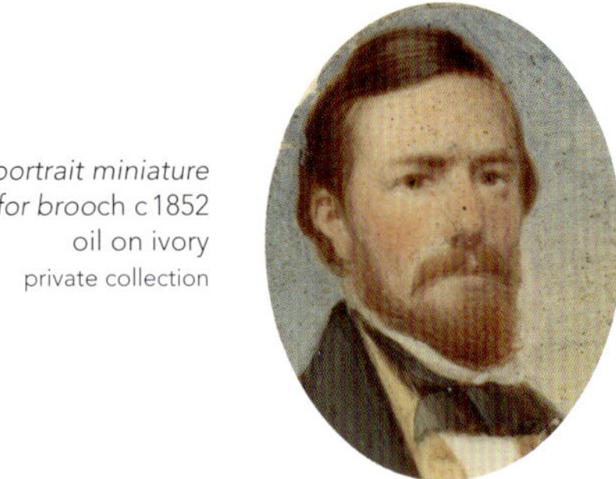

Self-portrait miniature for brooch c 1852
oil on ivory
private collection

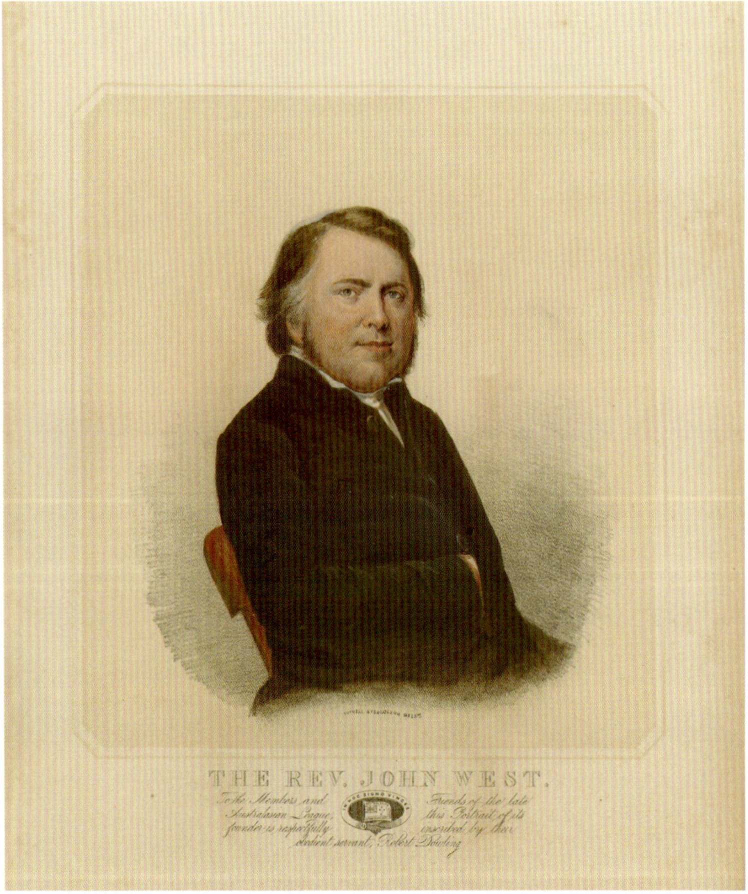

THE REV. JOHN WEST.
To the Members and Friends of the late Australasian League, this Portrait of its founder is respectfully inscribed by their obedient servant, Robert Dowling

Robert Dowling (artist)
Campbell & Ferguson (lithographer)
The Reverend John West 1852
lithograph, printed in colour and hand-coloured with oil paint, on paper
private collection

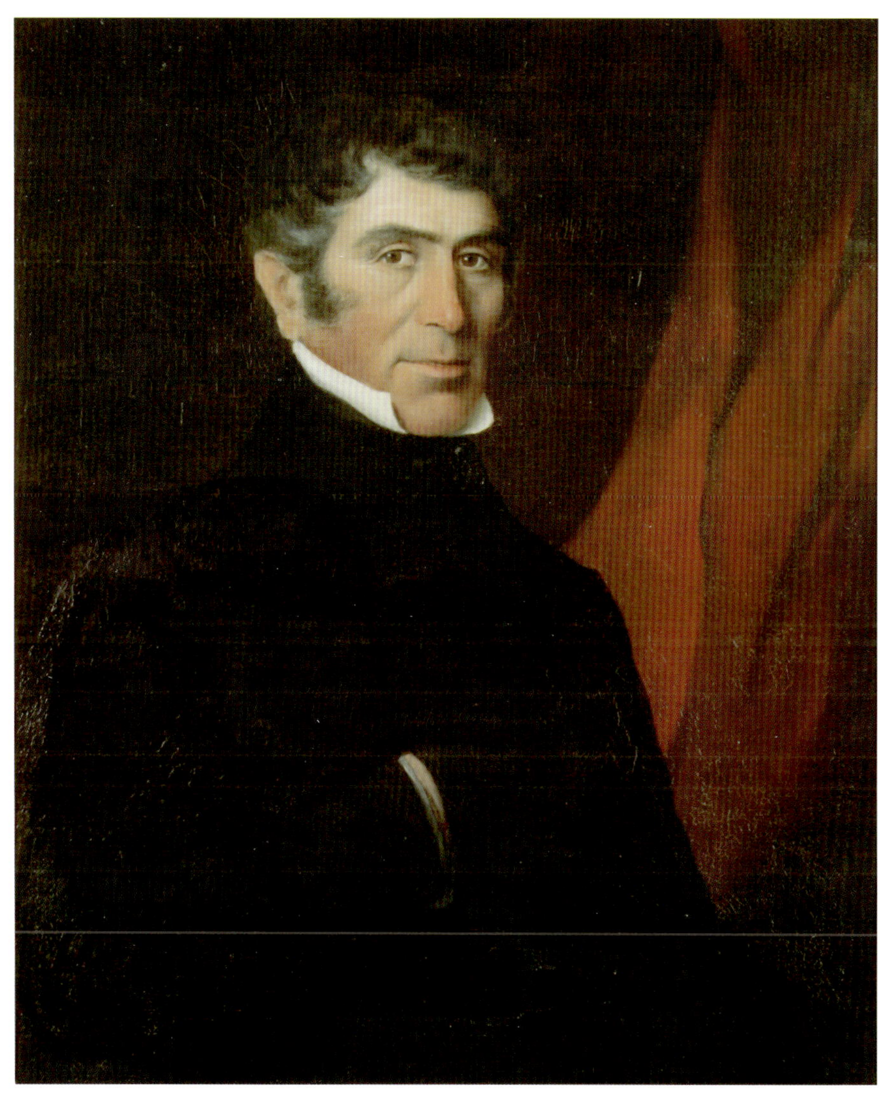

Mr WP Weston c 1852
oil on canvas
Queen Victoria Museum
and Art Gallery, Launceston

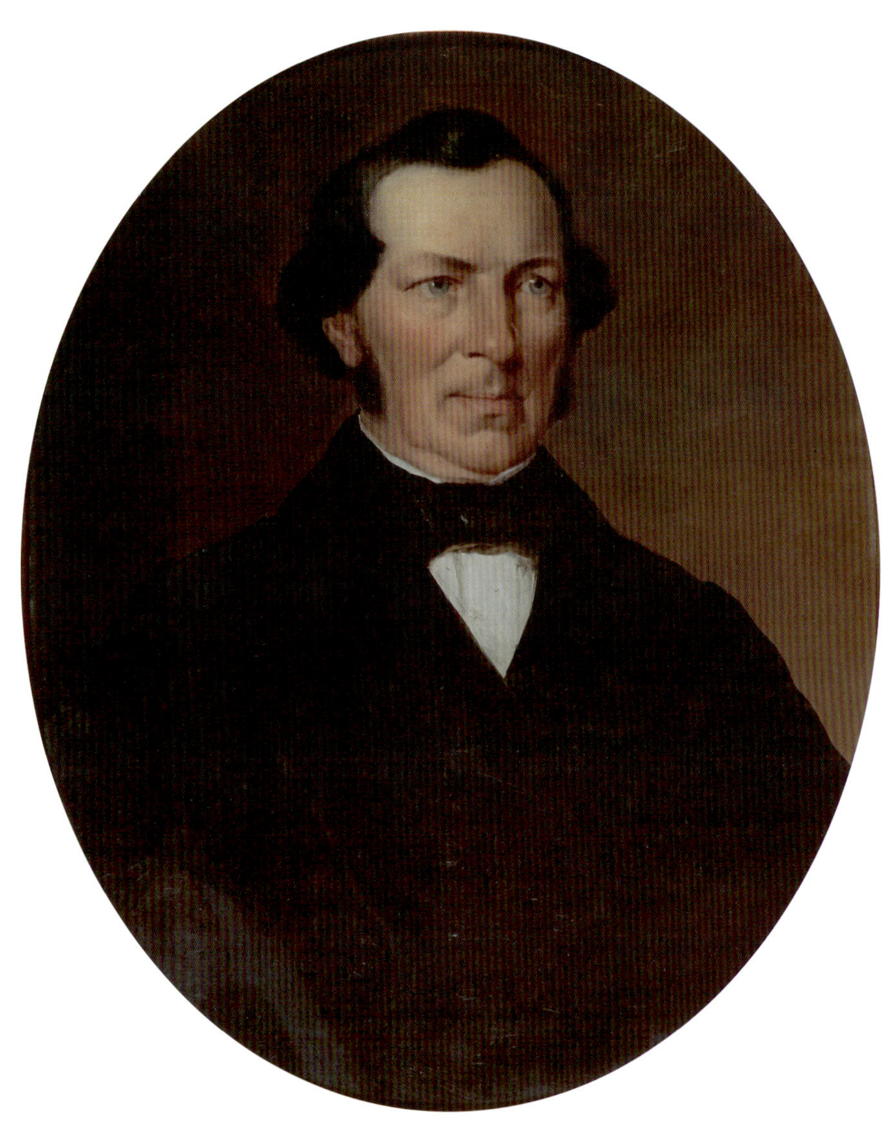

Jeremiah Ware Snr
c 1852–53
oil on board
Warrnambool Art Gallery, Victoria

Mrs Mary Ware c 1852–53
oil on board
Warrnambool Art Gallery,
Victoria

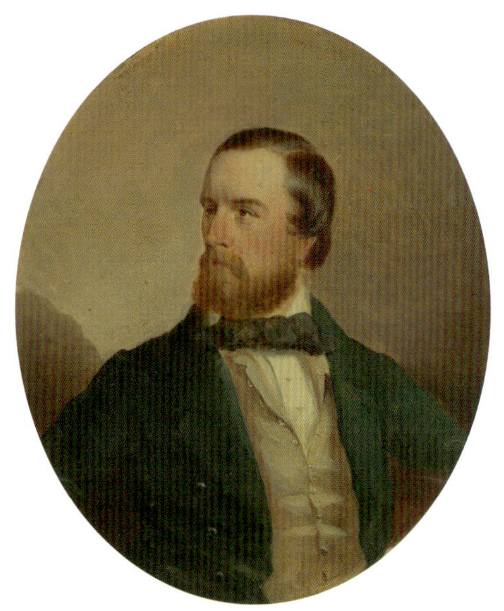

Self-portrait c 1852
oil on board
private collection

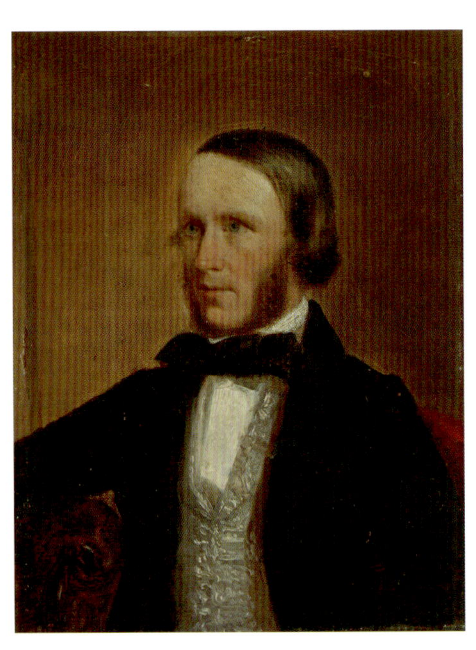

Skelton Buckley Emmett
c 1852–53
oil on cardboard
private collection

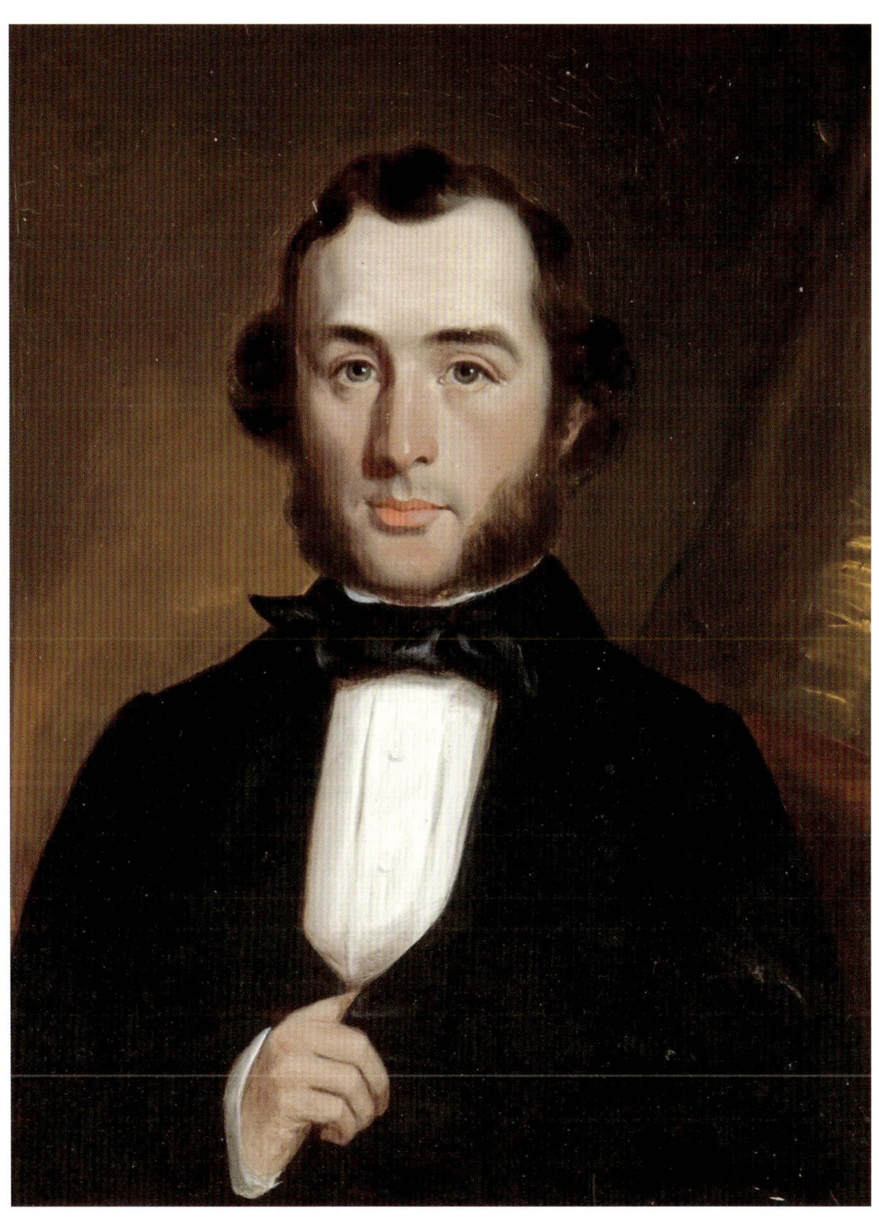

Francis Butler c 1853
oil on board
Art Gallery of South Australia,
Adelaide

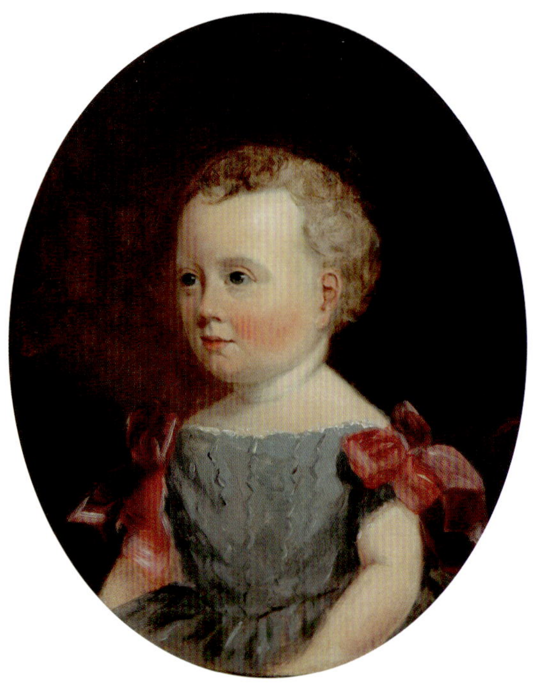

Master Harry Downing 1853
oil on cardboard
Queen Victoria Museum
and Art Gallery, Launceston

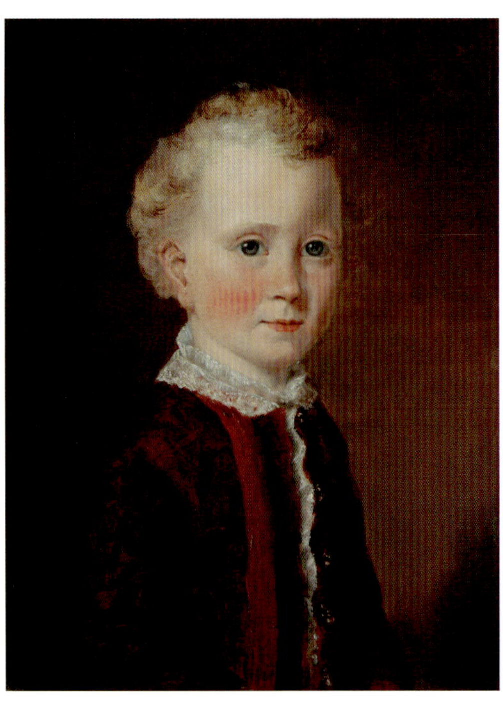

Master Ernest Downing 1853
oil on cardboard
Queen Victoria Museum
and Art Gallery, Launceston

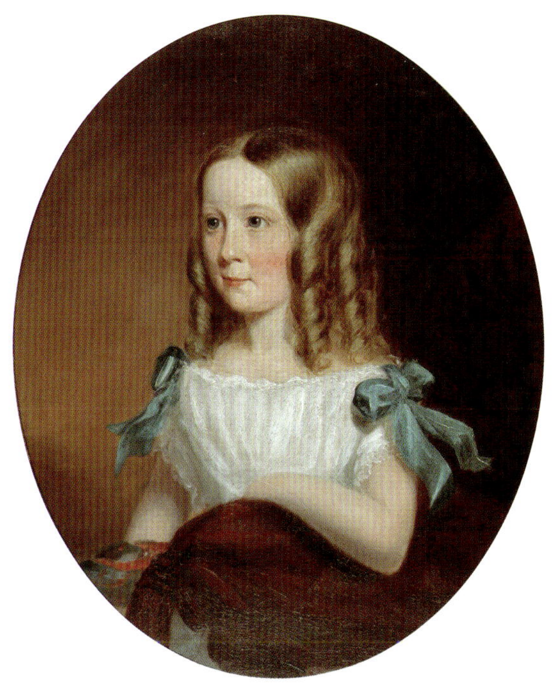

Miss Emily Downing 1853
oil on cardboard
Queen Victoria Museum
and Art Gallery, Launceston

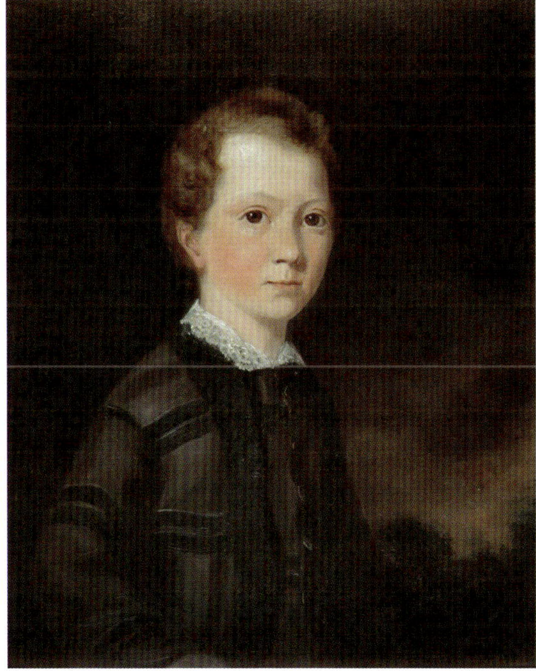

Master Albert Downing 1853
oil on cardboard
Queen Victoria Museum
and Art Gallery, Launceston

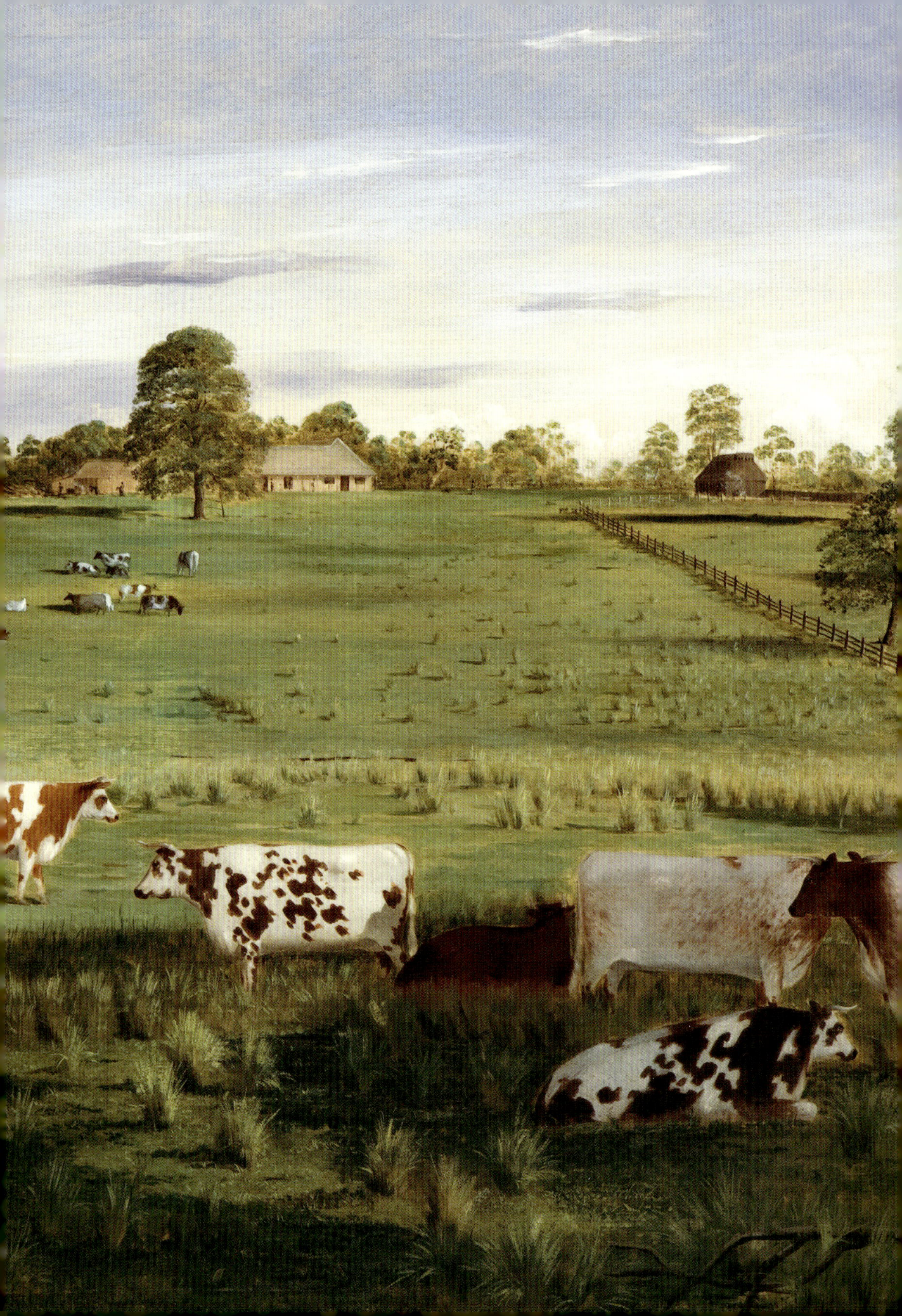

CHAPTER 2
Victoria 1854–56: Melbourne and Geelong

Jeremiah Ware's stock on Minjah Station 1856 (detail)
oil on canvas
Art Gallery of South Australia, Adelaide

On 18 September 1854 Robert and Arabella Dowling and their three-year-old daughter Marian boarded the Launceston Steam & Navigation Company steamer *Lady Bird* on one of its regular crossings between Launceston and Melbourne.[1]

On 26 September Dowling placed a notice in Melbourne's *The Argus*, announcing: 'Mr Robert Dowling, Portrait and Miniature Painter, Studio at Messrs Lush & Co's No. 31 Collins Street.'[2] He was attempting to establish a career in the Melbourne of the mid 1850s, an attractive place for an artist, considering the great wealth that a gold rush had brought to the newly separate colony of Victoria and its capital city. By 1855 the population of Victoria would be 300 000. In this influx were artists recently arrived from Britain, elsewhere in Europe, and other Australian colonies. Some were highly trained, among them the painters William Strutt, Eugene von Guérard, Nicholas Chevalier and Thomas Clark, and the Pre-Raphaelite sculptor Thomas Woolner. Interestingly, Woolner's departure for Melbourne inspired that most famous of emigration-subject images, Ford Madox Brown's *The last of England* (1852–55), the principal version of which is in the Birmingham Museum & Art Gallery. In 1852, artists attracted to Victoria from South Australia included J A Gilfillan and S T Gill. In 1853 the briefly Sydney-based British portrait and religious painter, Marshall Claxton, visited Melbourne, where he executed a major commission and exhibited. The itinerant portraitists Conway Hart and Frederick Hutton were also practising and advertising their presence in Melbourne in 1853. The previous year an exceptionally fine portrait and landscape painter, the German Ludwig Becker, had arrived in Victoria after a short time in Tasmania. Georgiana McCrae, a gifted watercolour portraitist and landscape artist had been active in Melbourne since the mid 1840s. John Botterill, a brilliant miniaturist and photographer, had been working in Melbourne since the early 1850s. All were part of a varied milieu from which emerged a Victorian Fine Arts Society and its inaugural exhibition in Melbourne in August 1853, a year before Robert Dowling's arrival. Although a great deal of their artistic production was landscape and other genres, the city had more than a surfeit of talented portrait painters.

Dowling found difficulty in obtaining patronage. New money and new men were supplanting the powerful pastoralists of the 1840s, and Melbourne at the time of Dowling's arrival perhaps lacked the settled urbanity of the Tasmanian middle class that had been the mainstay of his support in Launceston and Hobart. The rival portrait medium of photography was also in ascendance.

However, Dowling did find some commissions. His portrait of the pastoralist George Evans, of Emu Bottom near Sunbury on the outskirts of Melbourne (Pictures Collection, State Library of Victoria, Melbourne), may date from late 1854; the subject was one of the Tasmanian associates of J P Fawkner, whose expedition had settled Melbourne from Launceston twenty years earlier. Dowling also had dealings with the printers Campbell & Ferguson and his lithograph of Charles Perry, first Bishop of Melbourne (Melbourne Grammar School Collection), may have been published in 1854. Campbell & Ferguson's imprint would confirm a date for the lithograph prior to 1855, which is when the firm became known as Hamel & Ferguson.

By November 1854, Dowling had settled in Noble Street, Newtown, a suburb of Geelong, the second-largest town in Victoria.[3] By December, he had found secure employment. It proved to be a provident relocation for the Tasmanian artist; he was now in closer geographical proximity to the pastoral families to whom he was related.

The first settlement of Victoria, or the Port Phillip District of New South Wales as it was known before separation in 1851, was largely a product of Tasmanian pastoralists seeking 'unoccupied' grazing land after the pastures in Van Diemen's Land were fully taken. In November 1834, Edward Henty had sailed in the *Thistle* from Launceston and had established a pastoral settlement at Portland Bay. Melbourne was subsequently founded in 1835, again from Launceston, by two rival parties, one of which was led by Fawkner in the

Enterprise. The following year another Tasmanian, George Russell, settled in the Geelong area.

After the New South Wales Surveyor-General Thomas Mitchell's official expedition to the area in 1836 and the publication of his findings on the riches of what he called Australia Felix, many settlers from New South Wales began to overland south, heading for the rich plains to the west of Geelong. By 1840 these grasslands were effectively settled. Geelong itself was first gazetted as a town in late 1838 and through the 1840s became the gateway and port for the growing wool industry of the Western District.

The discovery of gold in 1851 in the newly proclaimed Colony of Victoria, and subsequent gold rushes to Ballarat, Castlemaine and Bendigo, dramatically affected its social and economic structure. Eugene von Guérard, a German who became perhaps Australia's greatest colonial painter, in 1852 was among the flood of immigrant gold-seekers who used Geelong as the principal route to the Ballarat diggings. The place was recalled by him in 1854 in two paintings, *Barter*, also known as *The Barwon River, Geelong*, and *Aborigines met on the road to the diggings*. By the time Robert Dowling arrived in Geelong it had a population of 23 000 and, though smaller than Hobart, was larger than Launceston. The young cities of Victoria lacked the elegance of the older towns in Tasmania, but Geelong was a pretty settlement, captured from 1853 in watercolour views by the house-painter Alexander Webb. More important than these was the large panoramic view across Geelong and Corio Bay to the You Yangs, painted after von Guérard revisited the city in 1856. This work, *The country near Geelong* (Geelong Gallery), was purchased by Frederick Dalgety, whose bush-merchandise and wool-trade firm was headquartered in Geelong. Other artists were associated with the area. Previously, John Skinner Prout had briefly worked there in the late 1840s, and the Tasmanian portraitist, landscapist, set designer and marine artist William Duke lived in Geelong from 1851 until his death in 1853, as is recorded in Duke's painting *Geelong from Mr Hiatt's, Burrabool Hills* 1851. At the Geelong Mechanics' Institute Exhibition of paintings in 1857 there were works by Robert Dowling, Conway Hart (who signed his 1854 portrait of Marcus Sievewright 'Conway Hart of Geelong'), along with Ludwig Becker and Thomas Robertson, a ship artist and the captain of the *Lady Bird* which brought the Dowlings from Launceston to Melbourne.

The secure employment that Dowling found in Geelong late in 1854 was with a commercial gallery run by a French-born daguerreotypist, Amand August Fortune La Moile (1798–1883), at the premises of the chemist, Henry Goulter[4], in Yarra Street. On 14 December 1854 *The Geelong Advertiser* displayed the following notice:

> Public Gallery of Daguerreotypes, Paintings, objects of art, science etc, Yarra Street North and at Emerald Street, Little Scotland. Mr. La Moile begs to inform the public that he has opened the above for the taking of daguerreotypes and oil painting portraits, groups including children, horses, dogs etc, copies of pictures … Objects of arts, science, industry productions that may attract, awake and create a taste for the fine arts will be received for exhibition or sale …[5]

Robert Dowling is described in this advertisement as 'conducting the oil painting'. He also had the miniaturist skills to handle the delicate powder-tinting of contemporary daguerreotype and ambrotype photographs, as had Thomas Bock in Tasmania, who made daguerreotype portraits with painted backgrounds from 1848. In Geelong, La Moile is likely to have employed Dowling in this way, as well as provide prospective clients with painted oil portraits. That Dowling was involved in photography is confirmed by his brother Henry, who in 1860 lent 'Specimens of coloured Photographic Portraits tinted by R. Dowling' to an art exhibition at the Launceston Mechanics' Institute.[6] None of Dowling's tinted photographs have yet been identified.

La Moile's notice appeared again in *The Geelong Advertiser* on 2 January 1855 but oil portrait commissions for Dowling seem to have come slowly. The only Geelong portraits identified so far are the modest, cabinet-sized pair of the chemist, printer and later politician, Charles Kernot, and his wife Mary, painted in 1854. The Kernots, Congregationalists from Essex, would have been known to the Dowling family from links back in Colchester twenty years earlier. Charles Kernot's son William, founding Professor of Engineering at the University of Melbourne, and sometime President of the Baptist Union of Victoria and Royal Society of Victoria, would later acquire from the artist, in Melbourne in the 1880s, six preliminary oil sketches for Dowling's large London paintings of Tasmanian Aborigines (pp 102–103). Because of their ethnographic interest, in 1909 he bequeathed the sketches to the Royal

Society of Victoria; they are now in the National Library of Australia. Charles Kernot was the lender of Dowling's *Minjah in the Old Time* (p 96–97) to the Geelong Mechanics' Institute Exhibition in 1857. Twenty years later his spinster daughters, the Misses W and C Kernot of Parkville, Melbourne, were among the subscribers to the appeal for the National Gallery of Victoria to acquire Dowling's big Orientalist painting of a street ceremony in Cairo (pp 138–39).

Little else is known of Dowling's life in Geelong. He and Arabella attended the local Aberdeen Street Baptist Church. In 1855, his father, the Reverend Henry Dowling, visited Geelong and stayed with his son and daughter-in-law at Noble Street. The old man, 'certainly indefatigable in preaching', ministered to the Baptist congregation in Geelong, 'who had never heard the truth so clearly preached and … one woman had found salvation'.[7] The Reverend Henry would certainly have taken the opportunity to see his other son Thomas and daughter-in-law Maria, visiting their sheep station Jellalabad near Darlington in the Western District.

This western hinterland of Geelong was country inhabited by a pastoral establishment to which Dowling was connected through his brother Thomas and the Wares, and which had been settled by other family friends like the de Littles. They proved a more reliable and fruitful source of patronage than the new merchants, civil servants and professional men of urban Melbourne or Geelong. In fact the number and quality of Dowling's Western District commissions make them the most substantial body of colonial portrait work from the 1850s in Victoria. They can be compared favourably with the lord mayoral portraits commissioned for Melbourne Town Hall, which include Ludwig Becker's superb 1855 full-length oil portrait of Mayor John Hodgson, and other full-lengths by William Strutt of Andrew Russell and Augustus Reeves, the latter two sadly destroyed, along with some forty-four later paintings, in the Town Hall fire of 1925.[8]

The modest Kernot portraits follow the format of Dowling's smaller Tasmanian works. The subsequent Western District portraits greatly extend his previous range and include for the first time large three-quarter-length images that recall the work of Henry Mundy. They are also more complex: Strutt and Claxton had painted group portraits but Dowling is the first in Victoria to paint group portraits that include Europeans and Aborigines together in extensive landscape settings.

After their marriage in Hobart in 1842, Robert's brother Thomas and his wife Maria had farmed in Tasmania, but in 1849 moved across Bass Strait to Victoria. In 1853 Thomas purchased Jellalabad, on Mount Emu Creek, from his brother-in-law Jeremiah George Ware. He went on to become one of the most famous breeders of merino sheep in Victoria and later served in the Victorian Legislative Council; Thomas and Maria's son Charles married his cousin Sarah, daughter of Henry Dowling junior of Launceston. The exact chronology of Robert Dowling's Western District paintings is difficult to chart but probably his *Thomas Dowling* and *Maria Dowling* may be the earliest, and date from 1855. This handsome pair of portraits of his brother and sister-in-law display the same fine character delineation as Dowling's best Tasmanian work. The couple may have sat for the artist in Geelong, where Thomas had business interests. The current elaborate gilt framing of the portraits by the Melbourne framer Isaac Whitehead would have taken place later, when Jellalabad was extensively renovated in the early 1860s.

The *Jeremiah George Ware* and *Anne Ware* portraits (Warrnambool Art Gallery, Warrnambool) (opposite) probably date from later in 1855 and could have been painted at Koort-Koort-Nong, also on Mount Emu Creek, and finished in the artist's studio in Yarra Street, Geelong. They are similar in format to the Jellalabad pair. The portrait of Jeremiah George, senior partner among the Ware brothers, was replicated by Dowling in at least one other version. John Ware, of Yalla-y-Poora, a major patron of Eugene von Guérard, also owned a later copy of Dowling's portrait of his brother, probably by the Ballarat artist Thomas Flintoff (NGV). The strong, bold and feckless character of Jeremiah George Ware is captured in Dowling's 1855 portrait of the skilled cattle breeder and brilliant horseman. Four years later in 1859, at the age of forty-one, he died in a fatal fall from his four-in-hand dog-cart. It is generally assumed that the two 1860 views of his station Koort-Koort-Nong, by Eugene von Guérard, were commissioned in memoriam by his devastated brothers Joseph and John.

Robert Dowling also painted portraits of the McArthur family of Meningoort, neighbours of Jeremiah and Anne Ware, near Camperdown. The existence of an

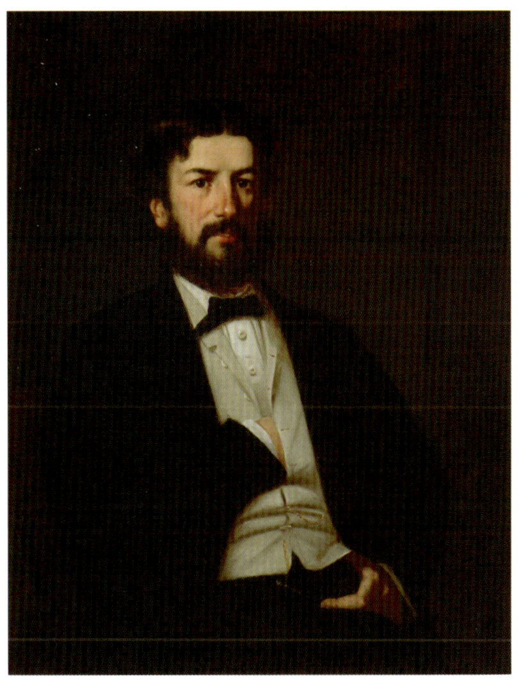

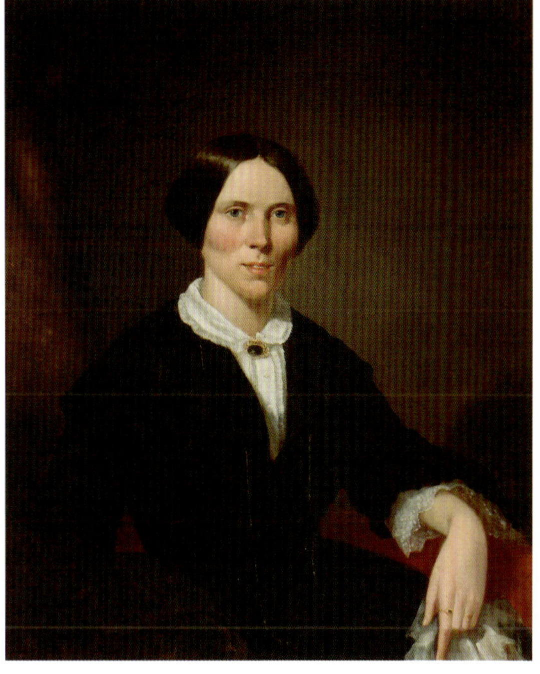

image of Peter McArthur himself has never been established. There is a modest portrait of his bachelor brother Gilbert (private collection), which is more informal than Dowling's usual traditionally structured portraits, more modern and anecdotal, perhaps influenced by photography. It depicts the bespectacled squatter engrossed in a Melbourne agricultural journal, *Bear's Weekly Circular and Rural Economist*, which merged in 1869 into the quintessentially rural *Weekly Times*. In comparison, the three-quarter-length portrait of Gilbert's future sister-in-law, Margaret, recalls the pictorial conventions of the 1840s and in particular Henry Mundy's grand Tasmanian images, complete with architectural accoutrements, of the Lette, Dowling and Field families. Margaret McArthur's portrait is ambitious and one that succeeds in capturing the strong character and quick humour of this Lanarkshire-born Scot. It is a handsome record of a woman whose descendants would give distinguished service to Australia's public life. Robert Dowling was at Meningoort in 1856, painting the resident Aborigine 'King Tom', last of the Mount Elephant Tribe (National Library of Australia, Canberra) (p 94). Peter and Margaret McArthur's marriage

Robert Dowling
Portrait of Jeremiah George Ware
oil on canvas
90.5 x 70.5 cm
Warrnambool Art Gallery
acquired c 1945

Robert Dowling
Portrait of Anne Ware
oil on canvas
74 x 60.5 cm
Warrnambool Art Gallery
acquired c 1945

took place in Geelong in December 1856, some months after Dowling's return to Launceston, so her portrait would pre-date the marriage, perhaps from the time of their engagement. Her portrait was probably Dowling's last commission from those years in Victoria.

Prior to this, from further out and closer to Warrnambool, are two group portraits from late 1855 or early 1856. The first, *Mrs Adolphus Sceales with Black Jimmie on Merrang Station* (NGA) (pp 64–65), was painted on that Hopkins River property near Hexham. The other, the children of Joseph and Barbara Ware, *Masters George, William and Miss Harriet Ware with the Aborigine Jamie Ware* (NGV) (pp 68–69) was painted on neighbouring Minjah. Both are set in landscapes, Merrang's especially extensive and specific to the place. More importantly, because they record social interaction between European and Indigenous Australians, rarely glimpsed in Australian painting of the period, they are perhaps the most fascinating of all Australian group portraits.

The Merrang picture, painted while Dowling was staying with Joseph Ware at Minjah, is much more than a portrait. Adolphus Sceales died in 1855; sometime in late 1855 or early 1856 his young widow, Jane, mother of two small girls, took the rare opportunity of having a professional artist close at hand and commissioned the work; she would have had some say in its complex structure. Wearing a riding habit in full-mourning black, the widow's weeds of the mid-nineteenth century, she stands beside her horse ready to mount, with her springer spaniel at her feet. Another horse, a large chestnut gelding hunter, her late husband's favourite, is saddled up for an absent male rider and held by the Aboriginal groom, Black Jimmie. His late master's mastiff stands nearby. Dowling has created a memento mori: a sort of requiem or poetic tableau set in an elegiac landscape, yet recognisably that of Merrang. The view looks west from the homestead, past haystack and stables, across paddocks dotted with red gums. We know a great deal about Jane, the future matriarch of the Hood family. The young widow was remarried in December 1856 to Robert Hood, who acquired not only a wife but also purchased her late husband's station from the Sceales trustees. We know little about the stable groom in the painting except that he was one of many Indigenous people employed on this large 18 860-acre (7632 ha) station. Another Aboriginal employee was Jeanie, Jane's long-serving housemaid, who died at Merrang in 1899. The local Mopor Aborigines were skilled workers with stock and farm animals, and Jimmie cared for a stable of some twenty-four horses.[9] The work's charm lies in a juxtaposition of sophistication and naivety. The finely painted portrait heads are indicative of Dowling's earlier Tasmanian experience, though their unusual smallness within the composition has more the look of the collaged photographs that James Shaw, in the next decade in Adelaide, would paste onto an oil painting of the South Australian parliament. The painstaking delineation of the figures and animals, in strangely close alignment with the horizon, tells of an artist reaching for a subject bigger than his portraitist training but not beyond his artistic capability. It is unique in Australian colonial art, an image of marital affection and a shared pioneering life cut short.

The similarly engaging group portrait of the children of Joseph and Barbara Ware was painted on Minjah station in the summer of 1856. It is a disarming summer record of the Wares' children: George (born 1851 at Minjah), the standing, centrally placed young heir to the property and its famous Shorthorn stud; his brother William (born 1852); and their two-year-old sister Harriet Kate (born 1854)—who is affectionately seated beside the Mopor Aborigine, Jamie Ware (born c 1819). Their pet dog is included. The painting is testament to the mutual trust and intimacy between the children and Jamie, and by implication their unseen parents. Beneath a great gum tree, the boys are dressed in identical jackets and short skirts, then the fashion for male children. Harriet is wearing a summer frock and holding a hat. The Aborigine Jamie is also dressed in European fashion with trousers, shirt, bow tie and cap, for he worked, according to family tradition, as some sort of guardian for the children and as their father's batman.[10] He remained with Joseph Ware throughout his life until the sale of Minjah to the Affleck family and Ware's death in 1894 in Melbourne. Jamie died in Warrnambool in 1902, aged over eighty, unmarried and without known Aboriginal relatives. He was buried as James Ware, in a public grave in the Warrnambool Cemetery; the funeral was a lonely service conducted by the photographer and naive painter Daniel Clarke (1837–1928), one-time Superintendent to the Church of England Aboriginal Mission at nearby Framlingham and warmly regarded by the Mopor Aborigines.[11]

This children's portrait at Minjah presents many of the same pictorial idiosyncrasies as the mourning portrait at Merrang. There is a similar mixture of sophistication and naivety, the heads delineated with assuredness and photographic clarity, particularly that of Jamie Ware. They are in miniature, though more realistic than the similarly scaled heads in William Strutt's *Maria Elizabeth O'Mullane and her children* c 1854 (NGV), a group portrait painted in a similar oval format a year earlier in Melbourne. There may be an echo of the longstanding British tradition for portrait miniatures—small, painted, personal images on ivory, a fashion then on the wane. Or the manner may be a reflection of the similarly small, but new, daguerreotype portrait images that replaced miniature painting, and with which Dowling was associated. The resolved head studies of the Ware children and their Aboriginal companion contrast with the flat, almost doll-like representation of their bodies—which was no dilemma for the much more sophisticated French-trained William Strutt. Dowling's bodies lack form or substance and were an obvious challenge to his technical skills. Unlike Strutt, he had no art-school or life-class experience. In spite of this, however, sincere warmth and happiness is overwhelmingly expressed in the image. It stands as testament to the family's identification with this Aboriginal man, and his with them.

Ron Radford agrees that Dowling's mid-1850s figure groups, such as this and the Merrang commission, are caught in a transition between the dying art of miniature painting, of which Dowling was a practitioner, and the new rising art of the photographic portrait, with which Dowling was associated as a photographic colourist. Radford believes,[12] though no evidence survives, that Dowling may have used photographs, as he later used Bock's watercolours for his Tasmanian Aboriginal images, in the creation of the faces and perhaps figures of these works painted in Victoria in 1856.

The children's homestead is visible in the distant background of the painting *Jeremiah Ware's stock on Minjah Station* 1856 (AGSA) (pp 66–67), another commission to Dowling from Joseph Ware. Homestead portraits are common in the work of Eugene von Guérard, Thomas Clark and Nicholas Chevalier in Victoria, of Conrad Martens in New South Wales, and before them of John Glover in Tasmania. This example of the type is unique in Dowling's oeuvre.

The modest station complex at Minjah was replaced in 1870 by architect Andrew Kerr's Italianate mansion, in whose drawing-room Dowling's later religious paintings from London were to hang. At the same time, the house paddocks were transformed into a park, laid out in the English manner by the curator of the Warrnambool Botanic Gardens, Charles Scoborio. Dowling's painting records the surroundings prior to that gentrification, and depicts the same lush Western District pastures as in his Aboriginal subjects of the period. The time of day is late afternoon but the homestead is still a hive of bustling activity. Dowling's view of Joseph Ware's station property has none of the Romantic grandeur or dramatic sweep of landscape found in Eugene von Guérard's views of his brothers' two stations: John Ware's *Yalla-y-Poora* 1864 (NGV); and the reciprocal pair of 1860 views of Jeremiah's station *Koort-Koort-Nong homestead, near Camperdown, Victoria* together with *Koort-Koort-Nong homestead, near Camperdown, Victoria, with Mount Elephant in the distance* (NGA). However, it shares with them an invitation for close inspection; in such paintings detail is as much a pictorial element as any overview. Dowling, with a miniaturist's skill, but with less variety than von Guérard or Glover, documents the mechanics of a great working estate. Beneath the distant homestead verandah we can discern figures, including a woman and child enjoying the sunshine. To the left of the homestead is an outbuilding where a woman stokes a fire and another carries a basket of washing; to the right, a farm labourer and dog walk toward a stable. But most important and most prominent in the foreground are portraits of livestock owned by the squatter's brother, pastured not at Jeremiah's Koort-Koort-Nong but at Joseph's Minjah. The Wares were renowned cattle breeders. A horse, and specimens of their famous herd of Shorthorns and Ayrshires, graze frieze-like and side-viewed like cardboard cut-outs, in the paddocks.[13] The most celebrated of these beasts, the bull Master Butterfly, purchased in England for a huge sum on behalf of Jeremiah Ware, died in Australia of heat stroke and was posthumously and prominently recorded by von Guérard in one of his two 1860 views of Koort-Koort-Nong.

Prize livestock portraits and homestead station paintings generally celebrate a 'wilderness' transformed and made productive by their new owners. As well as dynastic memorials, they can be seen as celebrations of colonial progress and possession. They record a new history of the Western District of Victoria, the dynamic of which was to result in the destruction of the way of life of its Indigenous inhabitants.[14] Dowling's more matter-of-fact, less poetic, image of Minjah and its livestock records the same reality as von Guérard's many homestead portraits. Both painters document our European Australian past. Though the history and social mystique of the Western District still survives today, the great landholdings that Dowling and von Guérard painted have long since been broken up, and few survive in original hands. These paintings have become mementoes to another and very different age.

Robert Dowling, who grew up in a colony where the Tasmanian Aborigines had been completely dispossessed twenty years before, was now recording the Victorian Aborigines while they faced a similar, if less horrific, displacement.

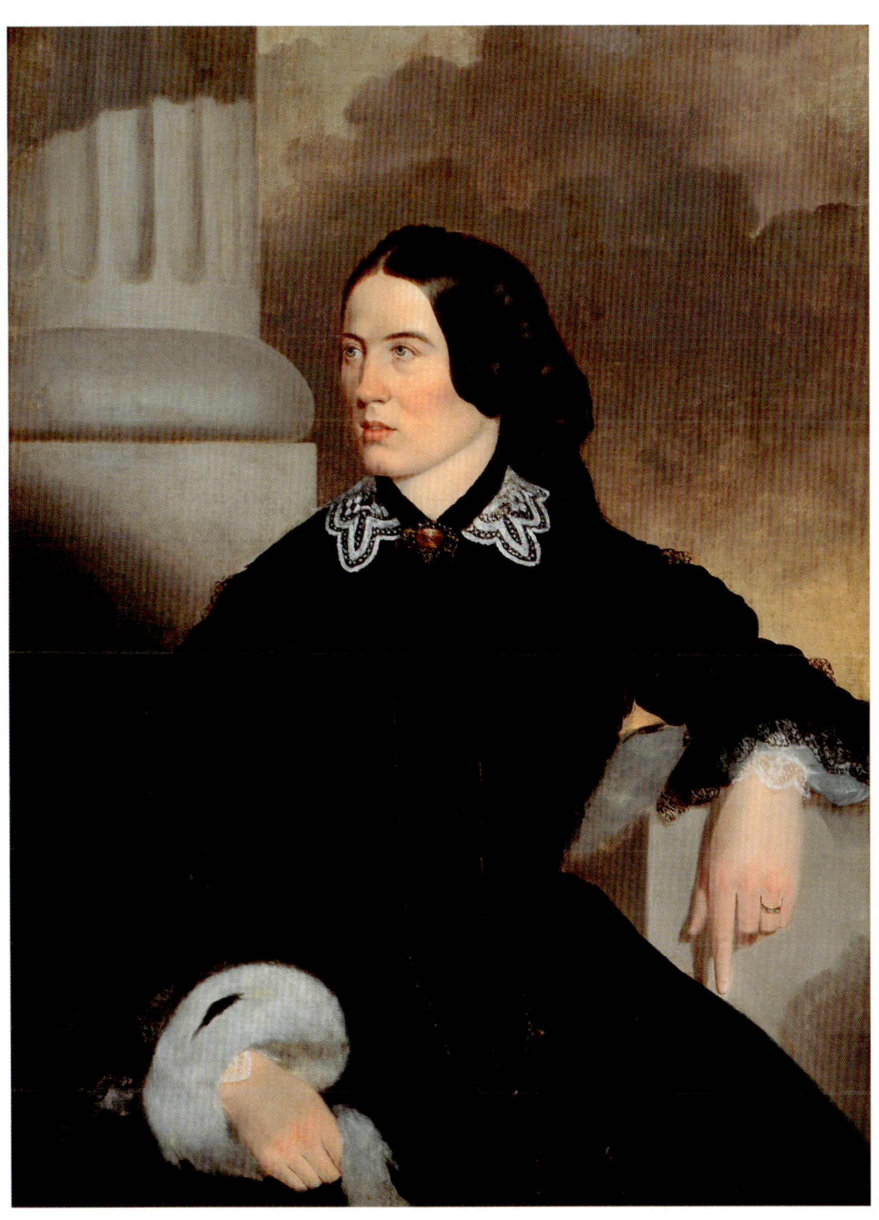

Mrs Margaret McArthur of Meningoort 1856
oil on canvas
Geelong Gallery, Victoria

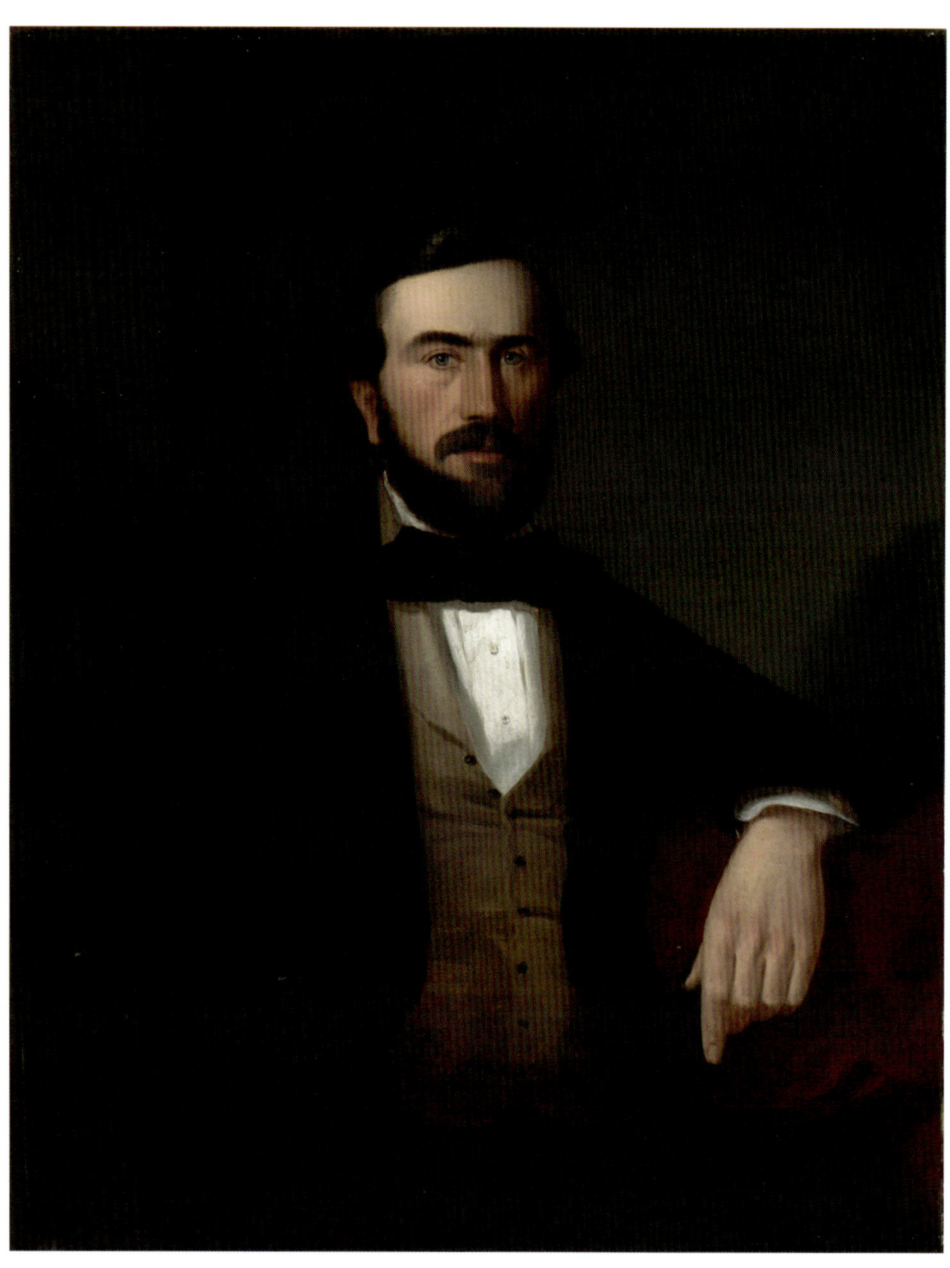

The Hon Thomas Dowling 1855
oil on canvas
National Library of Australia,
Canberra

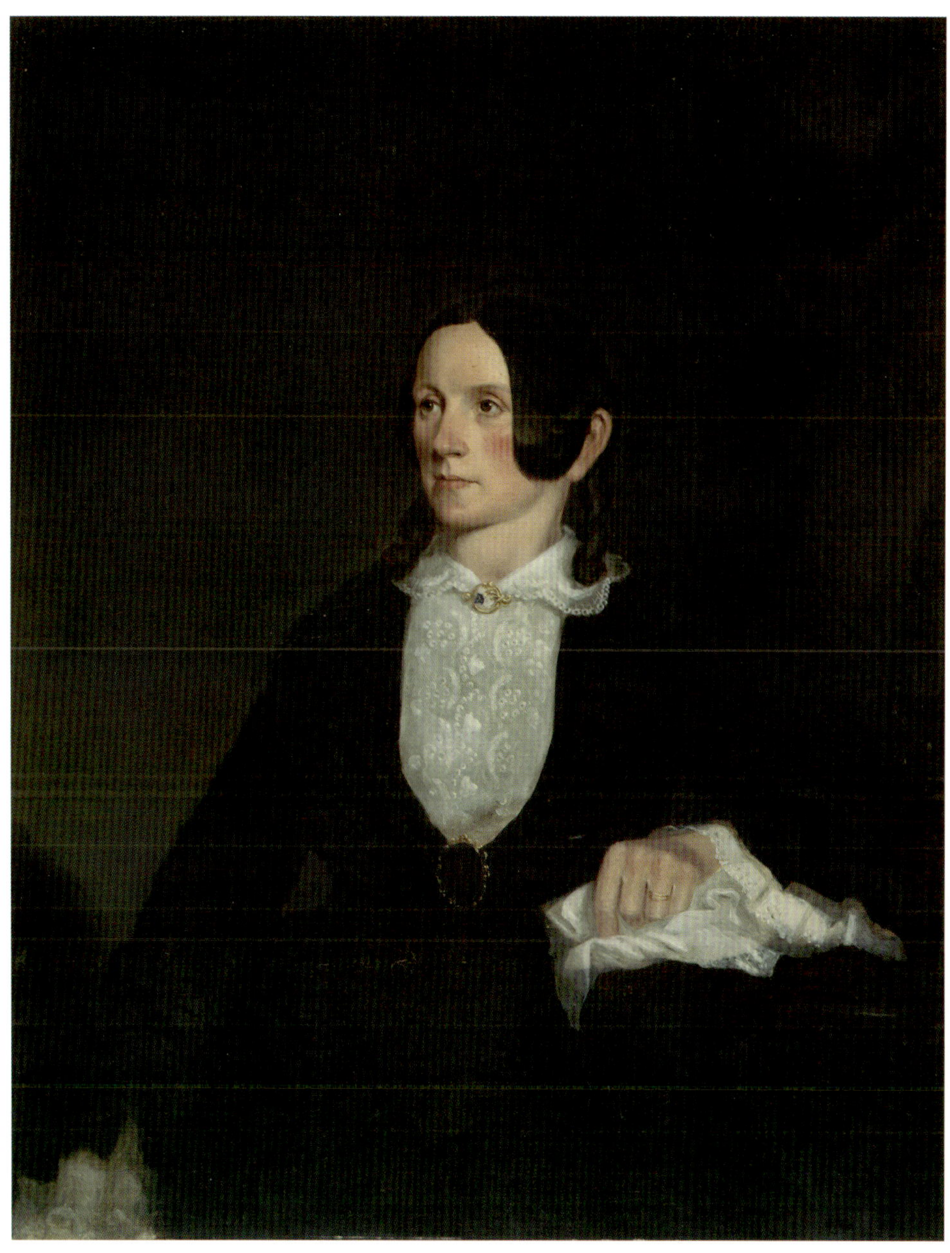

Mrs Maria Dowling 1855
oil on canvas
National Library of Australia,
Canberra

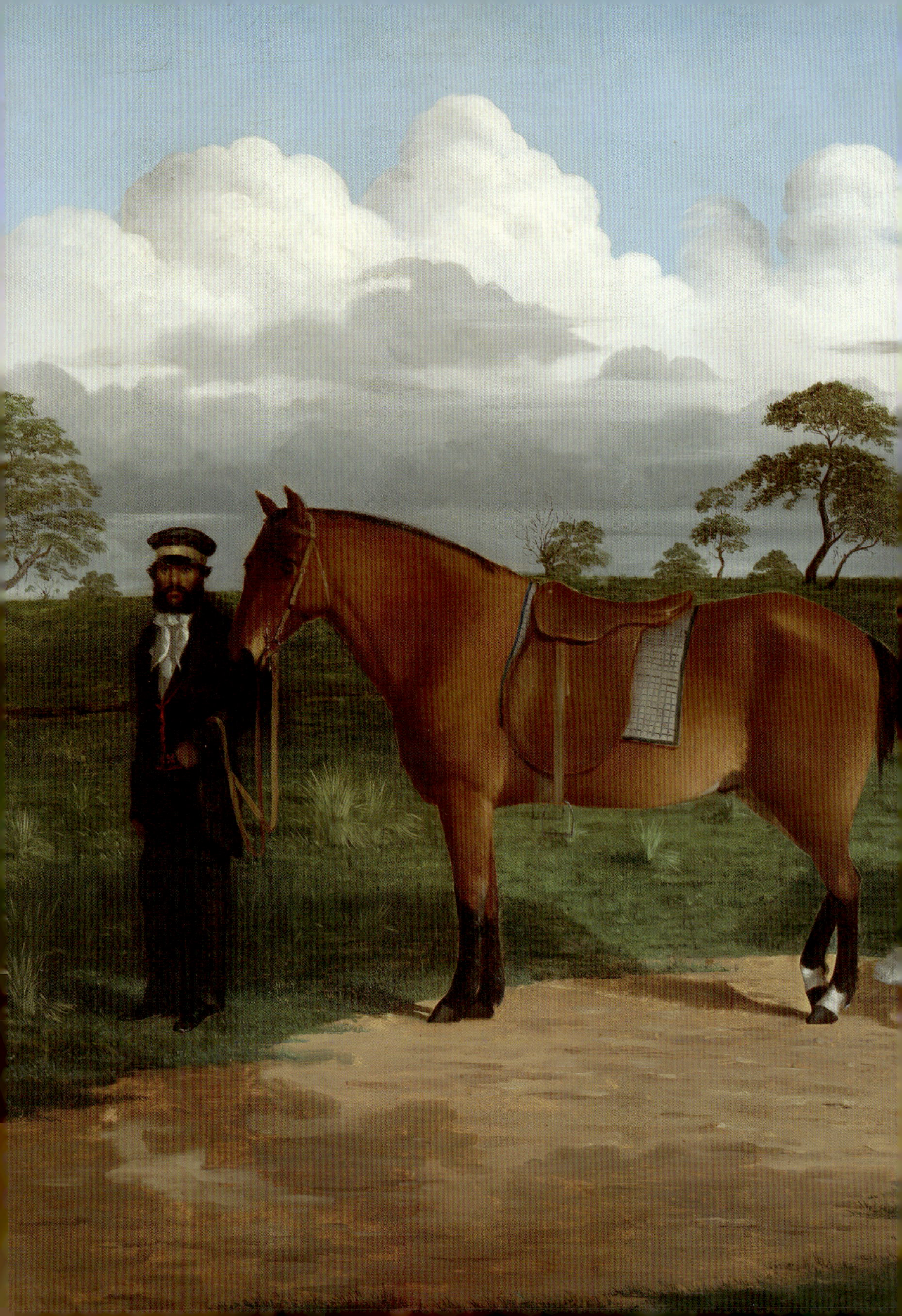

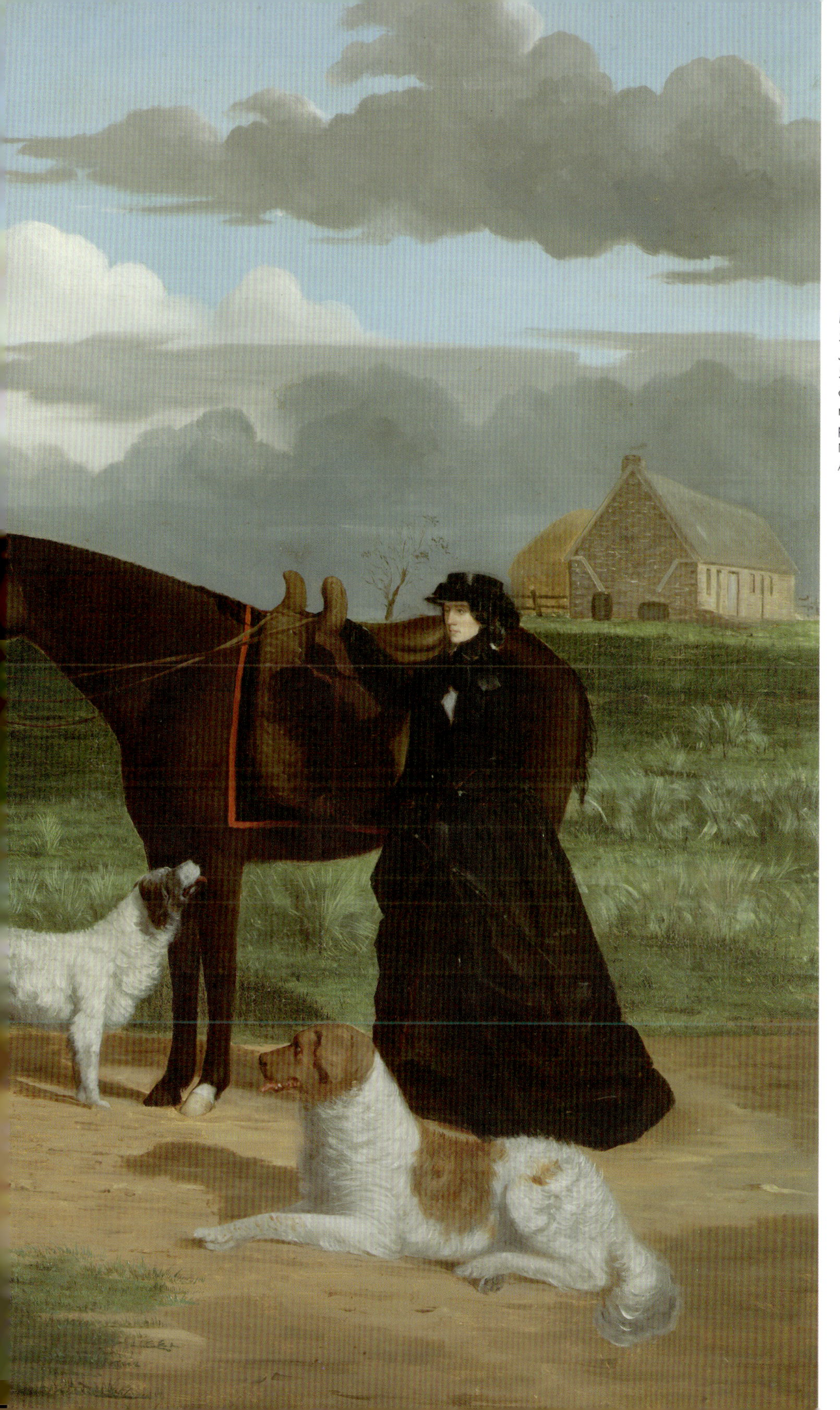

Mrs Adolphus Sceales with Black Jimmie on Merrang Station 1856
oil on canvas mounted on plywood
National Gallery of Australia, Canberra

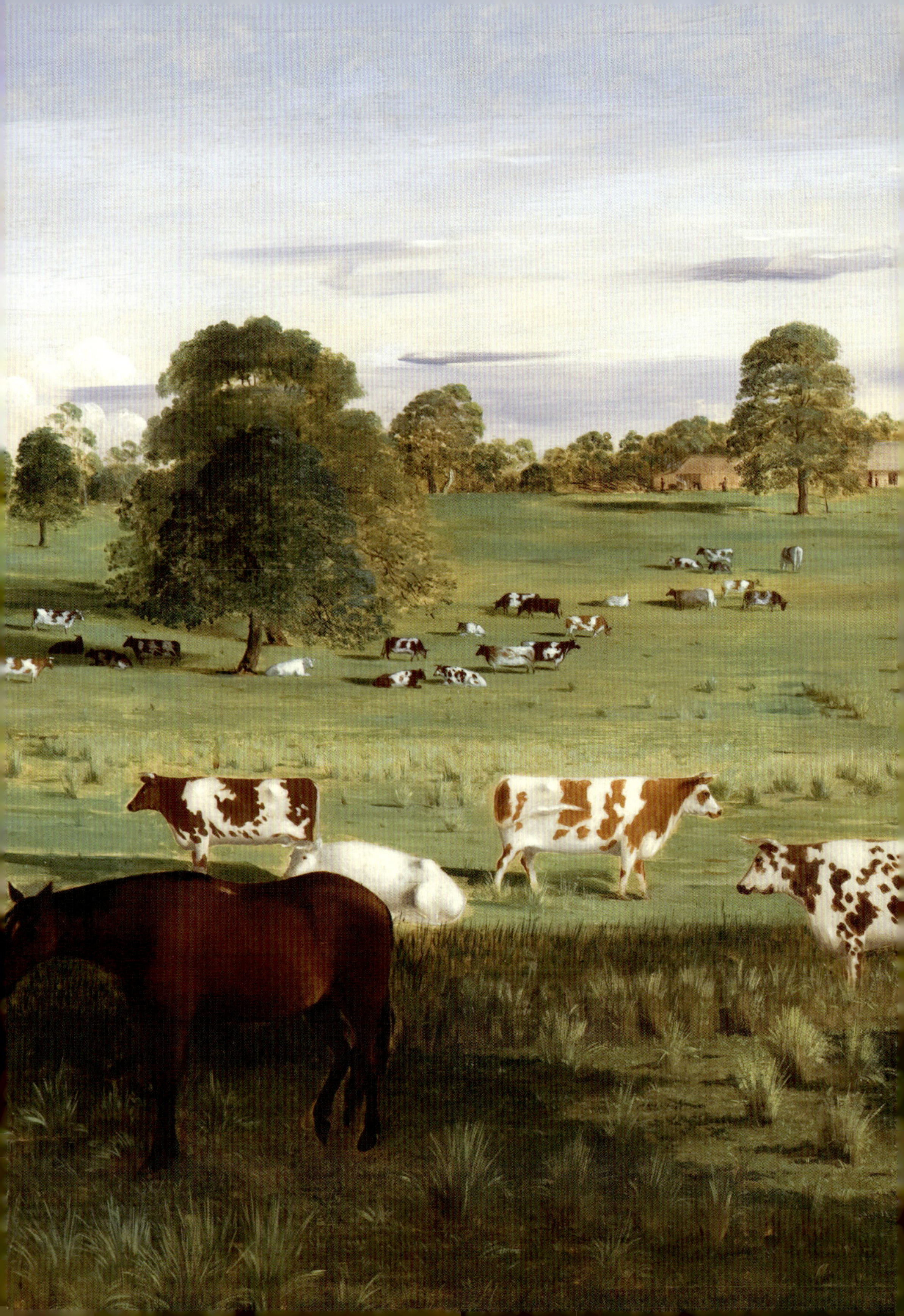

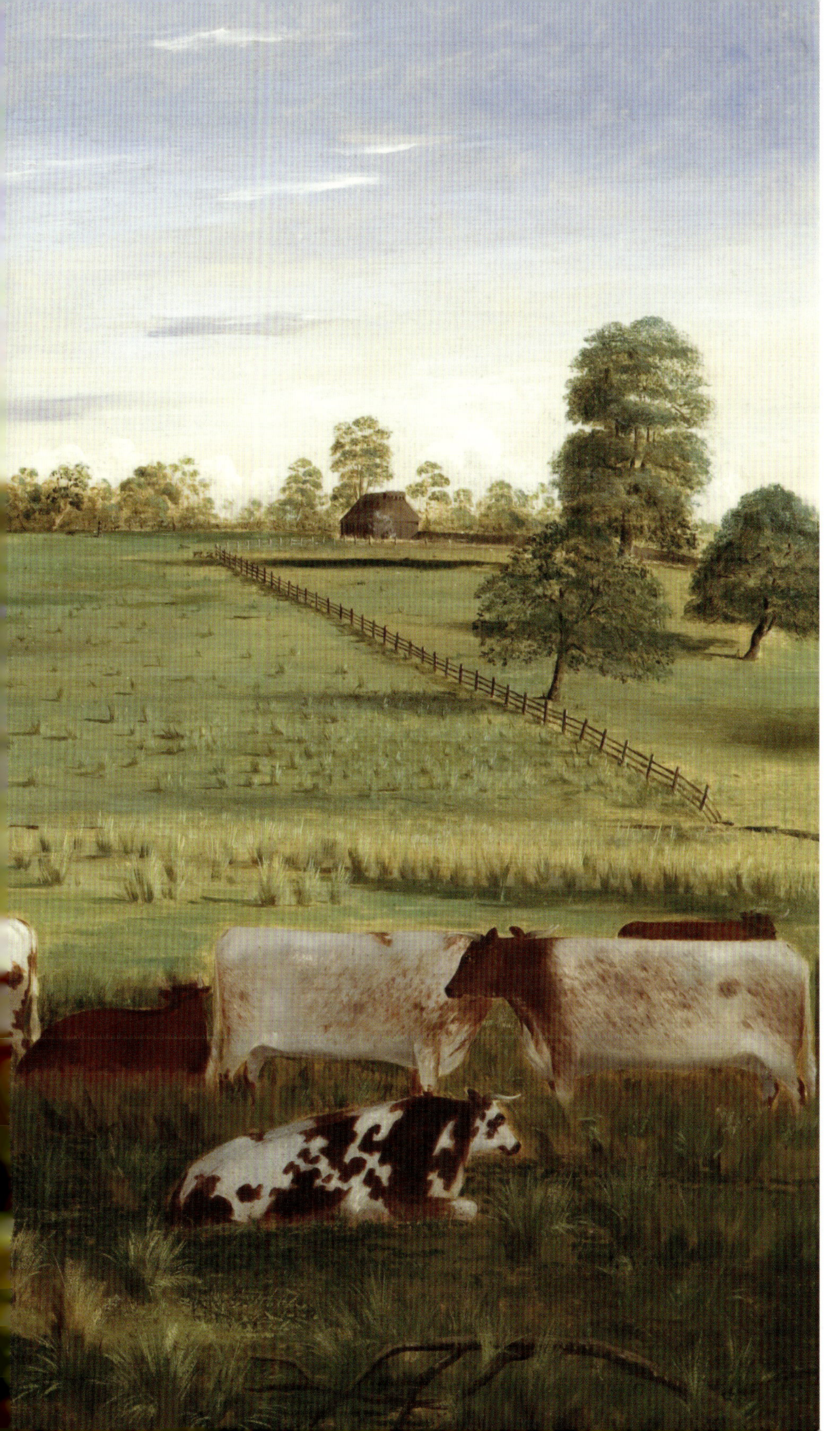

Jeremiah Ware's stock on Minjah Station 1856
oil on canvas
Art Gallery of South Australia, Adelaide

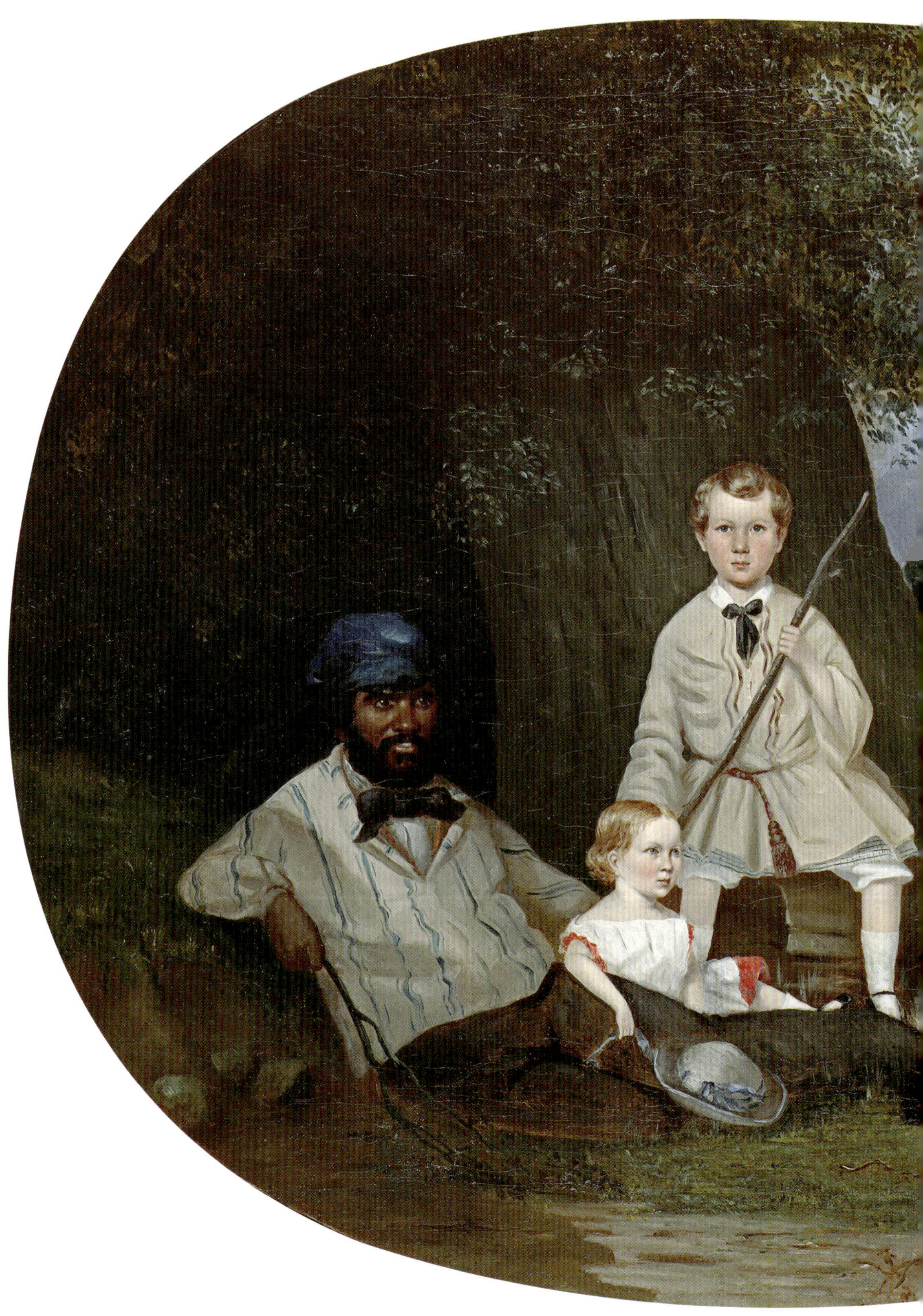

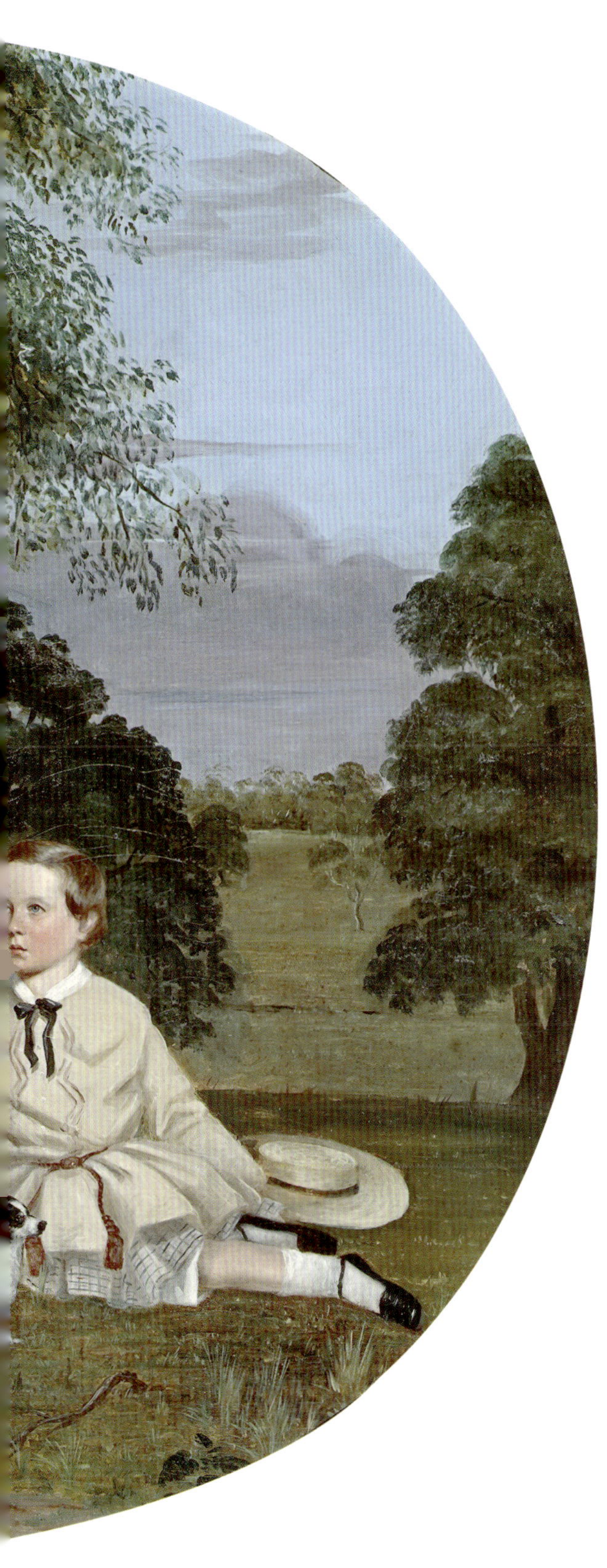

Masters George, William and Miss Harriet Ware with the Aborigine Jamie Ware 1856
oil on canvas
National Gallery of Victoria, Melbourne

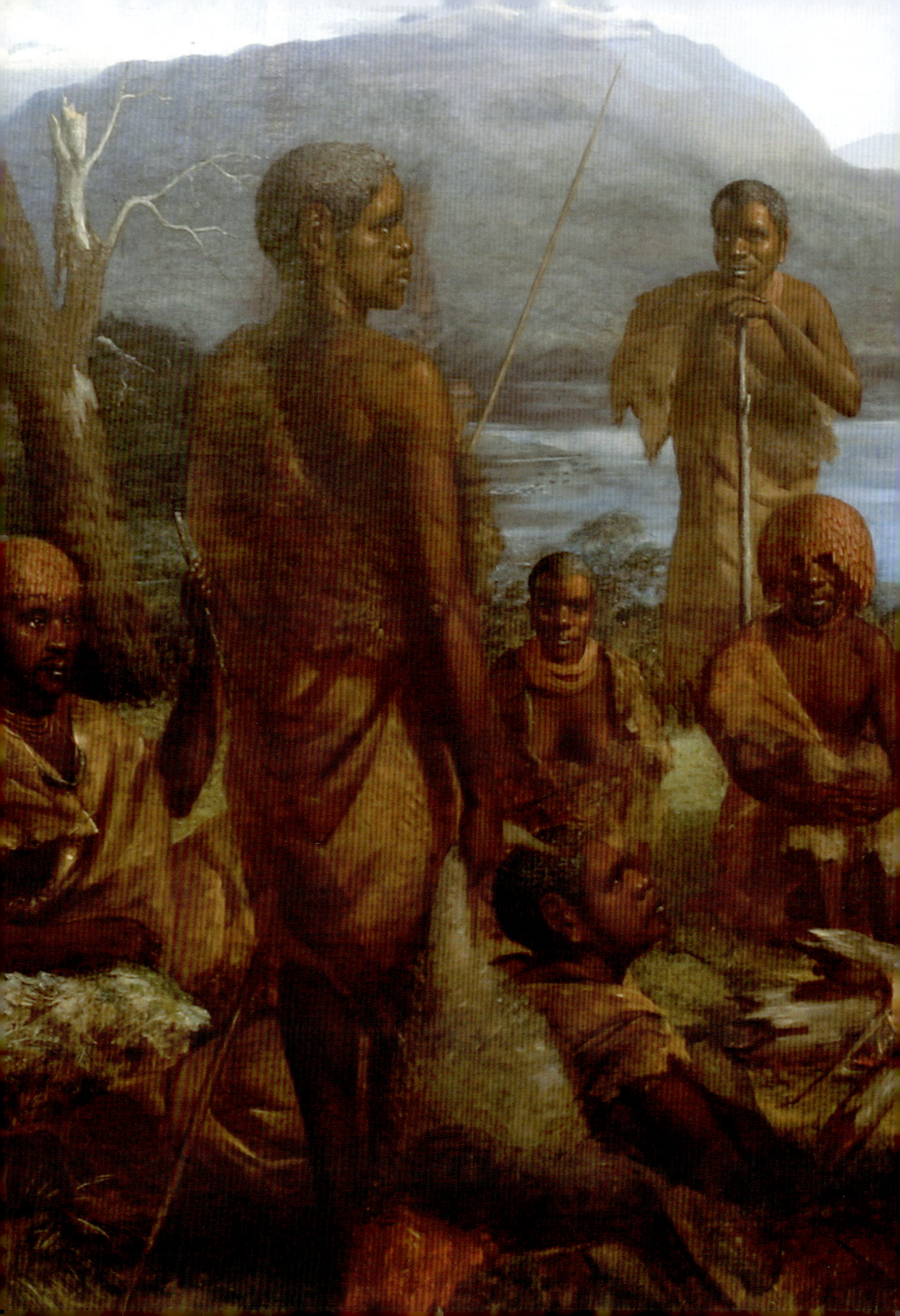

CHAPTER 3

Australian Aborigines: Victoria, Tasmania and London 1856–60

Aborigines of Tasmania 1859 (detail)
oil on canvas
Queen Victoria Museum and Art Gallery, Launceston

Robert Dowling's images of the Indigenous people of Victoria and Tasmania belong to a long tradition. Depictions of the Aboriginal inhabitants of Australia were a preoccupation of European artists, both professional and amateur, in their early voyages of discovery and from the days of Australia's 'First Settlement' in 1788.

Before and around that date are found many anthropological or romanticised images of Aborigines by artists who accompanied the late-eighteenth-century marine explorers, particularly the portraits by John Webber, who accompanied James Cook on his third Pacific voyage of 1776–79. Science was still the principal interest of artists on later post-settlement expeditions: William Westall and Ferdinand Bauer on Matthew Flinders's voyages of 1801–03 and the French artists Charles-Alexandre Lesueur and Nicolas-Martin Petit on Nicolas Baudin's voyages of the same years.

With settlement and direct contact, these images change. Some were still of natural-history interest, some were tawdry satirical cartoons, but most were personal recordings by artists of the Aboriginal people as they saw them, living in their diminishing natural state or in close and wretched contact with the new European communities. Nearly all are works on paper. Among the finest were Thomas Bock's famous 1830s watercolour portraits of the Tasmanian Aborigines, Charles Rodius's 1834 lithographic head studies of the Aborigines of New South Wales, Ludwig Becker's beautiful 1850s drawings of Aborigines around Melbourne, George French Angas's studies of South Australian Aborigines of the 1840s, and Georgiana McCrae's delicate watercolour portraits of the Bunurong people closely involved in the McCraes' life at Arthur's Seat on the Mornington Peninsula south of Melbourne. In a different medium are the miniature wax medallion relief sculptures by Theresa Walker, of South Australian Aborigines in the 1830s and 1840s. These she exhibited at the Royal Academy in London in 1841, the first resident Australian artist whose work was accepted there, some nineteen years before Robert Dowling's painting of Australian Aborigines, *Early effort—art in Australia* (p 95) appeared at that institution in 1860. Other sculptured images of these people were Benjamin Law's Tasmanian works of 1836. Sometimes Aborigines are poetic figures in substantial landscape paintings by John Glover, Alexander Schramm or Eugene von Guérard, and there are fine early 1850s formal portraits by J M Crossland of South Australian Aborigines. It is only in Tasmania in the early 1830s that Aborigines become the subject of ambitious History Painting.

Benjamin Duterrau (1767–1851), a British portraitist, genre painter and printmaker of somewhat eccentric accomplishment, immigrated to Tasmania in 1832. He was supposed to become drawing master at Ellinthorp Hall, the colony's fashionable school for young ladies run by Mrs George Carr Clark, but was thwarted by the appointment of the artist Henry Mundy. The unlikely Duterrau became Australia's first History Painter on the grand scale, fully within the canons of that most elevated of classical late-eighteenth and early nineteenth-century traditions.

He came to Hobart during George Augustus Robinson's Tasmanian expeditions from 1830 to 1834, rounding up the 'wild' remnants of the colony's Aboriginal inhabitants and bringing them into captivity under a Protectorate. This Friendly Mission, at the end of the Black War, freed the European settlers from fear of harassment or worse, and ensured that the full colonisation and appropriation of Tasmania could take place without impediment.[1]

Duterrau initially responded to this tragic epic by painting, in 1833, four large oil portraits of Robinson's celebrated Aboriginal collaborators, Woureddy, Truggernana (Trucannini), Manalargenna and Tanleboyer (TMAG). These were later purchased by governor Sir John Franklin's new colonial administration in 1837, under pressure from some prominent settlers, and were originally hung in the Legislative Council Chamber in Hobart. This was partly to commemorate these compliant 'domesticated' Aborigines for posterity and also because the petitioners believed that as a race the Aborigines had suffered from contact with European settlement and would suffer further from confinement. One of Duterrau's supporters, the historian Henry Melville, believed 'that this race of human beings will soon become extinct altogether '.[2] Subsequently Duterrau embarked on his idea for a 'national picture' that would celebrate the fateful 'concordat' that Robinson achieved in 1834 between the British and Aboriginal nations. He pursued this fraught project and in 1843 realised it on a huge, now lost, canvas some ten feet high and fourteen feet wide (300 x 427 cm). We know something of its pictorial structure from the artist's own projections, in etchings and small relief sculptures, and from two preliminary works—the painting *Mr Robinson's first interview with Timmy* 1840 (NGA) and the slightly larger *The conciliation* 1840 (TMAG). The latter is a complicated figure group full of rhetorical convention and probably commemorates the surrender to Robinson in 1831 of the Big River and Oyster Bay native tribes. Though the artist's admirers hoped the painting would promote racial respect and harmony with the remnant people, it now can be seen conversely as a potent memorial to genocide.

Robert Dowling, growing up in the relatively small community of colonial Van Diemen's Land, would have known of these paintings, for his father, the Reverend Henry Dowling, was a friend of Robinson's. Perhaps, too, the young artist was aware of the sad sale of Duterrau's remaining works, including some fifteen Aboriginal subjects, in Hobart after Duterrau's death in 1851.

Duterrau was not the only artist to paint major oil paintings of the Indigenous Tasmanians in the 1830s. Thomas Napier (1802–1881), a little known Scottish-born painter, arrived in Hobart in 1832, the same year as Duterrau, and also painted substantial portraits: *Woureddy* and *Truggernana* (Trucannini) (TMAG), *Manalargen[n]a* (Savage Club, Melbourne) and the larger *A Tasmanian Aboriginal man* (previously known as *Alphonse the Tasmanian*) (QVMAG). Napier, a devout Baptist from Dundee, was an active member of the congregation in Hobart. He was among those who welcomed the Reverend Henry Dowling and his family to Van Diemen's Land in 1834.[3]

Robinson left Tasmania in 1839 to become Chief Protector of Aborigines on the Australian mainland. Like many other Tasmanian colonists before him—such as Thomas Napier in 1837—this meant relocation to the new settlement at Port Phillip. Napier eventually took up land near Melbourne, around present-day Moonee Ponds, and pursued a successful career as a builder. Throughout the 1840s, Napier continued his artistic interest in Aborigines, executing a portrait, one of many, of the Boonwurrung native '*Jack Weatherly*' (Royal Historical Society of Victoria, Melbourne). In 1843 he exhibited 'two oil paintings of Aborigines of Australia Felix in a bazaar at the Melbourne Mechanics' Institute in aid of the Wesleyan Chapel', along with a number of Aboriginal artefacts from Edward Parker's Loddon Protectorate at Mount Franklin near Daylesford.[4] Napier's paintings thus preceded Robert Dowling's oil portraits of Victorian Western District Aborigines by at least a decade. As late as 1869 Napier exhibited an oil painting, *A native of Melbourne* 1861, probably another Boonwurrung man, in the 1869 Art Treasures Exhibition at the Public Library of Victoria.[5]

The lofty pretensions of these paintings were most fully realised in the portrait sculptures produced in Hobart by Benjamin Law, of *Woureddy, an Aboriginal chief of Van Diemen's Land* 1835 and *Truggernana (Trucannini), wife of Woureddy* 1836 (NGA and other collections). With the encouragement of G A Robinson, the subjects agreed to sit for these portraits, which are Australia's most important sculptures of the early colonial period. They were created in plaster and exist in multiples, with either dark 'bronze' or light 'stone' patination. Their significance was recognised at the time, not just for their ethnographic value but, in their dignity and pathos, as works of High Art. That they shed lustre on the achievements of Tasmanian culture was acknowledged when they were shown in 1837 in the colony's first art exhibition.[6] Robert Dowling grew up with these sculptures close at hand; his brother Henry owned a pair, which he eventually donated in 1879 to the Launceston Mechanics' Institute.

Robinson was almost certainly behind the creation of Thomas Bock's first set of watercolour portraits of Tasmanian Aborigines.[7] Among the seven or so sets that Bock produced between 1831 and 1838, one belonged to Robert Dowling's brother Henry,[8] who knew these people personally.[9] Henry lent his set to Robert, who, at some time in the 1850s, copied the watercolours in small oil sketches, adding atmospheric and sometimes landscape elements. Dowling used these oil sketches to create a four-foot (120 cm) wide painting, *Tasmanian Aborigines* 1856–57 (NGV) (pp 100–101), executed in Launceston, and also as the portrait source for further sketches (NLA) preparatory to two London works—the extremely large painting *Aborigines of Tasmania* 1859 (QVMAG) (pp 102–103) and its small replica, *Group of natives of Tasmania* 1860 (AGSA) (pp 106–107).

If works by Duterrau and Law were the artistic antecedents, and Bock's watercolours the specific portrait sources, for Dowling's compositions of Tasmanian Aborigines, other influences must also be factored in. His Evangelical father, the Reverend Henry, his equally devout brother Henry, and their circle's Christian missionary concern for the wellbeing of all races, all influenced Robert Dowling's perceptions. For example, their friends and fellow Baptists, the Edgars of Hobart, when moving to Port Phillip in 1848, established the Merri Creek Aboriginal School to care for the needs of local Aboriginal children. This Christian concern for the treatment of the Aboriginal peoples was eloquently expounded by the Launceston Congregational minister, the Reverend John West.[10] West was commissioned by Henry Hopkins in 1846–47 to write a history of Tasmania. It was published in 1852, by Henry Dowling junior, in two volumes, the second of which deals with the Aborigines, Aboriginality, and their tragic history since European colonisation. Writing on the collective guilt of both government and settler in the dreadful saga, West noted:

> It is not in the nature of civilisation to exalt the savage. Chilled by the immensity of the distance he [the indigene] cannot be an equal: his relation to the white can only be that of an alien or a slave. By the time astonishment subsides, the power of civilised man is understood, and their encroachment is felt. Fine houses garrison his country, enclosures restrict his chase, and alternately fill him with rage and sadness. He steals across the land he once held in sovereignty, and sighs for the freedom and fearlessness of his ancestors: he flies the track of his invaders, or surprises them with his vengeance;—a savage he was found, and a savage he perishes![11]

West's is the voice of the nineteenth-century reformer, echoed in the Christian paternalism of men like the Archdeacon of Adelaide, the Venerable Mathew Hale, founder in 1850 of a Christian Mission to the South Australian Aborigines at Poonindie, near Port Lincoln. Hale commissioned J M Crossland in 1854 to paint two memorable portraits (NGA) of young natives 'civilised' at Poonindie.[12]

The Tasmanian genocide was so sweeping that Robert Dowling may possibly have seen Indigenous Australians only after moving to Victoria in 1854. Although consigned to history in the popular imagination of the Tasmanian settlers,[13] in Victoria the more populous remnants of the mainland tribes were very visible. Many of these Aborigines by 1854 were living near, and working for the new owners of, the great pastoral estates which, in the Western District, occupied their traditional lands. The distinctiveness of the Aboriginal situation in Victoria has been noted by Richard Broome.[14] Broome maintains that the situation in the new and later settlement of Port Phillip, without significant convict labour and with the presence of more God-fearing settlers, ameliorated earlier hard-line attitudes, and was different from the situation in Tasmania. These factors meant greater Aboriginal participation in the pre–Gold Rush pastoral economy. This was at a time when a modicum of Imperial conscience prevailed, for in 1837, under Evangelical pressure, Westminster ruled that in light of so rapid a territorial expansion, 'the adoption of any line of conduct, having for its avowed or secret object the extinction of the native race, could not fail to leave an indelible stain on the British Government'.[15] This led to the establishment of the short-lived Port Phillip Protectorate, the aim of which was to protect the various Aboriginal tribes, 'civilise' them, and minimise interracial conflict. It failed, and by 1849 the Protectorate was abolished.

This then was the setting for Dowling's paintings of the Victorian Aborigines of the 1850s. This body of work, in all his varied oeuvre, is perhaps the most engaging for the modern viewer.

Two commissioned group portraits, *Mrs Adolphus Sceales with Black Jimmie on Merrang Station* (NGA) (pp 64–65) and *Masters George, William and Miss Harriet Ware with the Aborigine Jamie Ware* (NGV) (pp 68–69), were painted in 1856. They exemplify in their subject matter a world in transition, and record the dynamics of interaction and interface between Aboriginal and European, as discussed in the previous chapter.

Dowling's first group portrait of Victorian Aborigines alone, the painting *Minjah in the Old Time* (Warrnambool) (pp 96–97), is thought to be another commission from Joseph Ware, along with the group of his children and his Aboriginal servant Jamie, and to have been painted in May of 1856.[16] The title, conferred later by Ware's family, denotes history, albeit European. The painting records and illustrates a post-invasion settlement, negotiated between black and white in a new cross-cultural world. The Aborigines depicted are Gunditjmara people of the Spring Creek or Mopor tribe.[17] Some of these people worked as paid labour on Minjah, which is situated on Spring Creek, a small tributary of the Merri River which reaches the coast at Warrnambool. Others were employed on stations nearby—Robert Hood's Merrang or, further out in the Port Fairy district, Paul de Castella's Quamby and James Dawson's Kangatong—as station labourers, wood cutters, stockmen and housemaids. Completing this hybrid readjustment, the Aborigines, encouraged earlier by George Augustus Robinson, took Christian names and the European surnames of the station owners—Jamie Ware, Johnny and Sarah Dawson, Henry Dawson, Johnny and Louise Castella, Jeanie Hood, or the boxer Albert (or Pompey) Austin. Many were evangelised and became Christians.

Robert Dowling's detailed oil sketches (British Museum, London) of the principal participants in this Minjah tableau were identified by him with their Aboriginal or European names, or by titles such as 'King' and 'Queen', or by location, for example 'Victorian native, Port Fairy'.[18] These designations were also used by James Dawson, conservationist, amateur ethnologist, and passionate protector and student of the Aborigines. Dawson's inscriptions can be found on a later series of carte-de-visite photographs by a 'J Harvey of Belfast' (now Port Fairy). Some of these photographs, a type issued for collectors of celebrities, were owned by pastoralist Edward Wilson, others by the Ritchie family (the photographs are now held by the SLV). Dowling's nomenclature for these people, and the hierarchic titles, most likely came from Dawson and suggest some involvement or interest by him in Dowling's project.

The central figure in *Minjah in the Old Time* is 'King Mopor' (Dowling used the spelling Marpoura), otherwise the Mopor 'chieftain' Weerat Kuyuut or 'Eel Spear', who was in his mid fifties. His daughter, 'Queen Mopor', Yarruum Parpurr Tarneen or 'Victorious', sits to his right. She was also known as Louise and was married to Wombeet Tuulawarn, also known as Johnny Castella. Beside her is Muularpurn Yuurong Yaar ('Kangaroo skins cut into stripes'). James Dawson and his daughter Isabella used Yarruum Parpurr Tarneen, Wombeet Tuulawarn, and another Aborigine, Kaawirn Kuunawarn ('King Davie'), as the principal sources for their later study of the customs and languages of the Western District Aborigines. The two standing Aborigines seem to be Johnny Dawson, the head stock-keeper at James Dawson's Kangatong, and his wife Sarah; these are identified in Dowling's oil sketches as 'King Laratong' and 'Queen Laratong' and the latter wears a bone nose-ornament omitted in the finished painting. Johnny Dawson was probably 'Johnny the artist', whom Eugene von Guérard met and sketched and who in turn sketched von Guérard at Kangatong in August 1855.[19]

The same paddocks and homestead complex seen in Dowling's painting *Jeremiah Ware's stock on Minjah Station* are depicted in *Minjah in the Old Time* but the view is from the rear. Aborigines and dogs sit around a smouldering campfire, echoed by the smoking chimneys of the house. Beneath a manna gum, two Aborigines shelter in a mia mia (a small shelter of branches, bark and grasses) beside another fire. The chieftain Weerat Kuyuut wears a hat and furs made from kangaroo or possum. The others wear a mixture of furs or government-ration blankets. Johnny Dawson, who carries an eel spear, boomerangs and a shield, and his wife Sarah, who holds a yam stick, appear as visitors to the campsite. As well as a descriptive record of the Aborigines' place in the new order, *Minjah in the Old Time* illustrates how closely Aboriginal and European people lived together.

The subsequent painting *Weerat Kuyuut and the Mopor people, Spring Creek, Victoria* 1856 (University of Queensland Art Museum, Brisbane) (pp 98–99) includes the same participants, similarly dressed and with much the same appurtenances. Wombeet Tuulawarn (Johnny Castella), is newly introduced and stands behind his wife Yarruum Parpurr Tarneen and father-in-law Weerat Kuyuut. The latter has adorned his hat with plumage, befitting his status. James Dawson later described Weerat Kuyuut as:

> Chief of the nations … a great warrior, and so much feared that he travelled alone all over the country unmolested. He was a professor of languages, astronomy and geography and teacher of the tribes between Portland and the River Leigh near Geelong and from the sea coast to the Grampians. The chief is now about 70 years of age and intends taking a young woman to himself as wife.[20]

Other new figures have been added. An Aborigine identified in Dowling's oil sketch as 'Jimmy of Blackman's River' sits at the right of Weerat Kuyuut as one views the picture. There are also two new, unidentified female figures, one reclining, the other standing with face ochred and holding a yam stick. To the right a mia mia shelters four men also wearing mourning ochre. The same two Aborigines from Kangatong appear on the left but the vegetation behind them is not readily identifiable. The format is much the same but the figure grouping and spatial organisation are more resolved. As in *Minjah in the Old Time*, the heads are fine, lively portrait studies, the result of the artist's Tasmanian training, but these cameos sit awkwardly on anatomically unresolved bodies. The poetic tenor of the grey sky enhances the poignancy of the Aborigines' mourning. Unlike *Minjah in the Old Time*, no European references intrude, apart from the Aborigines' piecemeal wearing of European clothing.

The landscape is beautifully observed, bathed in natural light and recognisably the rich plains of the Western District. The site is most likely that of the now drained Maramook Swamp, some four miles (6.5 km) west of the Minjah homestead.[21] This was the location, according to local European mythology, of 'King Mopor's throne' and the tribe's main meeting place, the heart of their country (in the Aboriginal understanding of that word). Did Dowling know this or did the participants request it? It is tempting to believe both possibilities. But if *Minjah in the Old Time* was indeed a commission, the motivation for this second Spring Creek work is unclear. Dowling's Tasmanian legacy has been discussed previously. Were there more immediate, locally Victorian factors influencing the artist in 1855–56? Was he encouraged by James Dawson to paint this subject matter?

Dawson could have met Robert Dowling in Melbourne or Geelong or when the artist was working in the Warrnambool area. The unusually Aboriginal-minded squatter had had contact with Eugene von Guérard, from whom he commissioned two paintings, the landscape *Tower Hill* 1855 (Warrnambool) and a cattle muster by Aboriginal stockmen, *Cutting out the cattle, Kangatong* 1855 (Benalla Art Gallery, Benalla) which Dowling may well have seen. Other works by von Guérard from 1854–55 might have had more resonance and impact on Dowling. Arriving in Victoria, he could have seen the paintings *Aborigines met on the road to the diggings* 1854 (NLA), a dramatic figure group of Aborigines hunting, and the Aboriginal genre painting *Barter* 1854 (Geelong)—both exhibited in November 1854 in the Melbourne Exhibition in conjunction with the Paris Exhibition 1855. Dowling could also have seen another painting, *Warrenheip Hills near Ballarat* 1854 (NGV), depicting Aborigines in their natural state in an idyllic landscape. This was displayed by von Guérard in September 1854 in Dr Frederick Wilkie's music shop in Collins Street, near where Dowling had briefly taken a studio. Von Guérard, too, had a studio in Collins Street, from 1854 to 1862.

Von Guérard's *Tower Hill* records, in a sweeping landscape, the primal state of that geological marvel near Warrnambool and so dear to Dawson. It was von Guérard's first panoramic and romantic landscape and includes a group of encamped Aborigines in the foreground—a figure-group device in the arcadian landscape tradition to catch a viewer's interest, but nevertheless one probably requested by the patron. The work received critical acclaim from James Smith, *The Argus* art critic, when shown in Melbourne. Dowling may have seen it there or at Kangatong, where von Guèrard was working in the autumn of 1856. That Robert Dowling met von Guérard is confirmed by his brother Henry: writing in 1877 to the trustees of the National Gallery of Victoria, who by then had appointed von Guérard as their curator, Henry Dowling mentions that the two knew each other.[22]

While Dowling was at work painting the Mopor Aborigines, an article appeared in the Melbourne *Argus* lamenting their fate and seemingly inevitable extinction:

> We assert that under the present circumstances this country has been shamelessly stolen from the blacks. We have made them outcasts from their own land and are rapidly consigning them to entire annihilation. This is what we should do for the few of them left, comparatively. We should feed and clothe every one of them. We would have local establishments constituted as centres for their concentration. We would give them medical assistance, protection and advice. We would educate them if we could—(Christianise them too, letting the meal-cask, the flour barrel and the sugar bag wait heavily upon the Bible).[23]

This view, and an awareness of the Protectorate's failure, was widely held by many of the Christian colonists in Victoria, including Dowling and his Western District family. It was not James Dawson's belief; he held that Aborigines should be able to move wherever they wanted, and be free to retain their traditional beliefs and customs. He dismissed the value of conversion.

Robert Dowling returned from Geelong to Launceston in late 1856, determined, and perhaps encouraged by his brother Henry, to turn the descriptive images of his Victorian experience into a significant memorial to the Aborigines of his homeland Tasmania.

This was first realised in his painting *Tasmanian Aborigines* 1856–57 (NGV). When that painting and *Weerat Kuyuut and the Mopor people, Spring Creek, Victoria* 1856, were shown together at Mr Tozer's watchmaker's shop in Launceston in March 1857, *The Examiner* noted that these groups of the

Aborigines of Victoria and Tasmania were portraits of well-known individuals and declared:

> We would like to see these pictures preserved in some public institution as memorials to the original occupiers of this land, who have all but disappeared before the onward progress of the white man.[24]

These paintings eventually achieved the status of memorials in honour of the Aboriginal inhabitants of Australia.

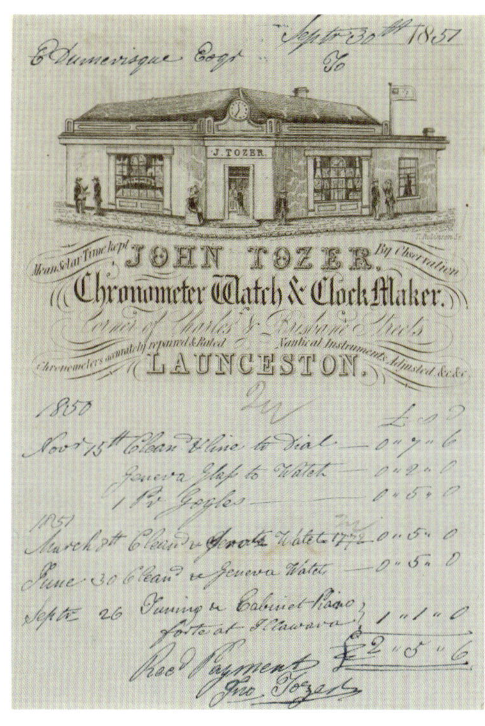

Thomas Robinson
Billhead: John Tozer, Chronometer, watch and clock maker, Launceston 1851
line-engraving on paper,
16.1 x 11.4 cm
National Gallery of Australia, Canberra

After Dowling left Victoria, *Minjah in the Old Time* was lent, under Charles Kernot's name, to the Geelong Mechanics' Institute exhibition in April 1857.[25] Kernot was perhaps acting for Joseph Ware or jointly with the artist, for it subsequently hung at Minjah, until given in 1886 by Ware to the newly established Warrnambool Art Gallery. The two other paintings, *Weerat Kuyuut and the Mopor people, Spring Creek, Victoria* and *Tasmanian Aborigines*, were never sold and remained in Dowling's family well into the twentieth century. The latter was purchased from the family in 1948 by the Director, Daryl Lindsay, for the National Gallery of Victoria. The former, after rejection by the State Library of Victoria, was given by Miss Marjorie Dowling to the 'Anthropological section' of the University of Queensland in 1952; it is now held by that university's art museum.

Of these two works, the Victorian composition was based on sketches made there from life in 1856, whereas the Tasmanian composition was recreated history. We do not know when Dowling made his oil studies from Thomas Bock's 1830s watercolours, for he had access to his brother's set over a long period of time. Stylistically Dowling's sketches date from the early 1850s, so they could have been made before the artist left Tasmania in 1854 or, being small and portable, while in Victoria in 1854–56, allowing him to embark on *Tasmanian Aborigines* on his return to Launceston in late 1856, and have the painting ready for exhibition there by March 1857.

Henry Dowling's set of Bock watercolours of the Tasmanian Aborigines comprised nine portraits and five monochrome blue profiles. Dowling copied them in oil sketches which correspond with Bock's watercolours; some of the profiles and the portrait of Manalargenna, who appears in the finished oil, have not survived among Dowling's copies. They differ from Bock's originals in some colour aspects but, more importantly, by the addition of atmospheric or landscape backgrounds. Two of the oil sketches, the arch-topped *Tunnerminnerwate* and *Problatena*, have full landscape settings with foliage, which suggests that Dowling planned from the start to realise them in a figure group in an extensive landscape.[26]

Ten figures constitute the central group in the 1856–57 *Tasmanian Aborigines.* These were identified by Dowling on the reverse of the canvas by name and 'country', the inscriptions revealed in recent conservation work by Michael Varcoe-Cocks of the National Gallery of Victoria. Those in frontal view are Woureddy, Bruny Island; his wife Truggernana ('Trucannini'), Recherche Bay; Larratong, Cape Grim; Tunnerminnerwate ('Jack'), Cape Grim; Problatena ('Jimmy'), Hampshire Hills; Manalargenna ('Chief'), East Coast. Those in profile are Maulboyheener ('Timmy'), East Coast; Numbloote ('Jinny'), Port Sorell; and Wortabowigee ('Jinny'), West Coast. One reclining figure is not identified.

As Terence Lane has observed,[27] it is a pictorially sophisticated work. The grouping is more complex than the previous compositions executed in Victoria; the figures are more resolved anatomically, integrated with the landscape, and posed with references to the Antique. Unlike the Victorians, the Tasmanians all wear traditional clothing and hair adornment. The landscape, a rock-strewn Tasmanian wilderness with a distant bright mountain range, has authority and resolve, its tonality recalling the work of von Guérard. The middle ground to the right is deeply shadowed and inhabited by numerous spectator Aborigines,[28] perhaps a symbolic reference by the artist to the whole Tasmanian race. This is History Painting, and was recognised as such by Dowling's contemporaries. *The Cornwall Chronicle* remarked upon the 1857 Launceston exhibition:

> Such works of art as these become more valuable with age, even now they must be looked on as Historical paintings, of the primitive state of society in these colonies, banished by the light and progress of civilization.[29]

Realisation of the sentiments expressed in the *The Examiner*'s review of the same exhibition, regarding worthy placement 'in some public institution', would come in the following years with two subsequent compositions, both painted in London. Dowling left Tasmania for England on the *Pharamond* in April 1857, with the assistance of a subscription from Launceston well-wishers, intending to study at the Royal Academy Schools. During 1858 and 1859, his time for academic study of the figure, he prepared a six-by-twelve-foot (1.8 by 3.6 m) heroic canvas, as a reciprocal gift to the citizens of Launceston. Its subject again was the Tasmanian Aborigines.

A munificent gesture to the place of his upbringing this painting may have been, but a sum of 350 guineas had to be raised by yet another local subscription for framing and freighting the work out to Tasmania. This subscription was adroitly and patriotically linked with a commission for Dowling to paint copies for Launceston of formal portraits of Queen Victoria and her Consort, Prince Albert.[30]

The huge new painting from London, *Aborigines of Tasmania* 1859, was intended for inclusion in the art exhibition that celebrated the opening of the new Hall of the Launceston Mechanics' Institute on 9 April 1860. It arrived on the *Seaflower* from England a little late and was unveiled on 23 April. *The Examiner* reported:

> The Tasmanian picture of the Aborigines by Robert Dowling consists of portraits, and the figures stand out with stereoscopic effect. This large painting is a gift to the institute, and contrasts strongly with the picture by the late Mr Duterau [*sic*] of Hobart Town.[31]

This contemporary comparison with Duterrau is illuminating. Dowling's large 1859 work was recognised as being in the elevated History Painting tradition of Duterrau's *The conciliation* 1840 and his lost 'National Picture' 1843. Dowling's work was seen as superior to these. On 28 August *The Examiner* declared:

> the improvement of Mr Robert Dowling in his art is something marvellous … the pictures he has painted since he reached England establish his right to rank highly among the artists of the day.[32]

In London, Dowling began his preparations by working up large oil sketches from his earlier oil-sketch copies of Bock's watercolour portraits.[33] He refined the anatomy and posing of the figures, using live models at hand, perhaps in Leigh's Academy,[34] to create a composition very different from the Launceston canvas of 1856–57. He enlarged the number of participants to twelve, 'all of whom however, have now passed away from this their native land' as *The Cornwall Chronicle* incorrectly noted in its 1860 review. Dowling added to the six depicted previously in frontal poses the figures of Wortabowigee and Maulboyheener. New profiles of Numbloote and Truggernana (Trucannini) supplement those of Maulboyheener and Manalargenna and the previous profile of Numbloote has been dropped. The artist has sometimes used the same person twice, either front or side view, to construct the figure group. The central, seated figures of Woureddy and Truggernana have been rearranged and the placement of the others radically broken up, creating a more complex but less satisfying composition. The standing figures of Maulboyheener, and the firestick-carrying Tunnerminnerwate, are markedly different in their poses. They, with the other standing figures, look inwards to the seated central group and campfire, nestled beside an ancient tree-stump and log. This creates the sense of inter-communication between figures, the 'stereoscopic' quality commented on in *The Examiner* review.[35]

Dowling had learnt the importance in London of narrative subject matter, so popular in contemporary British art. The painting tells a story. Maulboyheener has been hunting and carries a dead wallaby, soon to become the Aborigines' meal. His wife Numbloote carries a young child. Tunnerminnerwate, on the far right, carrying another wallaby or kangaroo, has been drawn from afar to the smoking campfire and smiles in greeting. A conversation is taking place between Manalargenna and other seated Aborigines.

The figures are much larger than in the 1856–57 painting and, filling the foreground rather than sitting deep within the pictorial space, their encampment dominates. Paint is more broadly handled, not only in the figure composition but also in the background, a wild Tasmanian coastal landscape of rugged mountain ranges to the sea. It is impressive in scale, intent and competence, but although the 1859 *Aborigines of Tasmania* is a more brooding and melancholic depiction of these people it lacks the freshness and clarity of Dowling's earlier Australian treatment of the subject. Distance in London may account for this. It also affects his depiction of the Tasmanian topography. The landscape setting of this painting may not be the specific wilderness location indicated by William Moore's 1930s usage of the title *Tasmanian Aborigines: scene in the Bay of Fires*,[36] which had some currency in Launceston for a number of years in the early twentieth century. Tasmania's landscape is often dramatic and unforgettable, but the Bay of Fires on Tasmania's far north-east coast is not mountainous like the south-east around Hobart, and this London painting is most likely 'a composition of the artist's memory and … purely Tasmanian', as Launceston's *The Cornwall Chronicle* put it in 1860.

Unlike the works by Duterrau, which on his death faded into obscurity until their revival in the 1960s, Dowling's *Aborigines of Tasmania* was at once given the institutional status and fame that Duterrau had sought in vain. This was achieved by Robert's presentation of the work to the Launceston Mechanics' Institute and the place of honour given to it in the Institute's great lecture hall. Later, in 1891, as contemporary photographs of the interior show, it was, with its massive gilt frame,[37] the key exhibit in Launceston's newly established Queen Victoria Museum & Art Gallery, where it continued to enjoy its position as 'the first national and historical painting possessed by the people of Launceston'.[38] And it was the whole of Tasmania's pride when prominently displayed in the Tasmanian Court at the Sydney International Exhibition of 1879 and the Melbourne International Exhibition the following year. In Launceston it has rarely been off public display.

Although some of Louis Buvelot's, Thomas Clark's and especially H J Johnstone's paintings were copied by others, Dowling's *Aborigines of Tasmania* is among the few Australian, certainly Tasmanian, colonial oil paintings to be copied on a substantial scale by another artist in the nineteenth century. The image was replicated by the Tasmanian artist and photographer Richard J Nicholas (working 1883 – c 1896), some time in the early 1880s.[39] Nicholas had his large copy framed in Melbourne by John Thallon, and exhibited it at the Melbourne Centennial Exhibition of 1888, two years after Dowling's death in 1886. That copy, its ownership insecure, is now in the collection storage of the National Gallery of Victoria.

In London in 1860, Dowling painted a small version of the great Launceston canvas.[40] This was purchased by the Ethnological Society, London. In it he made some minor modifications to the composition and altered the figure of Maulboyheener, giving him two boomerangs to hold in his right hand instead of the wallaby of the large version. Boomerangs, a common hunting tool and sometimes battle weapon on the mainland, were unknown to the Tasmanians. A photograph of this small 1860 canvas, an almost identical composition to the 1859 show-stopper, became available for purchase at Walch Bros in Launceston from 1861. With no local knowledge of this second version, Launceston locals in the 1890s were speculating that their large painting had been altered. It was assumed, mistakenly, that the adjustment had been made either by the artist or another hand, to conform to historical accuracy.[41] The Ethnological Society was formed in London in 1843, a breakaway group from an earlier Aborigines' Protection Society, founded in the aftermath of the early nineteenth-century British Quaker campaign against the African slave trade. This new society was formed to be a depository for the collection and systematisation of observations made on human races, and already had some Australian items in its collection. These included a set of seven of Thomas Bock's watercolours of Tasmanian Aborigines, purchased by its Secretary, William Cull, in 1851. At some stage they were supplemented by stone-coloured versions of Benjamin Law's busts of Truggernana and Woureddy. The Ethnological Society eventually morphed in 1871 into the Royal Anthropological Society of Great Britain & Ireland. In the 1980s, strapped for cash, the Society sold its Australian holdings: the Law busts went to the Art Gallery of Western Australia, and in 1988 Dowling's *Group of natives of Tasmania* 1860 was sold to the Art Gallery of South Australia, along with the remnants of the Bock watercolour set of Tasmanian Aborigines.

Also in 1860, Dowling painted his last work to include Australian Aborigines. This was his second Royal Academy exhibit, a complex autobiographical subject titled *Early effort—art in Australia* (NGV) (p 95).[42] It depicts two male and two female Aborigines posing outdoors for a young artist seated at an easel by the entrance to his family's home. One of the artist's models wears the bone nose-ornament seen on Sarah Dawson in one of Dowling's Victorian oil-sketch portraits; in the middle distance, tiny figures of Aborigines are moving around a campsite.[43] Unlike Dowling's other depictions of Aborigines, these four are not identifiable individuals but, rather, generic Noble Savages at the edge of an imaginary wilderness. That they are Australian is confirmed by the title of the painting and by various Indigenous paraphernalia: hair ornament of kangaroo claws, a woven reed carry-basket, and a spear and boomerangs. These were studio props that Dowling had collected in Australia and taken with him to Europe. (Von Guérard collected similar props.) Apart from this identification, the figures stand as any pre-settlement, hunter-gathering, warrior people of old, posed before a group of Europeans. In contrast, the Europeans are real, individuated people. In front of a settler's hut, Robert Dowling depicts himself as a young colonial artist at work surrounded by an encouraging family group, in which are recognisable his father, the Reverend Henry Dowling, and his brother Henry, with wife Eliza. Various nephews and nieces provide further anecdotal notes: a child plays with one of her uncle's paint brushes and smears her smock with a tube of oil paint. Towards the back of the group stands the artist's wife Arabella, holding their baby daughter Marian. The thirty-three-year-old artist's self-image as a youth emphasises that this composition is a public show of gratitude, at his moment of some metropolitan success, towards his always supportive family.

Whatever ideologies regarding interracial relations and present-day discourse on disempowerment and the Imperial agenda can be read into this strange work,[44] it is first and foremost a personal recording by the artist about himself and his professional journey. It is a statement about his budding career as a professional painter in the colonies, reinforced by the still-life details outside the cottage of saddle and equestrian equipment—references to his first employment as a saddler before turning to art. *Early effort—art in Australia* celebrates Dowling's colonial apotheosis. He had by 1860 created a series of works that realised his ambition of 1856 to depict the Indigenous peoples of Australia in images of national significance. He intended that this moving body of work should constitute a lasting memorial to the first Australians.[45]

Nevertheless, Dowling also painted *Early effort—art in Australia* to advertise himself in 1860 to the largest possible British audience. He was the first Australian-trained artist to exhibit at the Royal Academy. He was making a statement to his contemporaries in an over-crowded artistic world at the heart of Empire. He was claiming not only his individuality but also the exotic nature of his colonial background. In 1859 he had signed and inscribed *Sabbath in the country*, his first painting exhibited at the Royal Society of British Artists, as being by Robert Dowling 'from Tasmania'.[46]

Robert Dowling
after Thomas Bock
(1790–1855)
Larratong, of Cape Grim, Van Diemen's Land
1853–54 or 1854–56
oil on board
The British Museum, London

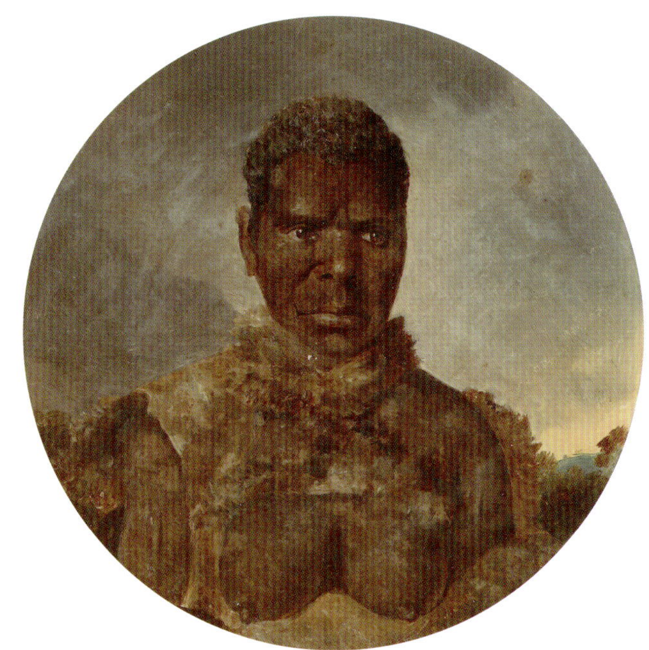

Robert Dowling
after Thomas Bock
(1790–1855)
Truggernana (*Trucannini*), *of Recherche Bay, Van Diemen's Land*
1853–54 or 1854–56
oil on board
The British Museum, London

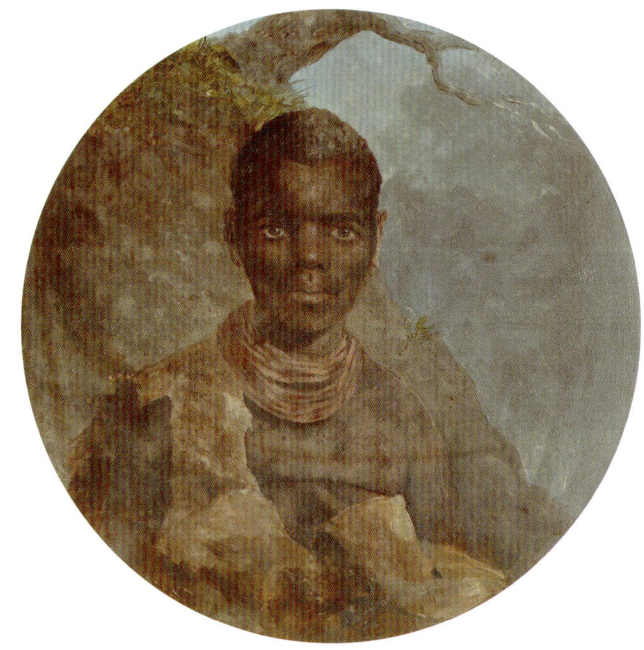

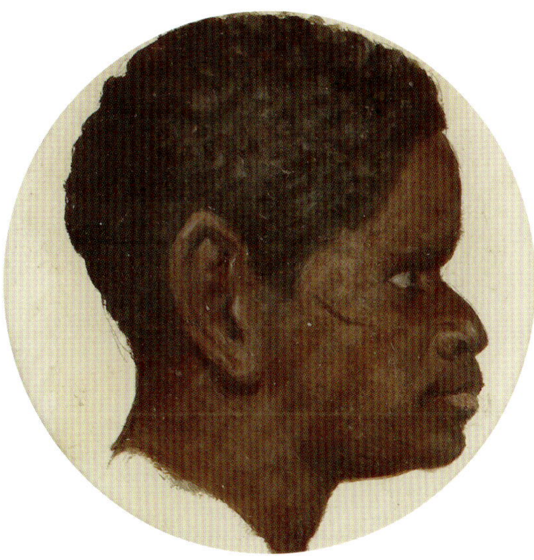

Robert Dowling
after Thomas Bock
(1790–1855)
Jinny, profile 1853–54
or 1854–56
oil on board
The British Museum, London

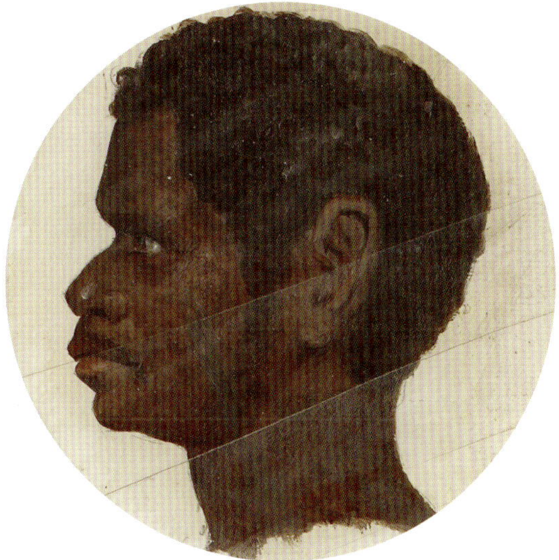

Robert Dowling
after Thomas Bock
(1790–1855)
Jimmy, profile 1853–54
or 1854–56
oil on board
The British Museum, London

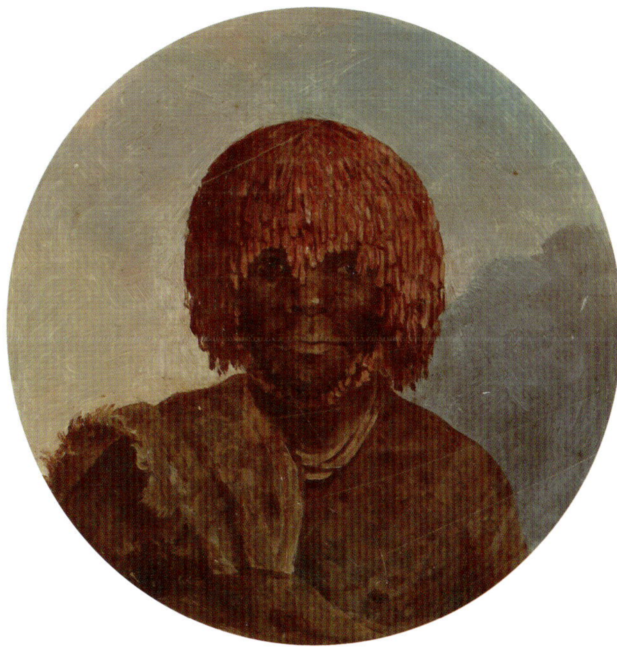

Robert Dowling
after Thomas Bock
(1790–1855)
Woureddy, of Bruny Island 1853–54
or 1854–56
oil on board
The British Museum, London

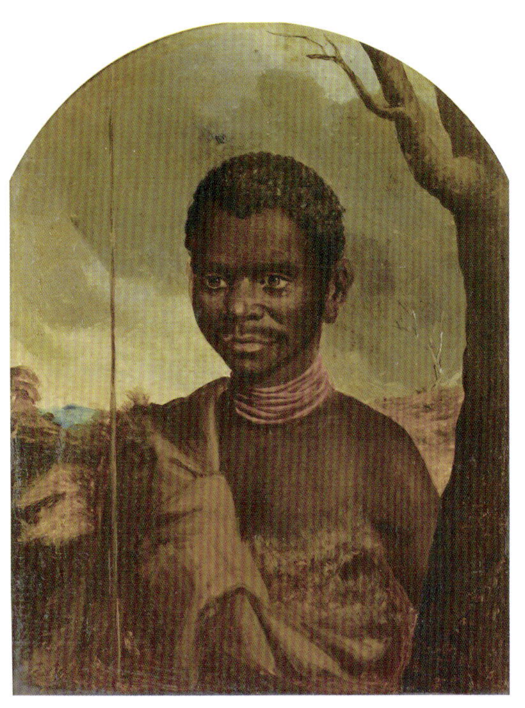

Robert Dowling
after **Thomas Bock** (1790–1855)
Jimmy, of Hampshire Hills, Van Diemen's Land 1853–54 or 1854–56
oil on canvas on board
The British Museum, London

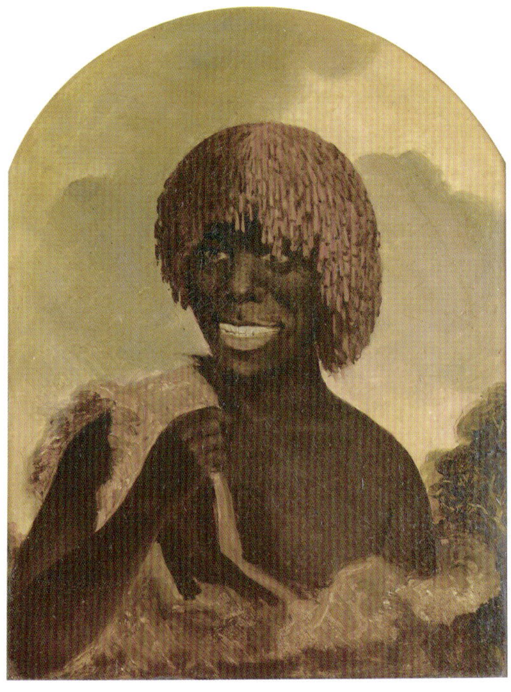

Robert Dowling
after **Thomas Bock** (1790–1855)
Jack, of Cape Grim, Van Diemen's Land 1853–54 or 1854–56
oil on canvas on board
The British Museum, London

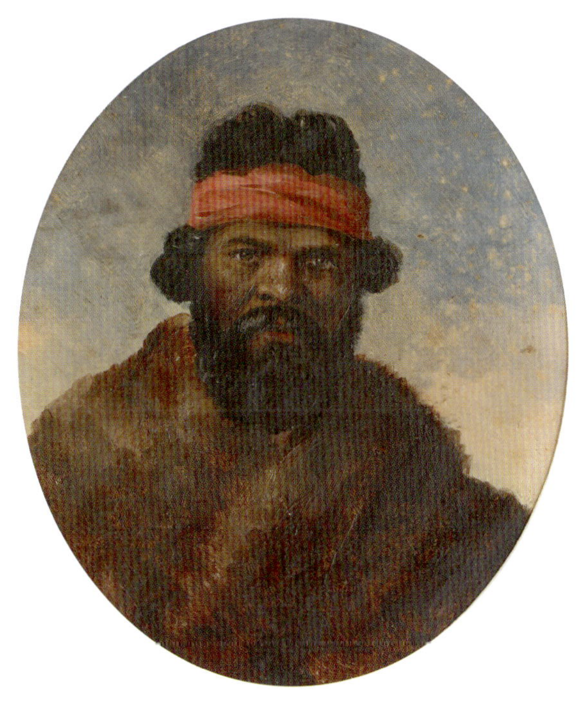

Robert Dowling
Man from Maria River
1856
oil on canvas on board
The British Museum, London

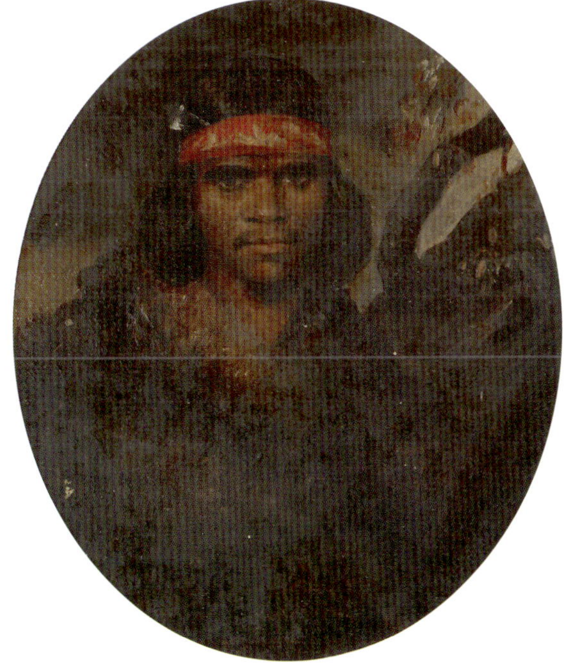

Robert Dowling
Woman from Maria River
1856
oil on canvas on board
The British Museum, London

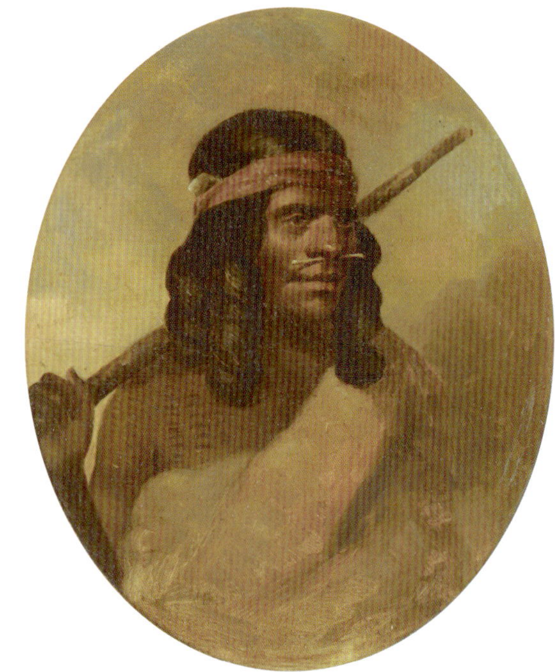

Queen Laratong, Spring Creek, Port Fairy, Victoria 1856
oil on canvas on board
The British Museum, London

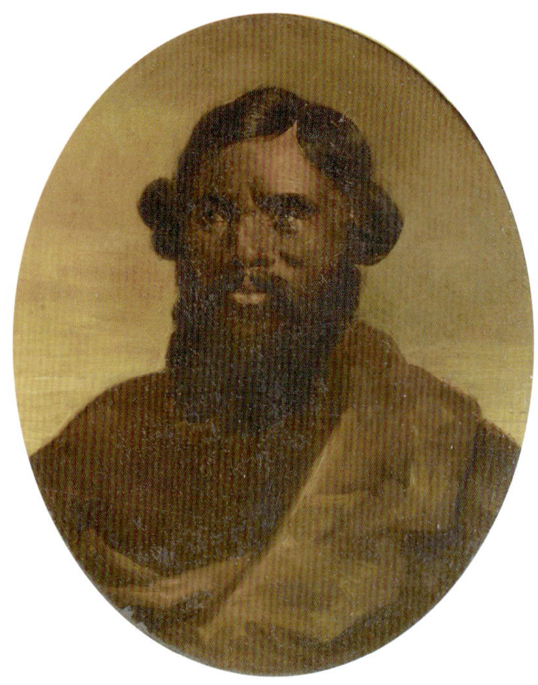

King Laratong, Spring Creek, Port Fairy, Victoria 1856
oil on canvas on board
The British Museum, London

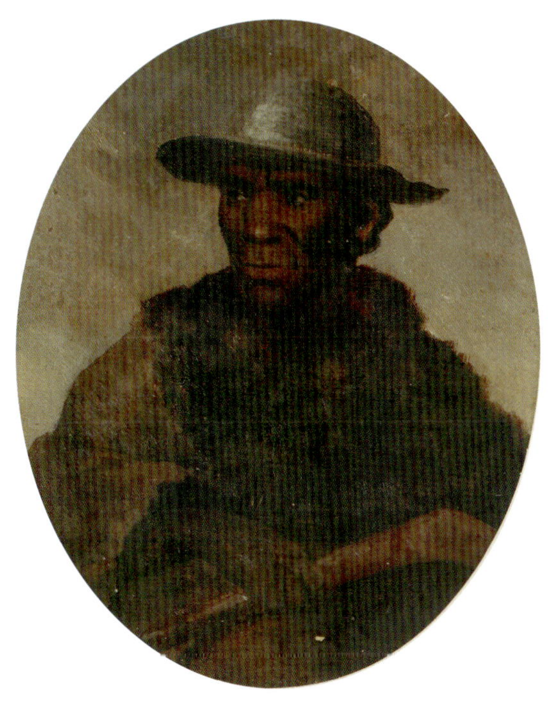

King Marpoura, Spring Creek, near Port Fairy, Victoria 1856
oil on canvas on board
The British Museum, London

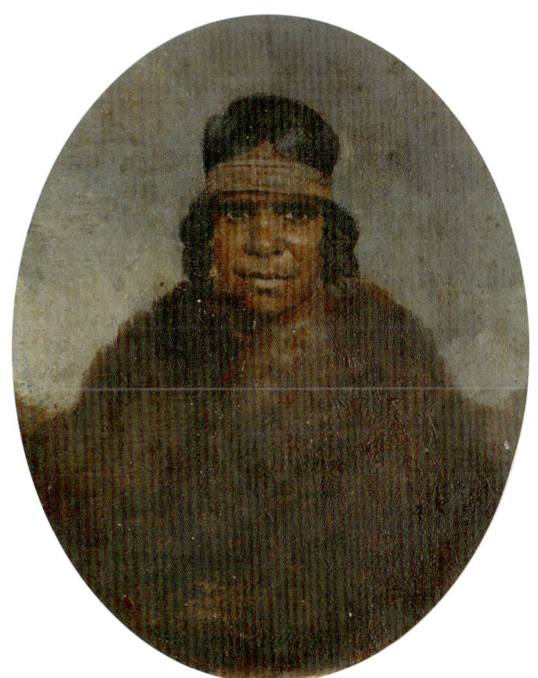

Queen Marpoura, Spring Creek, near Port Fairy, Victoria 1856
oil on canvas on board
The British Museum, London

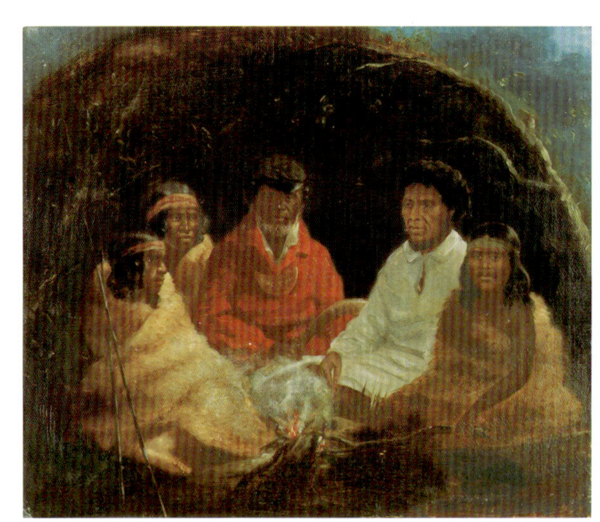

King Tom and the Mount Elephant tribe 1856
oil on board
National Library of Australia, Canberra

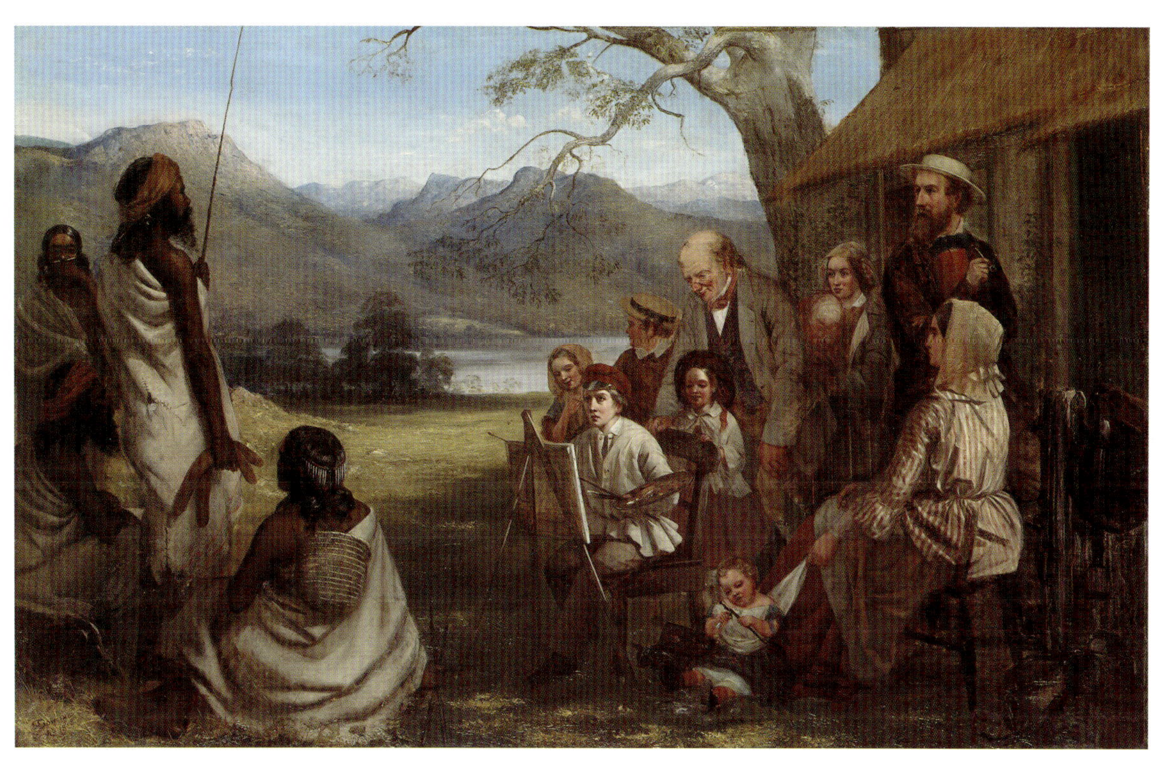

Early effort—art in Australia
1860
oil on canvas on board
National Gallery of Victoria,
Melbourne

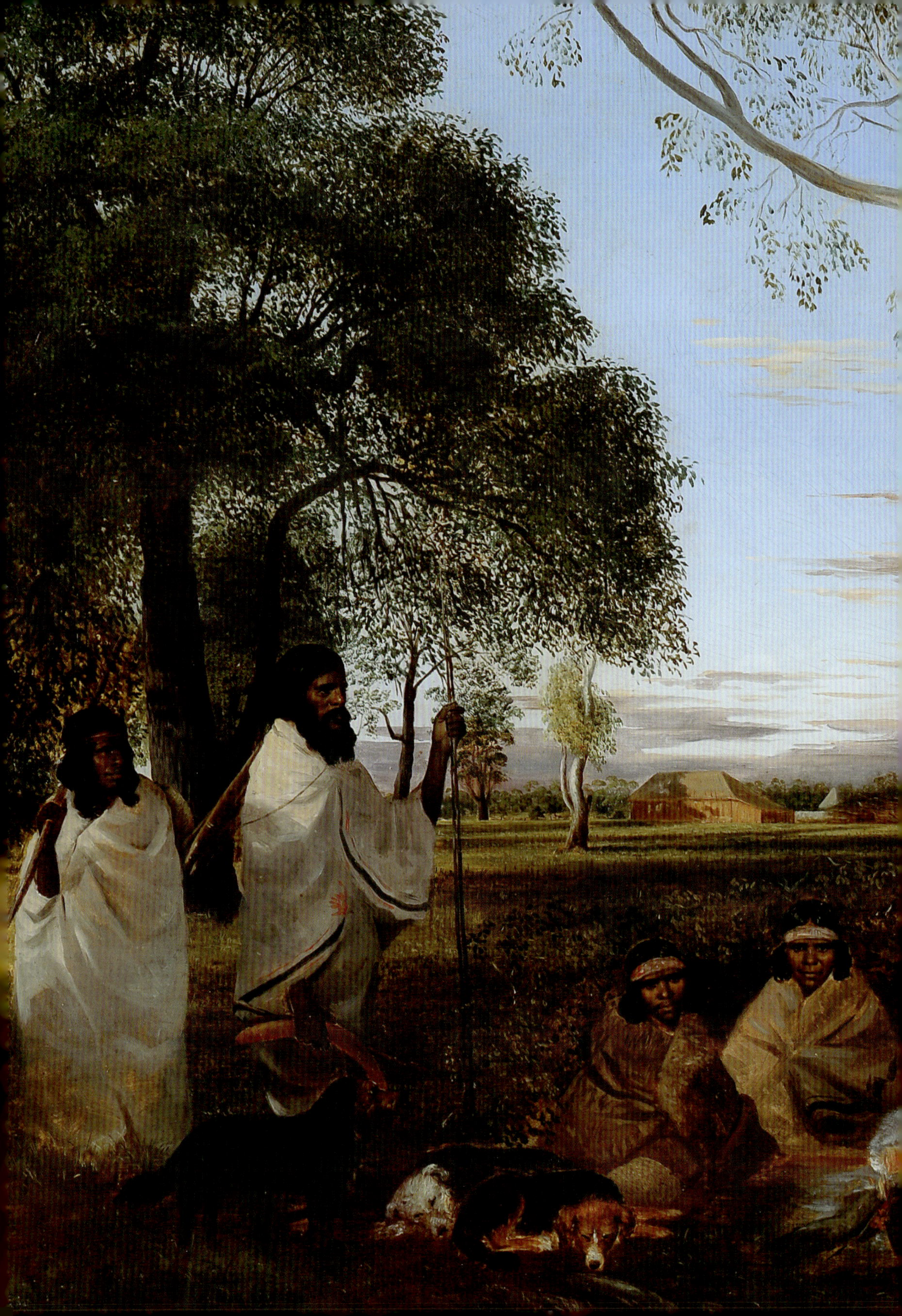

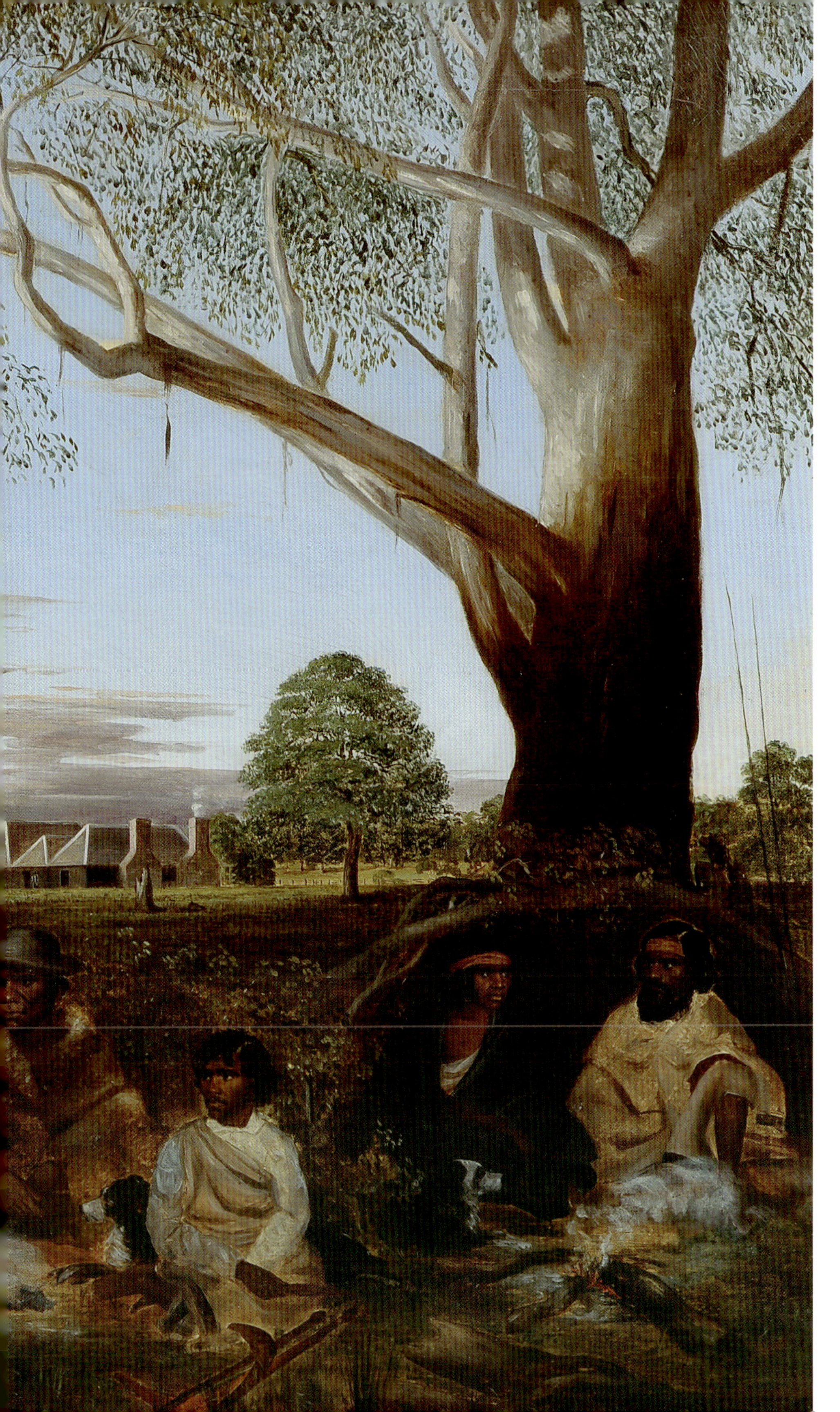

Minjah in the Old Time (Weerat Kuyuut and the Mopor people at Minjah Station)
1856
oil on canvas
Warrnambool Art Gallery, Victoria

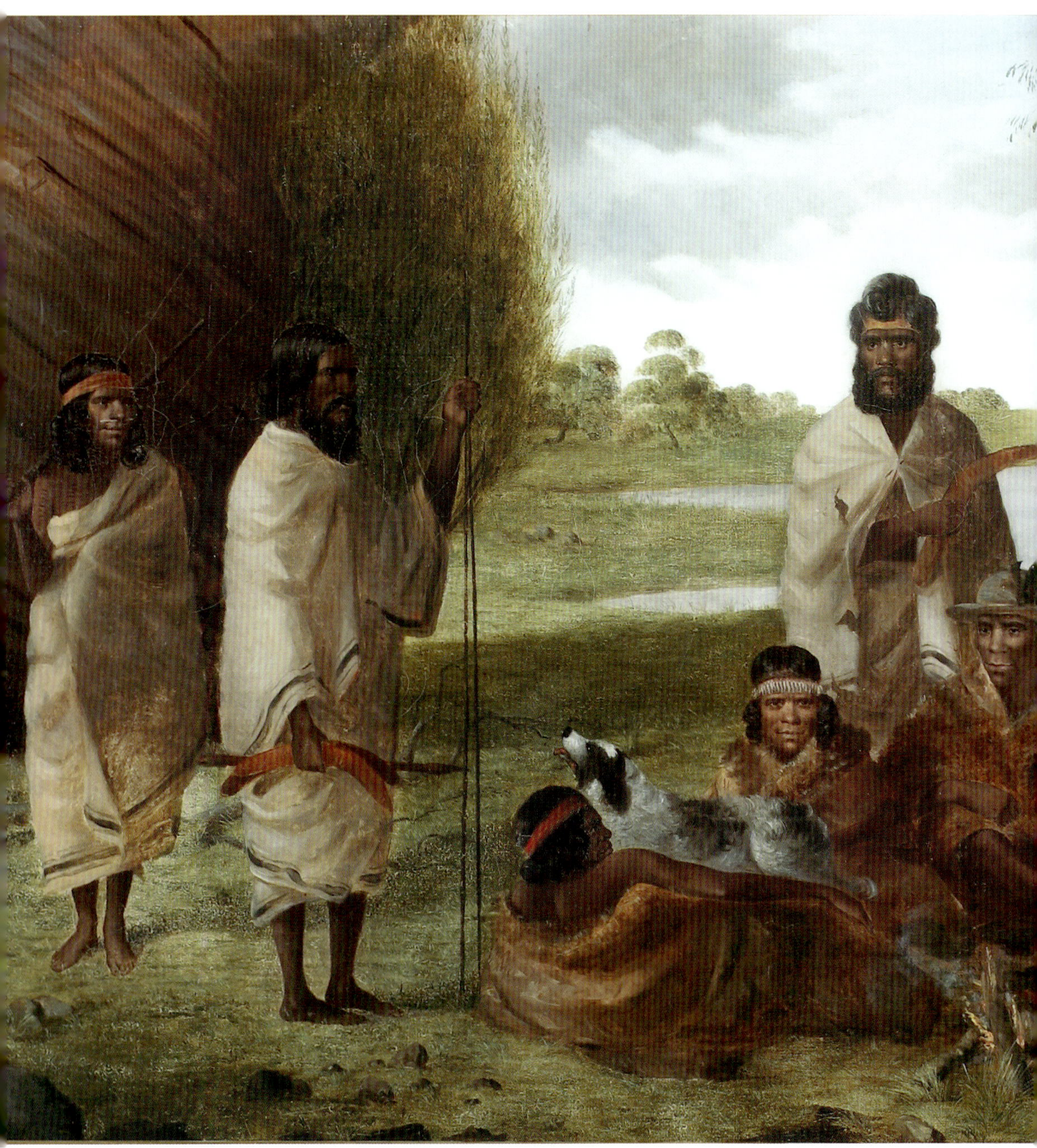

Weerat Kuyuut and the Mopor people, Spring Creek, Victoria
1856
oil on canvas
The University of Queensland Art Museum, Brisbane

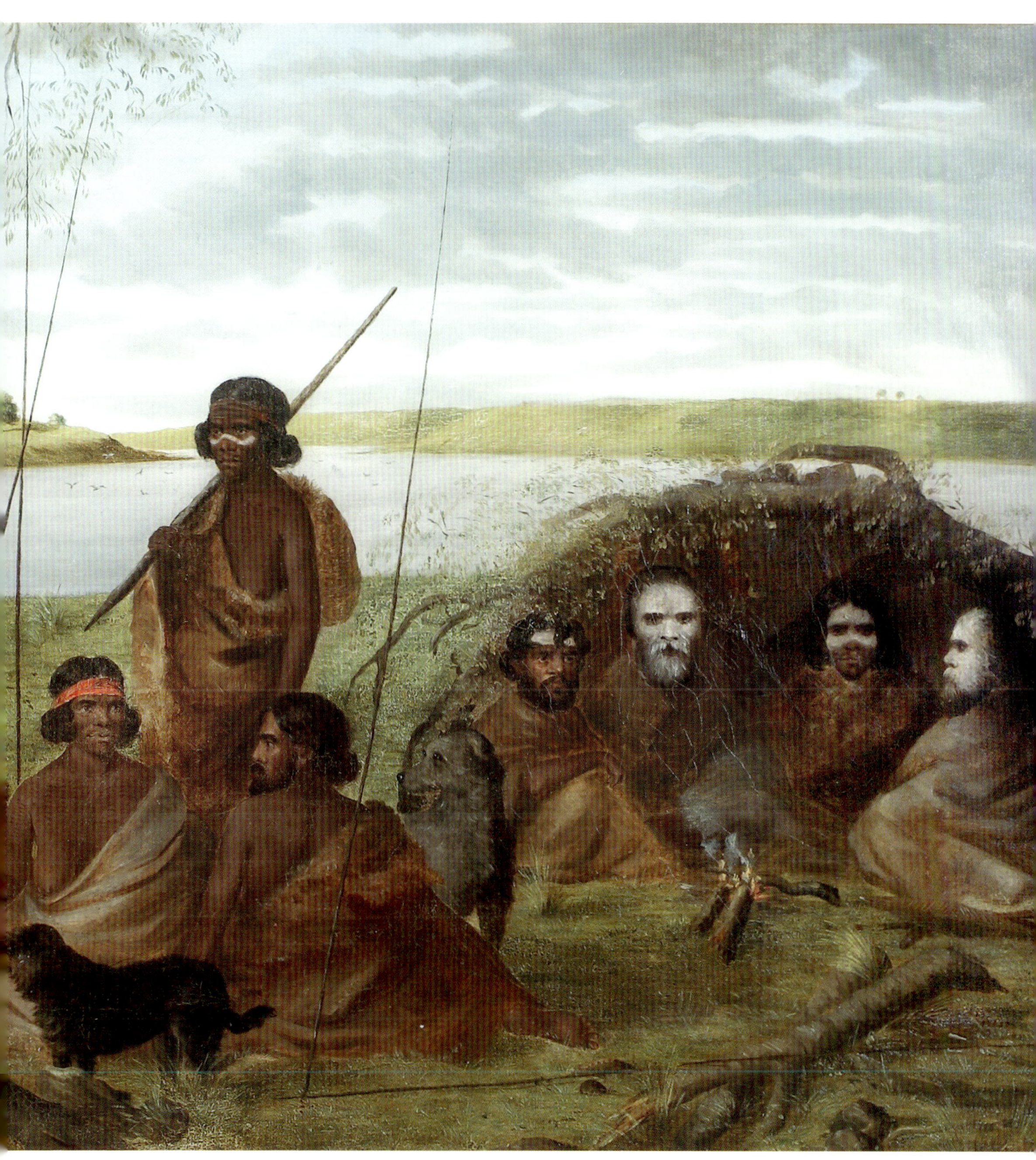

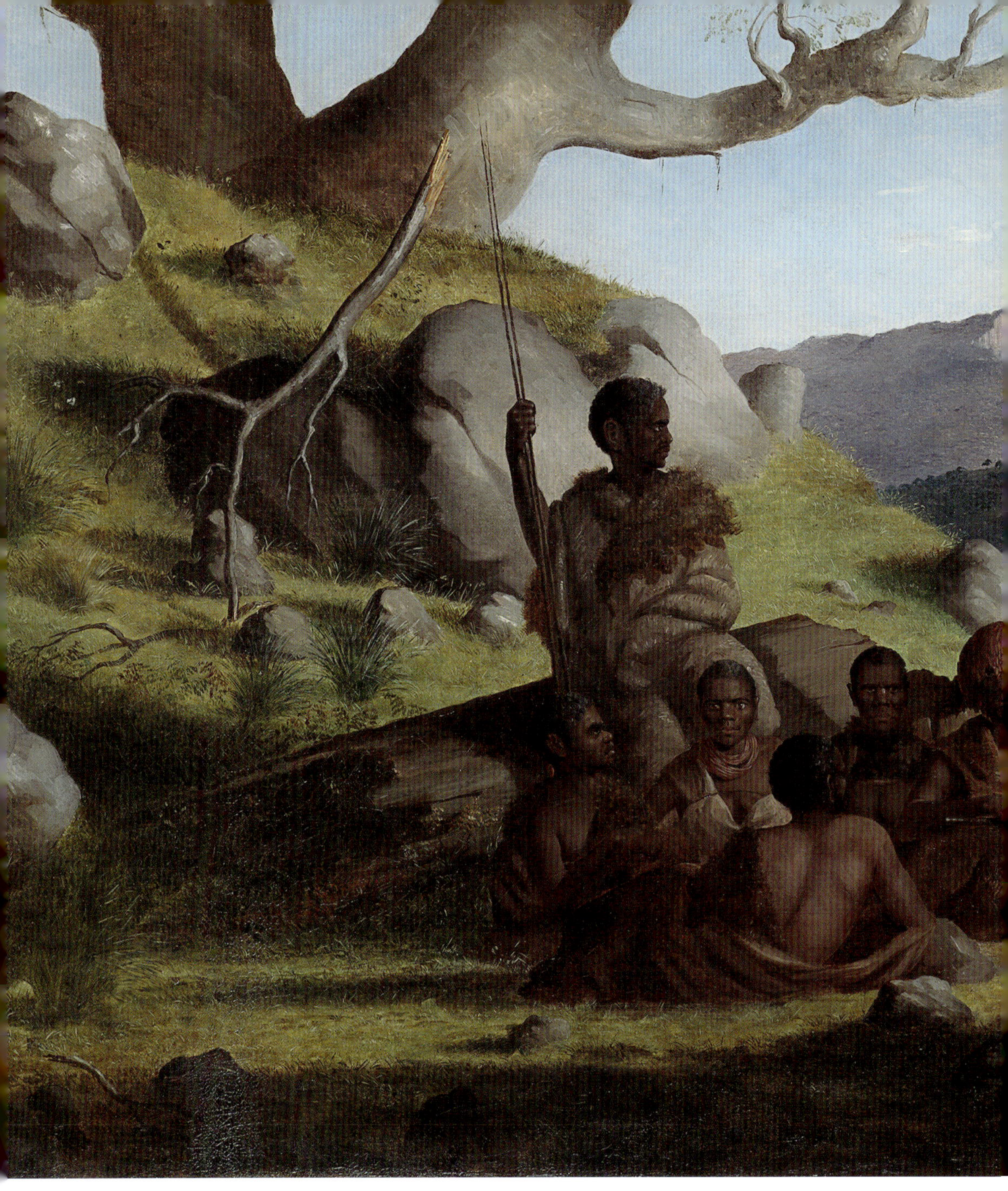

Tasmanian Aborigines 1856–57
oil on canvas
National Gallery of Victoria,
Melbourne

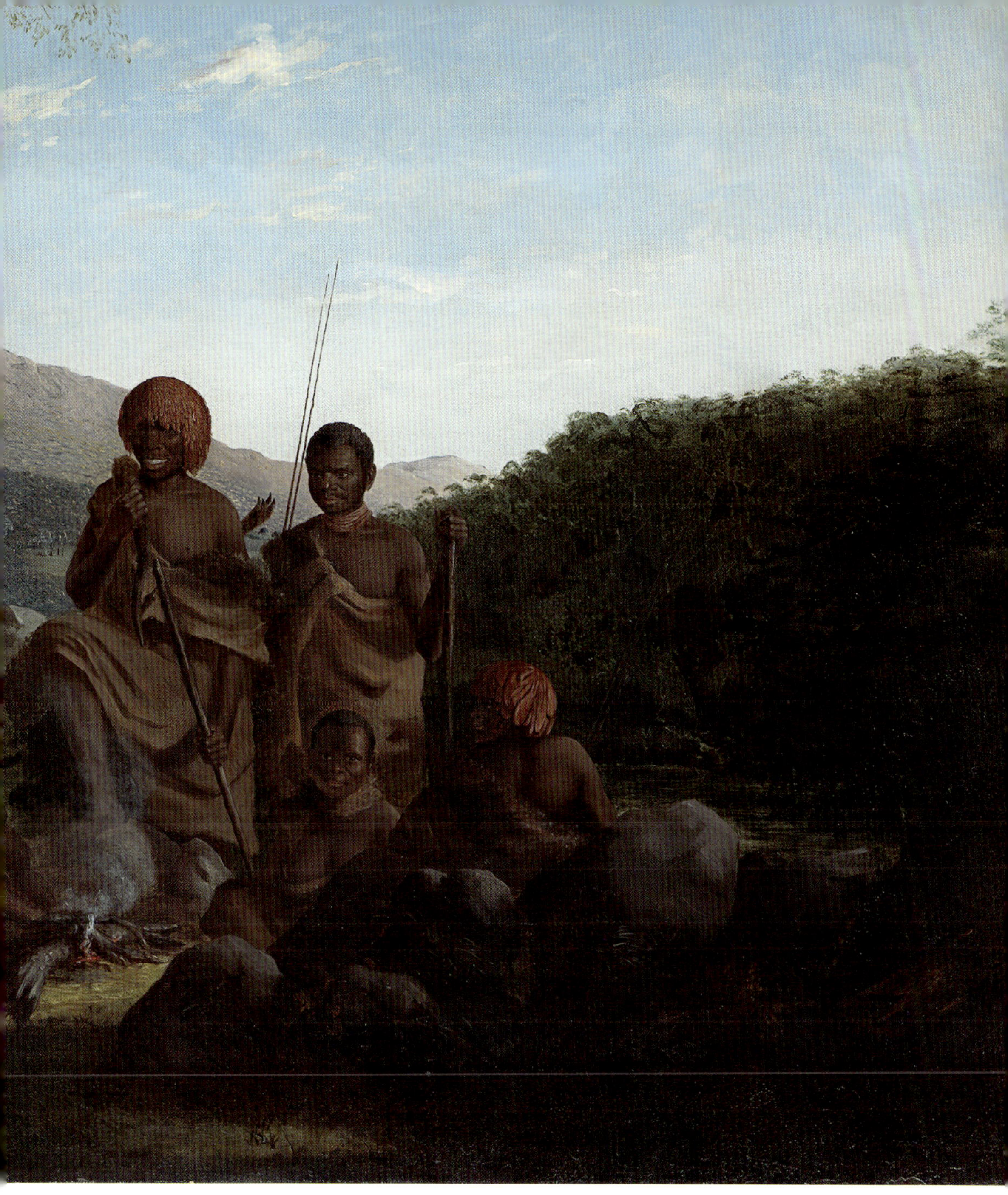

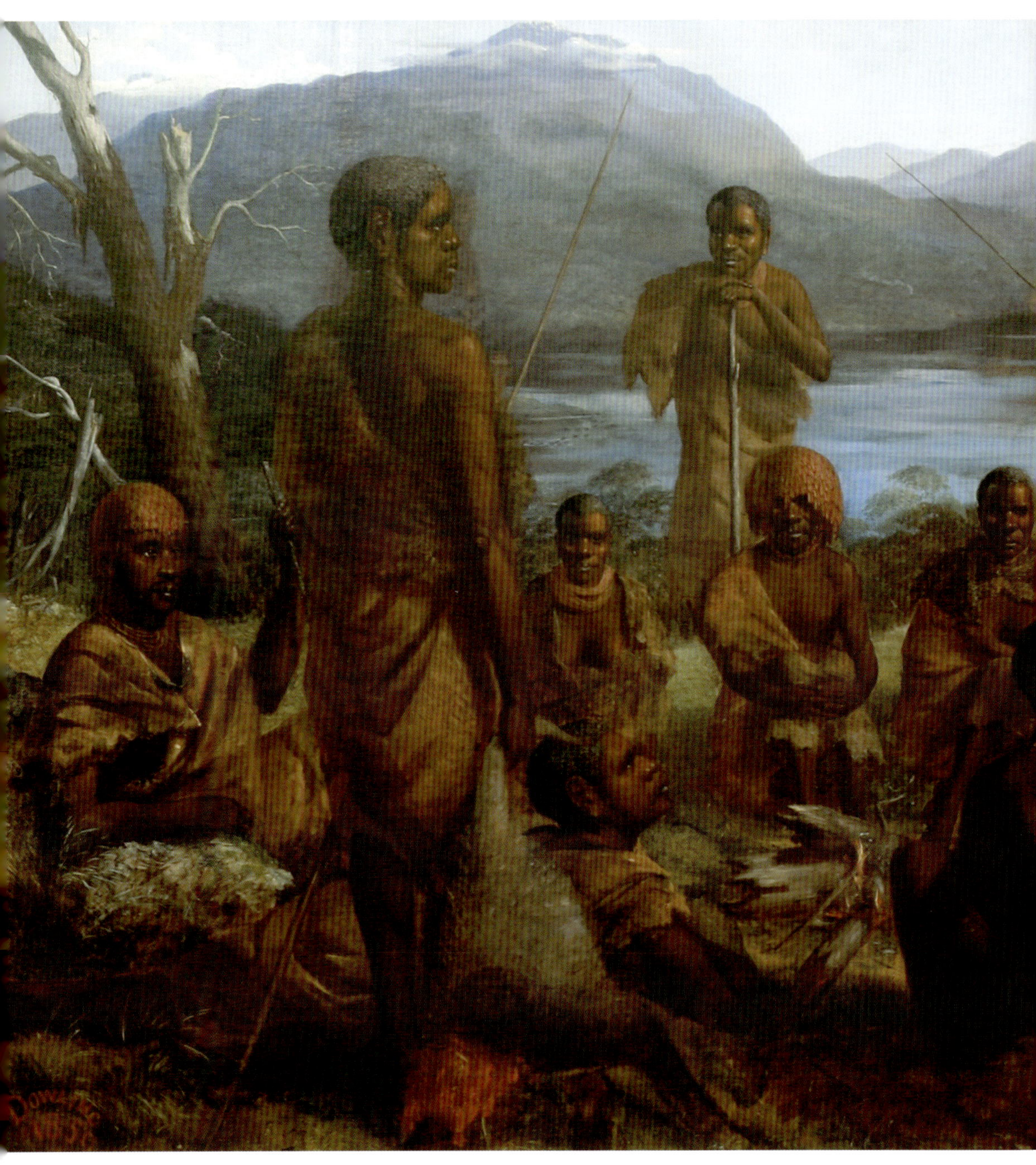

Aborigines of Tasmania
1859
oil on canvas
Queen Victoria Museum
and Art Gallery, Launceston

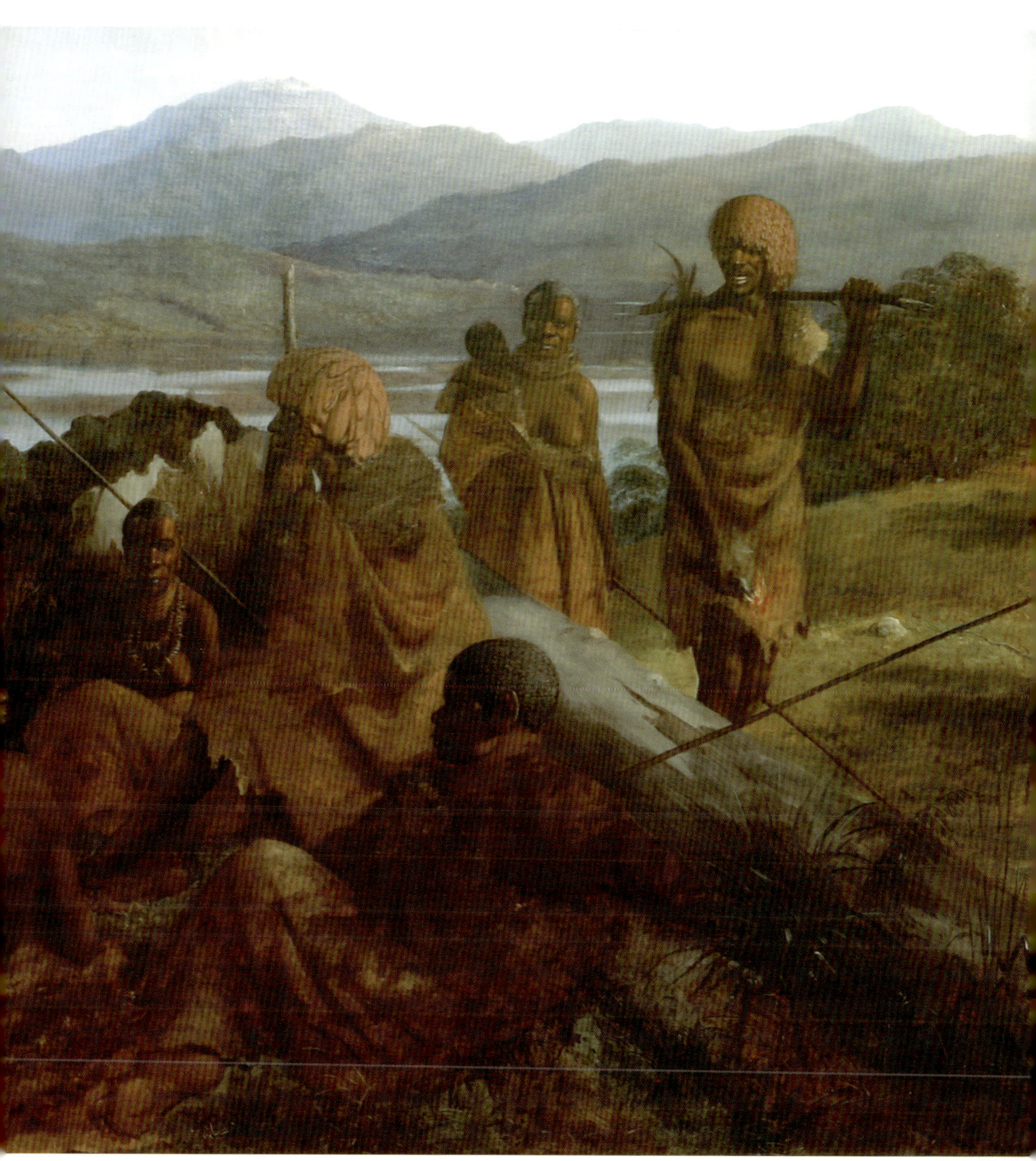

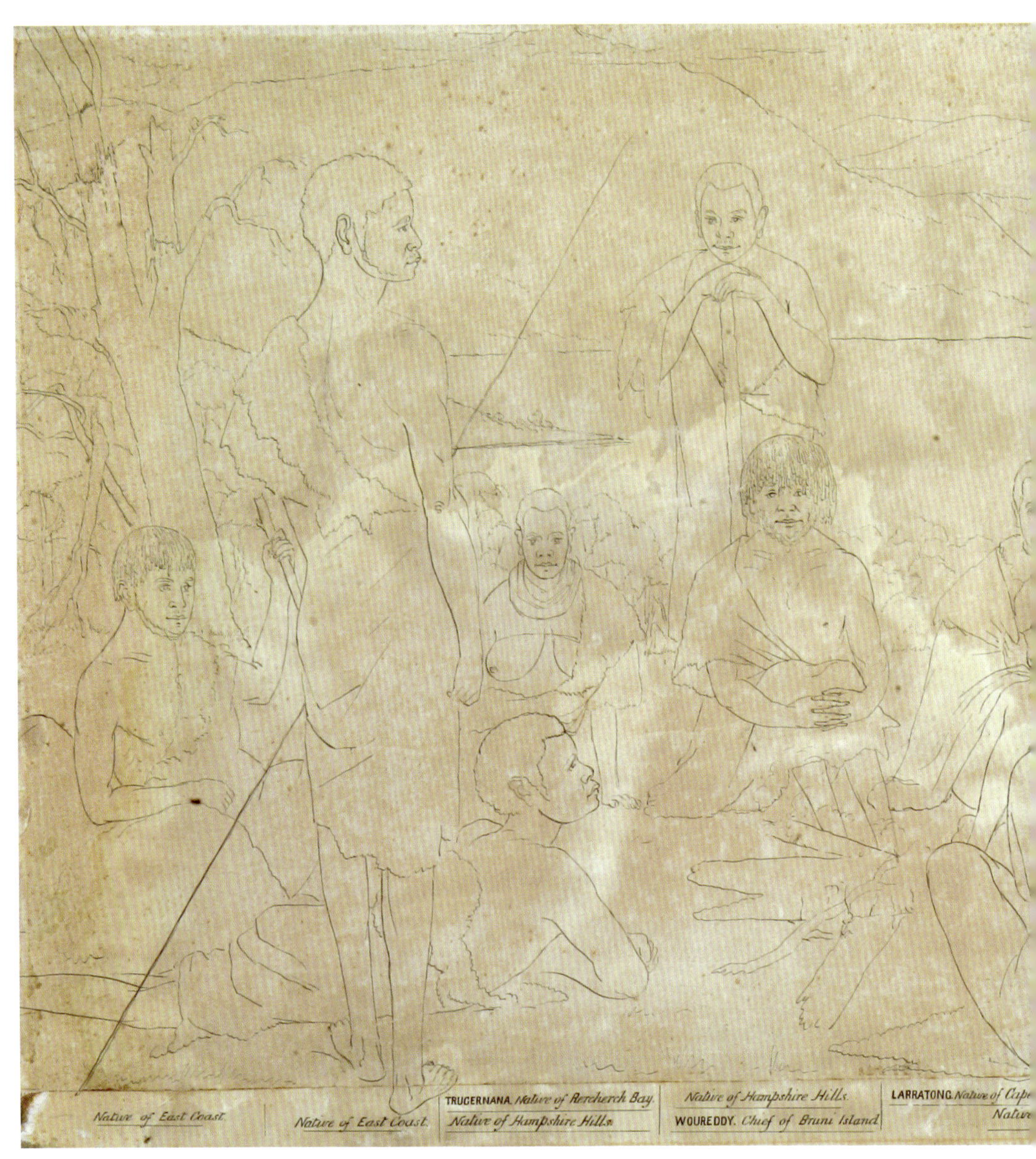

Key to *Aborigines of Tasmania* 1859
ink on paper
Queen Victoria Museum and Art Gallery, Launceston

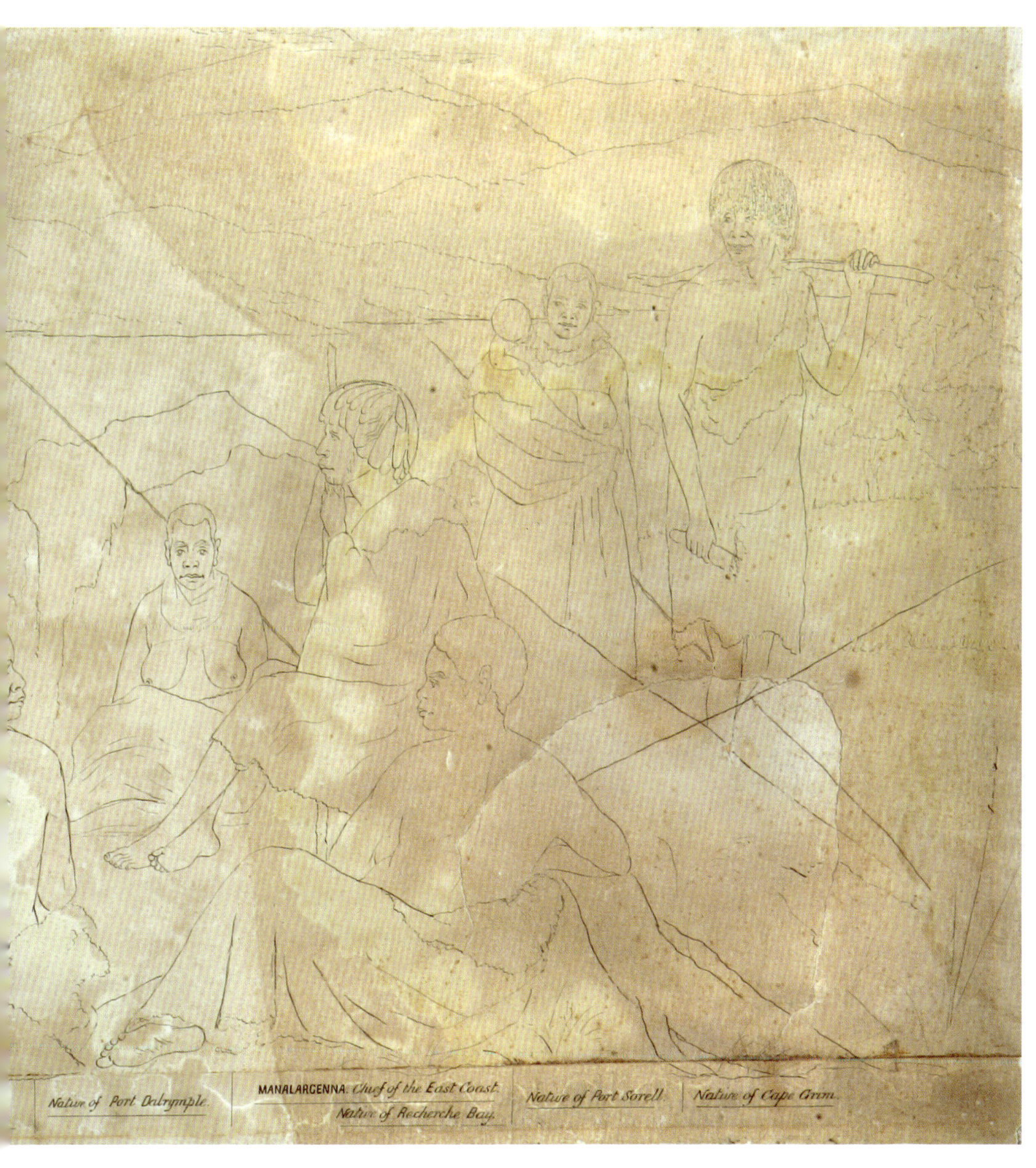
Native of Port Dalrymple.
MANALARGENNA. Chief of the East Coast.
Native of Recherche Bay.
Native of Port Sorell.
Native of Cape Grim.

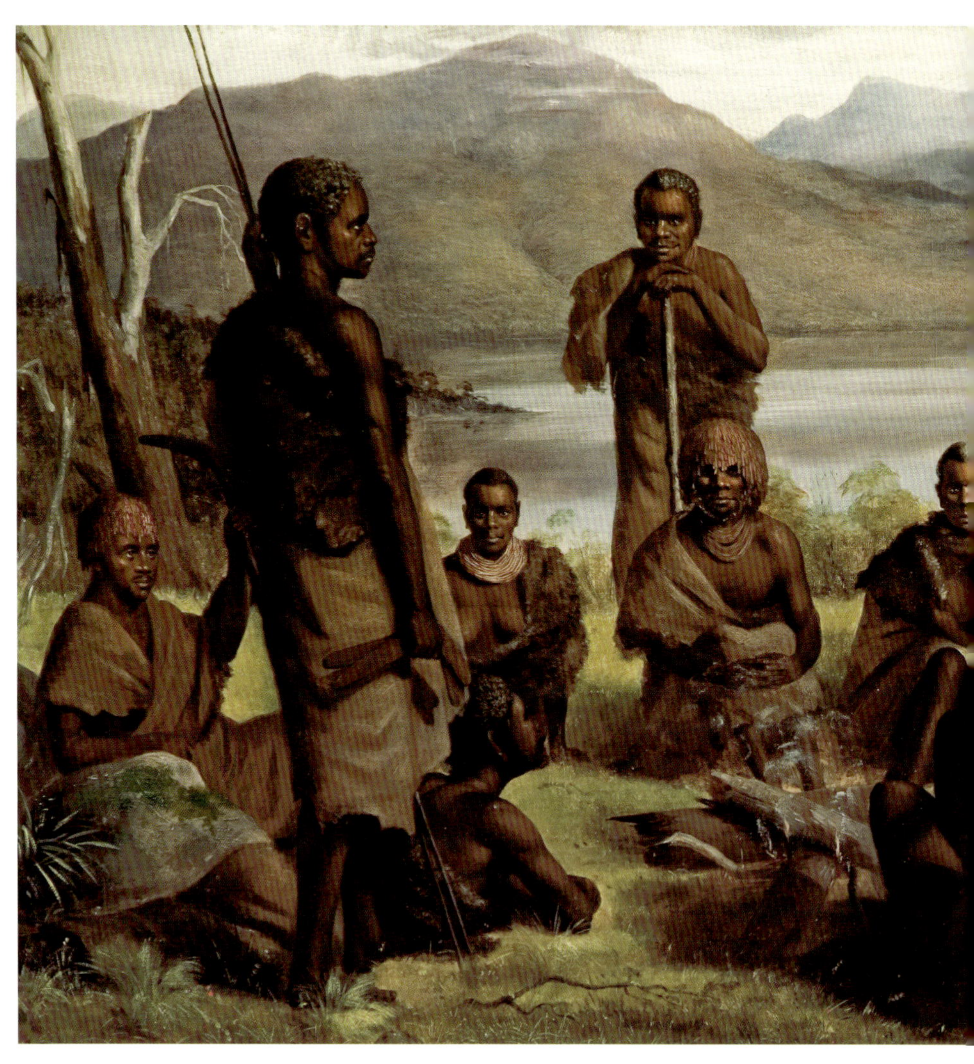

Group of natives of Tasmania
1860
oil on canvas
Art Gallery of South Australia, Adelaide

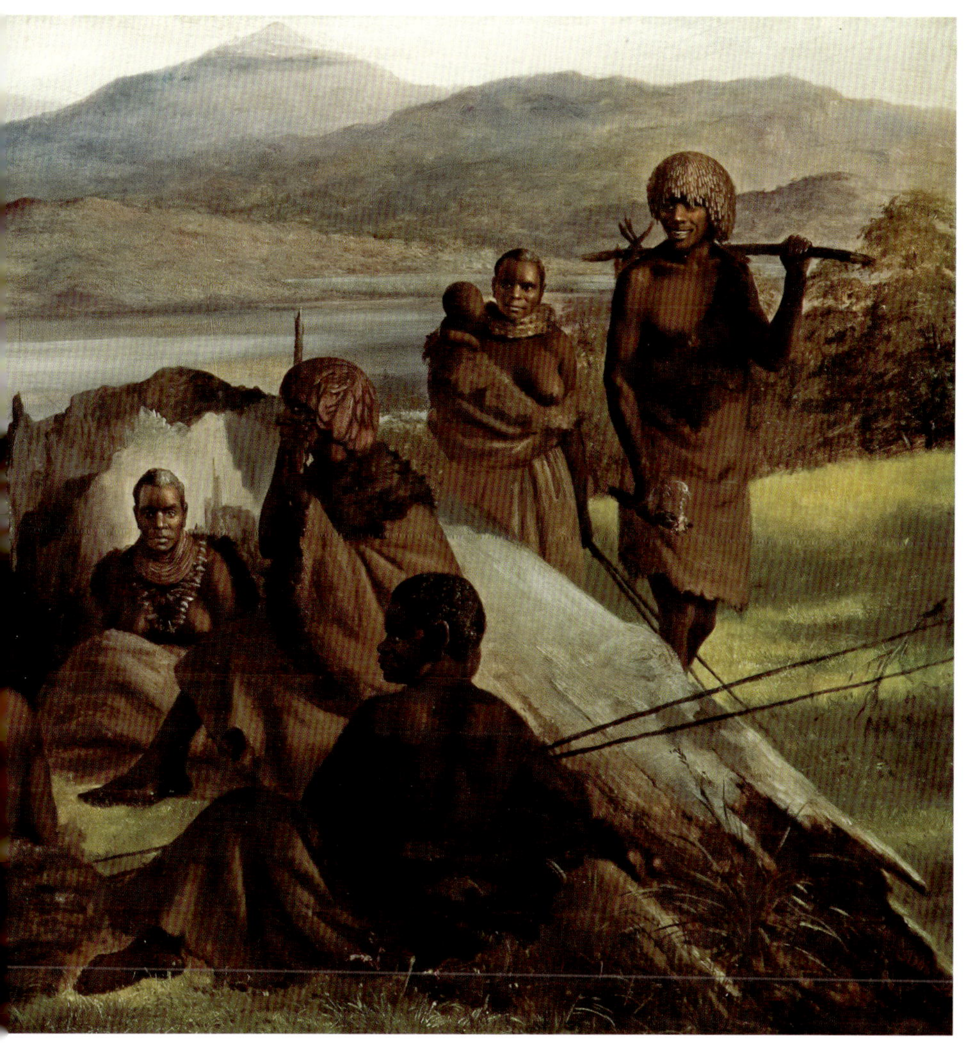

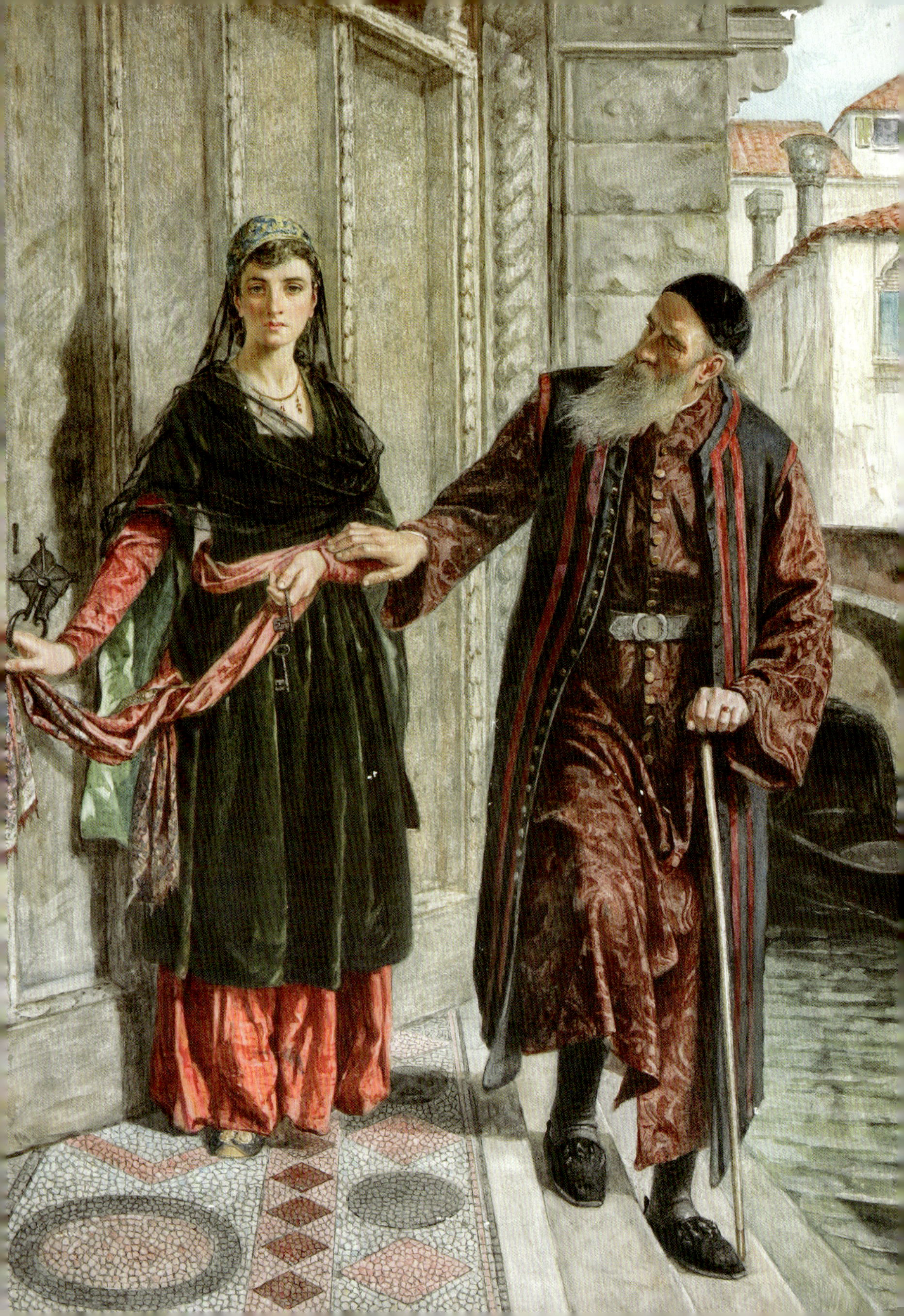

CHAPTER 4
London years 1857–84

Shylock and Jessica
1882
watercolour and bodycolour on paper on board
Queen Victoria Museum and Art Gallery, Launceston

On 29 April 1857, Robert Dowling, his wife and young daughter left Launceston on the French steamer *Pharamond* for England, arriving there on 3 September.

Dowling travelled to London on the proceeds from a public subscription by Launceston supporters, and the profits from portrait commissions. He took up residence at 56 Upper Charlotte Street, Fitzroy Square, and enrolled at James Matthew Leigh's Academy, 79 Newman Street. He seems to have remained solely with Leigh, who also prepared candidates for the Royal Academy Schools in South Kensington, for about two years. Before Leigh's death in 1860, among other students enrolled there were Laura Knight (1877–1970) and Edward Poynter (1836–1919), artists whose later work would be stylistically divergent.

Leigh's Academy, renamed Heatherley's after 1860, was a propitious choice for Dowling, rather than the arguably more famous preparatory academy run by Henry Sass. Leigh, a playwright and painter, and himself a student of painter William Etty (1787–1849), was noted for subjects of particular relevance to Dowling's later production of Scriptural, English Civil War, Walter Scott and Shakespearian genres.

At the beginning of 1860 an oval self-portrait was shipped to brother Henry in Launceston, along with collectors' photographs—for the artist's financial supporters—of the painting *Breakfasting out* (p 130), which in 1859 had been Robert's first work accepted for the annual Royal Academy exhibition. Henry exhibited the painting and the photograph, with earlier Australian work, at the Launceston Mechanics' Institute as before-and-after proof of the city's successful investment in their local artist. The self-portrait remained in the family and was eventually given to the Queen Victoria Museum & Art Gallery in 1930, by which time the reverse had acquired an inscription that apparently read 'Robert Dowling RA 1857' (the canvas was relined in 1983). The Tasmanian inscription misunderstands date and status both: the newly assured style, and comparison with securely dated work, confirm its date of execution as 1859; Dowling was never elected to the Royal Academy, either as Associate or full Academician, and never himself claimed the initials 'RA' as a distinction. After his success in 1859 with *Breakfasting out*, in 1860 Dowling submitted two new paintings to the Royal Academy, *Early effort—art in Australia* (p 95)and a religious subject, *The Presentation in the Temple*. Only the first of these was accepted.

Dowling next focused on official portraits of royalty. Coupled with, and in response to, his 1860 gift of *Aborigines of Tasmania* (pp 102–103) to the people of Launceston, he had received a commission from the Launceston Mechanics' Institute to replicate a pair of portraits of Queen Victoria and Albert the Prince Consort (QVMAG) (p 133). Previously, in 1855, the Tasmanian Government had commissioned the British artist John Prescott Knight (1803–1881) to copy the 1843 state portrait by Franz Xavier Winterhalter of Queen Victoria for Parliament House, Hobart. Not to be seen lagging in loyalty, Launceston also felt the need for an image of the Queen. It was proposed that Dowling, a Tasmanian now resident in London, be given a similar charge.

Impressive images of reigning monarchs were salient features of colonial administrative institutions throughout the nineteenth century and beyond. They can be found in many a government house or colonial parliament—for example in Government House, Adelaide, a William IV and Queen Adelaide pair, and in the State Parliament of Victoria in Melbourne a version of the same Winterhalter portrait of Queen Victoria that Dowling chose to copy for Launceston. Most are studio work or copies. Allan Ramsay's splendid c 1762 coronation portrait of the young George III and its pair of Queen Charlotte were personal favourites of that monarch. Winterhalter's majestic 1859 portraits of Queen Victoria and the Prince Consort not only pleased the sitters, but also resonated in the public's imagination, at home and in the colonies, as the sense and realisation of Empire evolved; they were an obvious choice for Dowling to copy. In November 1860, the president of the

Mechanics' Institute, Gavin Casey, could report that there had been a 'fair beginning' towards the £250 required to paint the portrait of Queen Victoria for Launceston.[1] Among the colonists who subscribed were Sir Richard Dry, Joseph Archer, Bishop Nixon and the Governor of Tasmania, Sir Henry Fox Young. George Carr Clark topped the list with a twelve-guinea donation. The artist's brother Henry, then Mayor of Launceston, eventually 'threw in' £50, as well as offering to pay for the copy of the accompanying portrait of Prince Albert, who had died in 1861. Access for the artist to Windsor Castle and permission to copy the portraits there was obtained via the services of the Tasmanian Governor. The completed paintings arrived in Launceston with much fanfare in February 1863.

On their unveiling, *The Cornwall Chronicle* declared: 'Her Majesty's face—unclouded—when she sat for the portrait—by grief is open, dignified, cheerful and very beautiful—the mouth displaying just sufficient of her pearly teeth is especially so.'[2] *The Examiner* reported:

> Whilst we [regard] with paramount interest the portrait of our beloved Sovereign, it was with scarcely less loyal devotion we contemplated the noble bearing … of Prince Albert, now, alas, no more. We may be allowed to congratulate Launceston on the possession of these authentic Royal portraits … the possession of which will be an object of envy in Australia.[3]

In a further gesture of loyalty, the Mechanics' Institute may have commissioned from Dowling another pair of royal portraits, but the circumstances are unclear. In 1863 the heir to the throne, Prince Edward, married Princess Alexandra of Denmark. A year later Dowling commenced work on *HRH Edward, Prince of Wales* 1864–66 and *HRH Alexandra, Princess of Wales* 1866 (QVMAG). The portrait of Prince Edward was exhibited at the Royal Academy in 1864, where Dowling described it as 'Painted for the Tasmanian Government', which was not the case. Unlike the 1860 commission, these portraits were 'taken from life'. They are impressive in scale but a little coarse and rather dull. When Dowling's paintings arrived in Australia they were promptly lent by his brother Henry to the British and Foreign Masters Court at the Inter-colonial Exhibition of Australia in Melbourne in 1866–67. Subsequently, according to the files of the Queen Victoria Museum & Art Gallery,[4] they were donated by Henry to the Launceston Mechanics' Institute—but the Mechanics' Institute archive has a different record of the Dowling donors.[5] The last in this series of Royal

Family images was the portrait *HRH Prince Alfred, Duke of Edinburgh* 1869 (QVMAG). Prince Alfred had toured the Australian colonies on the yacht *Galatea* during 1867 and 1868. While in Tasmania he turned the first sod for the Launceston & Western Railway of which company Henry Dowling was secretary. Again, some confusion surrounds the 'commissioning' of this portrait, but Prince Alfred did sit for it in London and Dowling exhibited the painting at the Royal Academy in 1869. When the portrait came out to Launceston, it was given to the Mechanics' Institute in 1871 by Messrs Overend & Robb, contractors to the Launceston & Western Railway.

Like the sculptor Charles Summers, working in Rome, Robert Dowling in London received portrait requests from Australians resident in or visiting Great Britain. In the early 1860s Dowling painted a portrait of fellow-Tasmanian Henry Reed, a wealthy landowner, merchant and philanthropic Evangelical. While maintaining his colonial business investments, Reed had relocated with his family from Launceston to England in 1847. His first wife and cousin Maria (née Grubb) died in 1860 and Dowling painted the two youngest of their eleven children. That portrait, *Masters Frederick and Arthur, sons of Henry Reed* (National Trust of Tasmania) (p 132), an attractive work in an extensive landscape—perhaps suggesting the landscaped park then being developed for Reed's mansion, Dunorlan,

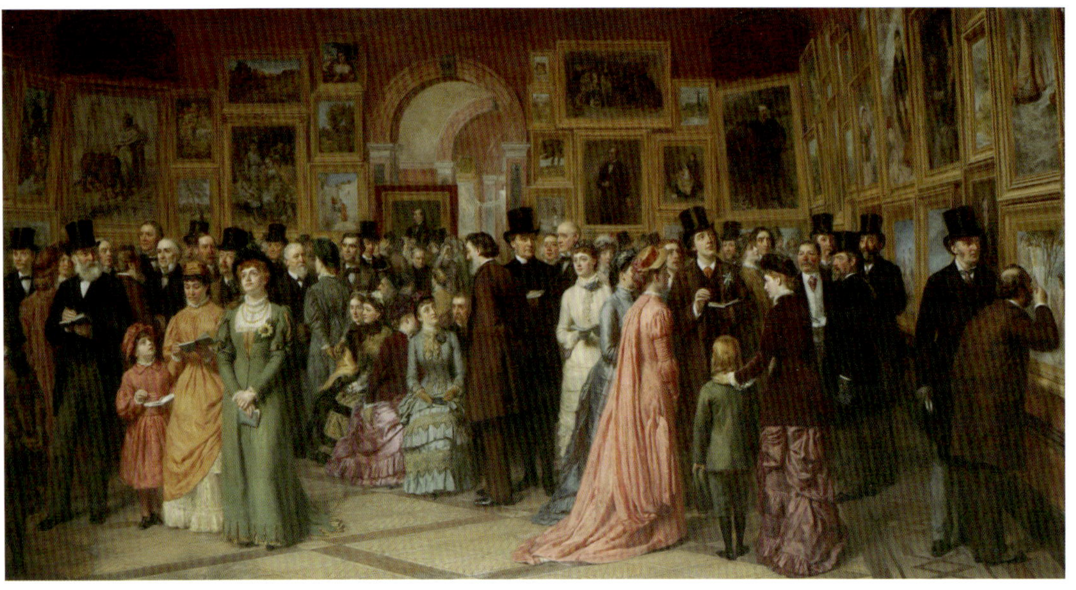

William Powell Frith
1819–1909
Private view at the Royal Academy, 1881
1883
oil on canvas,
60 × 114 cm
Royal Academy of Arts, London

at Royal Tunbridge Wells in Kent—has much of the charm of Dowling's 1856 Australian portrait of the Ware children, but after London life-class experience, the figures are better realised. Another portrait from the 1860s is *Lieutenant Harington Astley Trevelyan—survivor of the Charge of the Light Brigade*. Among later portraits of colonials visiting London were *Miss Mary Drysdale* 1879 (Queensland Art Gallery) and *Miss Annie Ware* 1882 (NGV), both the daughters of Western District pastoralists. In 1871 Dowling painted, from a photograph by Charles Woolley of Hobart, the first of two posthumous portraits of the late and much revered Tasmanian Premier Sir Richard Dry, who died in 1869; it became yet another gift from the artist's brother Henry to the Launceston Mechanics' Institute.

Other London portraits of this time remain untraced. They include, on an exotic note, Dowling's huge portrait, commissioned by the mayor of Southampton, of the Italian patriot and hero of the Risorgimento, Giuseppe Garibaldi, who had been triumphantly welcomed to England in 1864.[6] Also untraced is the last portrait that Dowling exhibited at the Royal Academy, in 1880: the Arctic explorer *Vice-Admiral Sir Leopold McClintock*. Leopold McClintock (1819–1907) was a characteristic 'Boy's Own' hero of the British Empire, famous for his discoveries in the Canadian Arctic Archipelago. In 1859, sponsored by a public subscription from Tasmania and with the support of Lady Franklin, McClintock, in the *Fox*, finally discovered the fate of Sir John Franklin and the North-West Passage Expedition of 1845–48; Sir John, a former Governor of Tasmania, remained a much-admired celebrity figure in the colony. As early as 1860 *The Examiner* reported: 'We understand that Mr R Dowling has been commissioned by Lady Franklin to paint a portrait of Captain McClintock.'[7] Some twenty years later a portrait appeared, five years after Lady Franklin's death and just four years before Admiral McClintock retired from the Royal Navy. There were other connections between the artist and this sitter, for McClintock acquired, from Dowling (or from his estate), the artist's oil studies of Tasmanian and Victorian Aborigines. These were donated by the Admiral's family to the British Museum in 1924.

In his first years in London, however, as his early submissions to the Royal Academy and Royal Society of British Artists indicate, Dowling was devoting his energies to narrative painting. This genre, in its various guises, was to be his abiding interest in the 1860s and 70s.

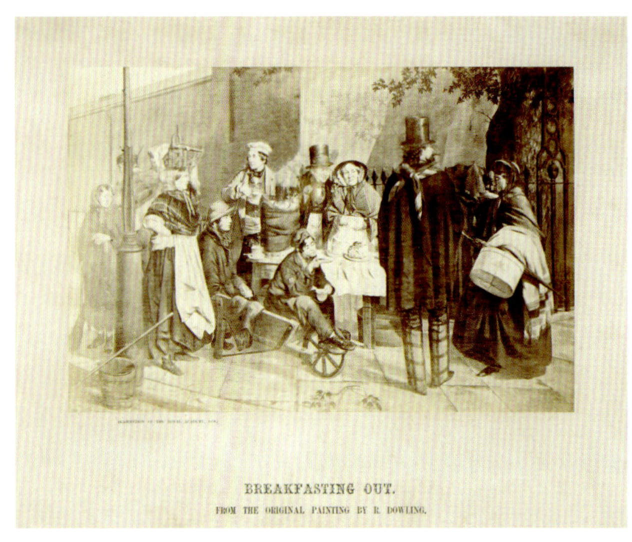

Robert Dowling
Breakfasting out
1859
photographed and published by HJ Betjemann & Son, London, 1860
Queen Victoria Museum & Art Gallery, Launceston

The acceptance of his painting *Breakfasting out* (Museum of London) by the 1859 Royal Academy exhibition was, for the young Australian artist, a milestone in his career. Dowling worked best on a small scale, of which this painting is an example. The subject is an early morning street scene, perhaps in Westminster, with a busy coffee stall and a small drama. Around the stall are people from all walks of life, full of Dickensian characterisation. A barrow-man sits with his boy, as their sack, stamped with the artist's inverted initials 'RD', spills straw onto the footpath; a girl, broom in hand and bucket nearby, looks askance at their mess. A young man with a coffee cup (a self-portrait of the artist?) stands to the left of a middle-aged coffee vendor and her friend. They, and a disapproving flower-seller, basket on her head, observe a predatory, top-hatted toff, who gazes fixedly at a pretty young milliner carrying a hat box. The unsuspecting girl is a potential victim for his seduction, and stands on the brink of a fall into vice—a sad narrative readily comprehended by Dowling's audience.[8] When J Walch & Sons of Launceston had photographs of the work for sale in 1861, they pointedly announced that a copy was 'worth purchasing by every father having marriageable daughters of the romantic age. A careful study of the photograph might prove to such as good as a sermon.'[9] At the Royal Academy in 1860 the painting had been noticed by the *Art Journal*:

> It is a street breakfast—the hour is 6 and the party a 'mixture' but the characters are judiciously selected and everywhere the painting and drawing are unexceptionable. The name is new to us, but the manner and art is sound, and bears promise and distinction.[10]

Dowling was buoyed by the positive assessment. A copy of the *Art Journal* review came with the photograph of the painting sent to Launceston for exhibition there in 1860. The photograph was published on a mount with a caption 'BREAKFASTING OUT. / FROM THE ORIGINAL PAINTING BY R. DOWLING' and a note of validation: 'EXHIBITION OF THE ROYAL ACADEMY, 1859'. Dowling's work was recognised, in the art centre of his world, fulfilling the faith of his hometown supporters in Tasmania.[11]

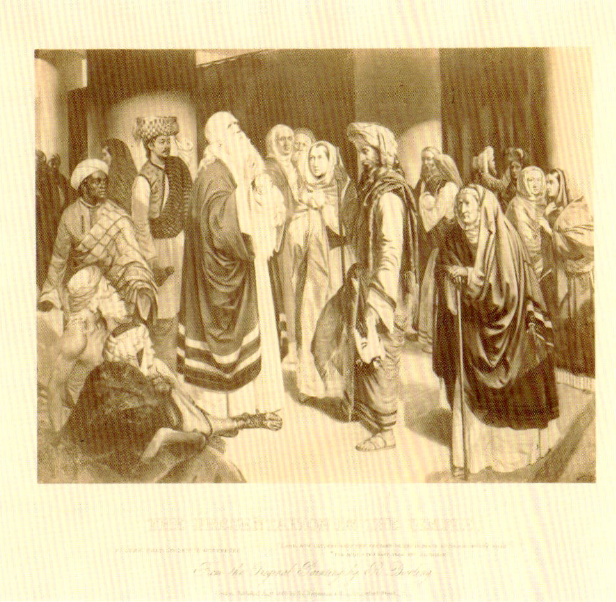

Robert Dowling
The Presentation in the Temple 1860
photographed and published by
H J Betjemann & Son, London, 1861
British Museum, London

The earlier-mentioned rejected Royal Academy submission of 1860 was a New Testament subject, *The Presentation in the Temple.* A less than successful composition, it was nonetheless sympathetically reviewed by *The Atlas.*[12] The painting was soon exhibited in Australia but its current whereabouts is unknown. We know the image—for the painting was exhibited at H J Betjemann & Son, 28 Oxford Street, London, and then published by Betjemann as a photograph 'mounted in imitation of an intaglio print'. That firm almost certainly produced the similarly mounted photographs *Tasmanian Aborigines* and *Breakfasting out*, sent to Launceston for subscribers in 1861.

Dowling's other Academy submission of 1860, *Early effort—art in Australia*, 'a picture of about the same size [as *The Presentation in the Temple*] but of less lofty pretensions [and] a comparative[ly] trivial work'[13] is discussed in chapter 3. Besides *Breakfasting out*, shown at the Royal Academy in 1859, Dowling had exhibited two other genre paintings at the Royal Society of British Artists: *Sabbath in the country* (p 129) and an untraced work, *Coming events.* Also untraced is a pair of paintings, *Summer* and *Winter,* submitted to the British institution that year.

Sabbath in the country has to be identified with the painting recently known as *An afternoon siesta* (private collection, previously Joseph Brown Collection), the carefully finished style of which is close to that of *Breakfasting out*, and which has the date 1859 inscribed on the reverse of the canvas. *Sabbath in the country* was in Melbourne in the nineteenth century and purchased by Sir Thomas Fitzgerald; *An afternoon siesta* is not a title recorded in Dowling's exhibition history, and this painting, once in the Joseph Brown Collection, sits easily with the recorded title of 1859. It tells a moral tale: on the Sabbath, 'the Lord's day of rest', an old farm labourer, scythe hanging on the wall above him, bread and an overturned mug of ale on the table, dozes off—his hard-earned reward and rest after the manual labour of the previous week. Dowling, despite his strict Sabbatarian background, had a quiet sense of humour.

One of Dowling's most successful modern-life subjects, *Grandfather's visit* 1864 (Art Gallery of Ballarat) (p 131), was also exhibited at the Royal Society of British Artists. It is another morality tale for the mid-Victorian age, a story his public would read with ease. The subject offers an intimate glimpse of domestic life, happy or otherwise: the proud grandfather; the invalid and ailing daughter, a cradle by her side; the healthy heir and grandchild; the caring nurse, her emotion indicated by a crumpled handkerchief held in her hand. The viewer asks, 'Where is the father?' Is he away on some far-flung, noble Imperial campaign in India, or is there a darker story? The painting *Grandfather's visit* depicts the virtues of faith and cohesive family love in adversity. Its story is an enduring theme of social comment in many English paintings from the Victorian period, and the very opposite of the 'fall into vice' suggested in Dowling's earlier *Breakfasting out*.[14]

Dowling continued to paint similar subjects into the early 1880s, even when the fashion for them was waning and the policy of the Royal Academy, after moving to Burlington House in 1869 and under Lord Leighton's presidency, was to discourage anecdotal subjects in favour of more elevated classical and poetic themes. Dowling's abiding interest in modern moral subjects can be seen in paintings such as *Jeanie's first born* 1882 and the Stanhope Forbes-like work, *Going out with the tide* of similar date, which presents emerging and dying generations of Cornish fishermen. Many other genre paintings are known only from exhibition records or photographs. Some were sent to Australia; others remained in England and have been lost to obscurity among the huge volume of comparable work by British artists of the time.

Dowling sent works from London for sale in Melbourne, Hobart and Launceston from 1861 onwards. This was largely organised in Australia by his entrepreneurial brother Henry. The first of these exports for sale, the painting *The Presentation in the Temple* 1860 was shown at 62 Liverpool Street, Hobart, in December 1861.[15] A month or so later, in February 1862, it was for sale at Charles Summers's Studio, Collins Street, Melbourne. In February 1866, coinciding with the loan of the portraits of the Prince and Princess of Wales to the Inter-colonial Exhibition, Melbourne, the artist consigned four paintings to William Cawston's Photographic Studio, Paterson Street, Launceston. Later they could be seen at Messrs Walch & Son and, failing to sell, were included in an Art Union lottery in August 1866.[16] This lottery comprised sixty tickets at two guineas each, the prizes being the four paintings: *The duet: Mary Queen of Scots and Rizzio* (a history subject); *Guinevere and the novice* (from Tennyson's 'The Idylls of the King'); *Miriam* (an Old Testament subject); and *Grandfather's visit*. The result of the lottery was that *The duet* and *Miriam* went to the Western District pastoralists Robert de Little of Carramut House, and Joseph Ware of Minjah respectively; *Guinevere and the novice* to Mr George Collins, a Launceston solicitor; and *Grandfather's visit* to northern Tasmanian pastoralist Mr Thomas Archer of Woolmers. This pattern of colonial exhibition and sale, with varying success, continued through into the 1870s.

In 1877 Dowling dispatched to Melbourne, 'as an experiment on public taste in the colony',[17] a mixed bunch of works, not necessarily new. These included the genre paintings *After the duel: the consultation* and *A domestic incident at Rouen*; the Orientalist paintings *The suburban barber, Cairo*, *A Moorish woman and favourite* and *The Italian Mission in Egypt*; and the Biblical paintings *Ruth and Boaz* and *Unequally yoked.* In May these were offered for sale through Gemmell & Tuckett in their rooms at 350–361 Collins Street West.[18] Henry Dowling worked hard to achieve results on his brother's behalf. Some of these works, *Unequally yoked*, *The suburban barber, Cairo* and *The Italian Mission in Egypt*, along with *A sheikh and his son entering Cairo, on their return from a pilgrimage to Mecca*, were subsequently lent to the National Gallery of Victoria.[19] *Unequally yoked* was eventually acquired by Joseph Ware. William Lynch of Brighton, a collector of mainly British landscapes, purchased *The Italian Mission in Egypt*,[20] and Frederick Sheppard Grimwade of Caulfield acquired *Ruth and Boaz* 1869 (he also owned the painting *Hagar* 1872–73).[21] Other paintings sent to Australia by Robert Dowling were purchased by John Ware of Yalla-y-Poora and AT Turner. In Melbourne, the noted collector of Munich School or other German paintings, RW Kinnear of Toorak, owned Dowling's *An incident in the siege of Gloucester 1643* 1867;[22] and the surgeon Sir Thomas Fitzgerald owned *Sabbath in the country* 1859.[23]

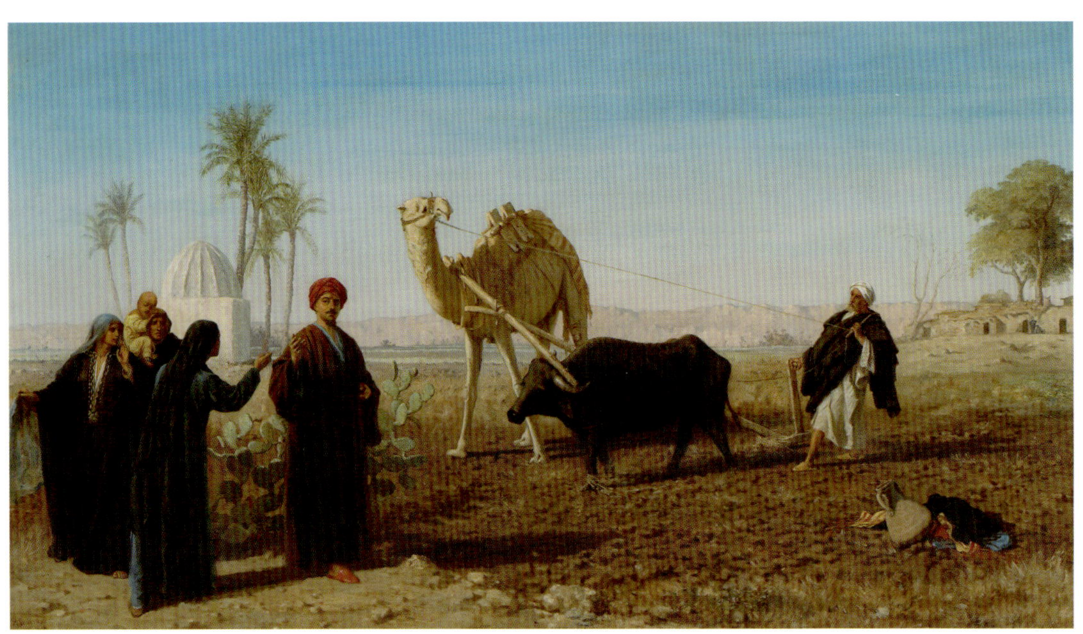

Robert Dowling
Unequally yoked
1874
oil on canvas,
81.5 x 145 cm
Warrnambool Art Gallery, Victoria, presented by Joseph Ware 1892

Dowling's biblical subjects were a major component of his career in England. He had been raised in a devout Christian home where the Bible was read daily, and these subjects had engaged him as a youth in Tasmania. In London, he pursued them throughout the 1860s, 70s and early 80s, sometimes on canvases that are the most ambitious in his oeuvre. Dowling's religious works are not devotional images, but Protestant Bible stories. They were created against the background of contemporary biblical study and archaeological excursions in Palestine and elsewhere in the Middle East. Historical authenticity characterised later-nineteenth-century biblical illustration, and earlier, from the late 1840s onwards, the avant-garde paintings by the Pre-Raphaelite Brotherhood. William Holman Hunt's *The Finding of the Saviour in the Temple* 1854–55, for example, was painted after the artist's first visit to Jerusalem, and widely disseminated by engraving. Holman Hunt's detailed historicism, in terms of place, architecture and costume, is reflected in Dowling's earliest identified religious painting, *The Presentation in the Temple* 1860.

Concern for authenticity is a strong element of the better composed, less complex painting, *Miriam* 1864 (Warrnambool) (p 136), a beautifully resolved work, and quite Pre-Raphaelite in colour and in its associations.

The subject comes from the Old Testament Book of Exodus where Miriam, the daughter of Jochebed, hides her brother Moses in the rushes of the Nile to avoid the impending slaughter of young Hebrew males by the Egyptian Pharaoh. The painting was exhibited at the Royal Society of British Artists, with the long title *Miriam. 'Should he escape, which yet I dare not hope, each sea-born monster: yet the winds and waves he cannot escape…' from Hannah More's Sacred Drama—Moses in the Bulrushes*. The reference is to the famous eighteenth-century religious writer, Sabbath School enthusiast and philanthropist, Hannah More (1745–1833). Her *Sacred dramas*, first published in 1782, were enormously popular and reprinted long into the nineteenth century. Dowling's painting follows her elaboration of the sacred text and precedes Miriam's action of concealment in preference for an exploration of the emotional drama of the event. It is the moment of decision and trust in Divine Providence. The mother Jochebed, her eyes raised heavenward, cradles Moses on her lap in a Pietà-like attitude. Miriam, acknowledging her mother's anguish, prepares to take the child and implement their plan for his survival. Bulrushes, the means for his concealment, litter the floor. In the doorway stands the shadowy figure of Moses's father, Amram.

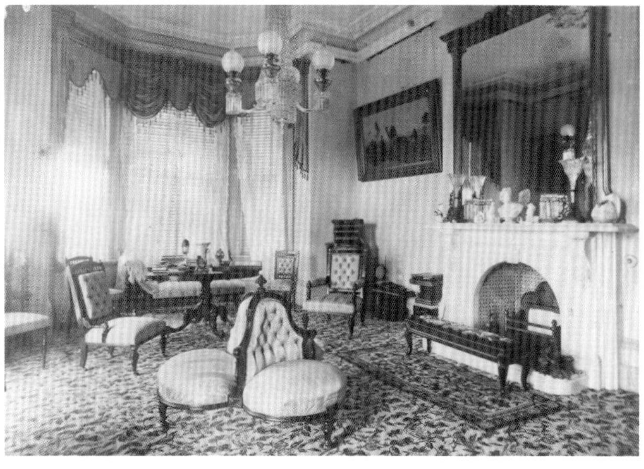

Drawing room at Minjah c 1880
On the wall left of the mirror hangs *Unequally yoked*. The painting *Miriam* is reflected in the mirror.
private collection

The year before, 1863, Dowling attempted a painting of the 'Baptism of Our Lord in the River Jordan', one of his most ambitious religious works. It existed in three states: *The Baptism of Christ*, 'a fourteen foot [high work] with life size figures', at one time belonging to Sir Peter Coats, but now lost;[24] a smaller version titled *Sketch for 'The Baptism of Christ'* (QVMAG) (p 134); and an engraving, *The Baptism of Our Lord* (Woolmers Estate, Longford, Tasmania) (p 135). Dowling was brought up in a denomination where the practice of adult baptism by immersion in water was a central tenet. This involved the adult's full immersion, rather than the more general baptism of infants by sprinkling, practised in other Christian denominations. The artist had witnessed this distinctive aspect of his father's ministry countless times.

His elder brother Henry, in 1844, and brothers John and Thomas, in 1845, all presented themselves to their father for this fundamental rite of the Baptist Church, conducted in a clay pit near their house in Launceston. Robert Dowling, aged twenty-four years, experienced his own baptism on 24 December 1851.

The large version of *The Baptism of Christ* was first shown at the premises of P & D Colnaghi & Co in Pall Mall in April 1865. The painting was favourably reviewed, at length, in *The Freeman*, 19 April 1865 and *The Art Journal*, June 1865, as 'much the best picture Mr Dowling has produced'.[25] Colnaghi subsequently published a widely popular steel-engraving of it by James Stephenson.

The smaller *Sketch for 'The Baptism of Christ'* was sent to Launceston two years earlier. It arrived in December 1864[26] and was exhibited there by Henry Dowling. He subsequently lent the work to the Exhibition of Paintings and Works in the Launceston Town Hall in July–August 1865 and, along with the portraits of the Prince and Princess of Wales, to The Inter-colonial Exhibition of Australasia held in Melbourne from October 1866 to February 1867. Over ten years later, in February–March 1879, Henry Dowling lent *Sketch for 'The Baptism of Christ'* to the Fine Arts Exhibition in Launceston.[27] It appears that Henry Dowling, a devout Baptist, owned the painting personally. His involvement is understandable, for the painting has a potency comparable with that of Holman Hunt's Christian-conversion subject, *The Light of the World* 1851–53 (and later versions), the most famous of all religious images in the English-speaking world. The inspiration for Dowling's painting comes from the New Testament, St Mark, chapter 1, verses 10–11:

> And straightway coming up out of the water, he saw the heavens open and the spirit like a dove descending upon him: And there came a voice from heaven saying, Thou art my beloved Son, in whom I am well pleased.

In 1866 an Australian religious poet, 'Theresa Tasmania' (Lucy Anna Edgar, 1838 — after 1875), writing in George Rolwegan's Hobart publication *The Tasmanian Messenger*, described her profound reaction to the painting (see opposite).

Thoughts Suggested by the Sight of Mr Robert Dowling's Painting 'The Baptism of Christ'

A WONDROUS PICTURE! full of tenderness,
Suggestive of so many touching thoughts,
That eye may gaze long at it, till the tears,
Slow-gathering, ease the full heart's overflow
Of deep emotion—holy, solemn, fond,
A picture wrought by a true Christian hand,
And striving to express the artist's sense
Of love and reverence. The canvas bears
Not merely the mute strokes of loveliness,—
A soul there lives and breathes! A heart beats there.
And like a gush of truest eloquence,
Feels for the gazer's heart and touches it.

A chill grey dawn just struggling o'er the heart
A solemn stillness at the river side
And on the great dark mountains far behind,
The stronghold of the cloud-king,
where he scowls
In sullen grandeur on this holy morn.
Behold his throne invaded! For the sun,
Stronger than he, forth from his chamber comes
And giant-like, crushes the darkness down.
The strong red light is fiercely still opposed
By proud black clouds that slowly, scornfully,
Give way to grey, which grasped in the embrace
Of the awak'ning monarch (who indeed
Turns all to gold at touch) are overlaid
With hues of vivid beauty that o'er leap
The dark dominions of receding night,
And gild the river as it wakes with joy
And sparkles into ripples at the touch.

Yet more. It ripples round the sacred form,
Kisses His dripping robes as slow he moves
Towards the nearer shore, a meek hand laid
Upon His sinless breast; His downcast lids
Shading those gracious eyes so full of love,
Of sympathy, and tears; His countenance
Of 'human face divine' the beau ideal,
A face of perfect beauty, with the God
Veiled in its human features, and as yet
Unmarred with griefs of a sad ministry;
Altho' the mouth in its pure comeliness
Seems rather formed of tender tones of woe,
And sympathy with sorrow, than for smiles.

Yet meek and lowly as the Saviour stands,
Having submitted to the first demand
On his obedience, His Messiahship—
Is witnessed by the Voice that opens Heaven,
And sheds a sudden stream of radiance down:
Upon His head, around His form, and o'er,
The bright'ning waters of fair Jordan's wave,
Until it quite illuminates the brow,
And rugged, grave, astonished face of John
Upgazing, boldly wet with reverent eyes,
And shielding careful finger, to the light,
And streaming glory of the Father's home.

Then on the face of that 'beloved Son',
The wand'ring glance concentrates, till rushes by,
Thoughts of the weary life He then began,
The saddest, sweetest life in history:
Thoughts of His mild compassion, and His love:
Thoughts of His noble dignity and power;
Thoughts of His patient sufferance of wrong;
Thoughts of His tender pity for His foes,
And more, pardon to His unfaithful friends;
Thoughts of His final agony and blood;
Thoughts of His glorious resurrection morn,
Thoughts of His coming once again with power;
To reign, the King confessed by every knee;
Until the glory that envelops Him
Absorbs the human in the artist's work,
And it becomes, like inspiration's breath,
A glass to view the Saviour's beauty in.[28]

'Theresa Tasmania' (Lucy Anna Edgar)

Dowling's *Sketch for 'The Baptism of Christ'* has had no presence in the annals of Australian art. The painting was out of the public arena for many years, hanging in the Paterson Street Wesleyan Church in Launceston and, even after its donation to the Queen Victoria Museum & Art Gallery in 1982, was rarely displayed. The number of religious images in colonial Australian art is very limited.[29] Dowling's painting of the Baptism of Christ is among the best of that small body and the most astonishing religious image in Australian art. Regardless of being painted in England, it came from the artist's own earlier Australian experience. When shown in Australia in the 1860s his contemporaries, like the poet Lucy Edgar, recognised its significance and responded to it.

The celebration of an Old Testament heroine in the painting *Miriam* 1864 was followed by others, among them *Ruth and Boaz* 1869, *Hagar* 1872 (Abraham's concubine and mother of his son Ishmael), *Ruth and Naomi; so they two went until they came to Bethlehem* 1874, *Ruth gleaning the cornfield of Boaz* c 1874, *Rebecca at the well*, and the New Testament subject, *The woman of Samaria* 1872. Ruth is probably also the subject of *The gleaner (An Egyptian woman)* 1873 (TMAG) (p 137). The Moabite heroine Ruth, the great-grandmother of King David, was a romantic figure whose famed beauty is celebrated in this painting, one of the best of Dowling's higher-keyed 'golden' works and a summer image of bountiful harvest, its white, sun-drenched tone reflecting the artist's experience in Egypt and Palestine.

Dowling countered these feminine images with patriarchal figures from the Old Testament. His large, approximately five-by-eight-foot (152 x 244 cm) canvas, *Moses viewing the Promised Land from Mount Nebo* (Paisley Museum & Art Gallery, Scotland) comes from the Book of Deuteronomy 34: 1–4. The painting was exhibited at the Royal Academy exhibition of 1878 and at the London Stereoscopic Company in Regent Street in 1879. There is a smaller watercolour version of the subject (private collection). The oil painting was described as 'being painted from the spot on which the prophet stands'.[30] This echoes Holman Hunt's earlier claim about his biblical painting, *The scapegoat* 1854, a canvas which was indeed partly painted at Osdoom on the Dead Sea and finished in his studio in Jerusalem. Dowling's very large canvas most likely comes from sketches made on Mount Nebo in 1872 or 1873 and conforms to the reality of that harsh, desert-like landscape at the northern edge of the Dead Sea. The lone, towering figure of the prophet Moses, having led the Israelites out of Egypt and through the wilderness for forty years, surveys the sweeping vista of the Promised Land of Canaan, where he will never tread. The native cyclamens flowering at his feet are sometimes read as the symbol of resignation and farewell. In 1880 the painting was sent to Australia from London, with a now lost work, *From Calvary to the Tomb* 1880, and exhibited that year in the Melbourne International Exhibition.

In 1884 Dowling brought with him to Melbourne another ambitious, six-by-four-foot (182.6 x 128.2 cm) canvas, *Daniel in the lions' den* 1882. The subject, taken from the Book of Daniel, 6: 4–27, was treated by other artists at that time. Dowling's treatment is melodramatic and very broad and it received mixed reactions when shown in the Victorians' Jubilee Exhibition in Melbourne. One reviewer responded:

> We do not greatly care for [it] … the God-sent angel [*sic*][31] that 'shut the lions' mouths' savours too much of the mawkish, modern German school of religious figure-drawing; while … the beasts appear to us a little out of scale, and of somewhat pantomimic anatomical construction.[32]

One found it 'noble'.[33] Another review compared the painting favourably with Briton Rivière's[34] popular and oft-reproduced painting *Daniel* 1872.[35] Dowling's *Daniel in the lions' den* returned to England after his death and found its way to the Convent of the Sacred Heart at Hove in Sussex. It is now in the collection of the Philadelphia Museum of Art, which acquired the painting believing it to be a work of the great nineteenth-century Bible illustrator Gustave Doré (1832–1883). Dowling's 1882 painting bears close resemblance to Doré's 1866 engraving *Daniel in the lions' den*.

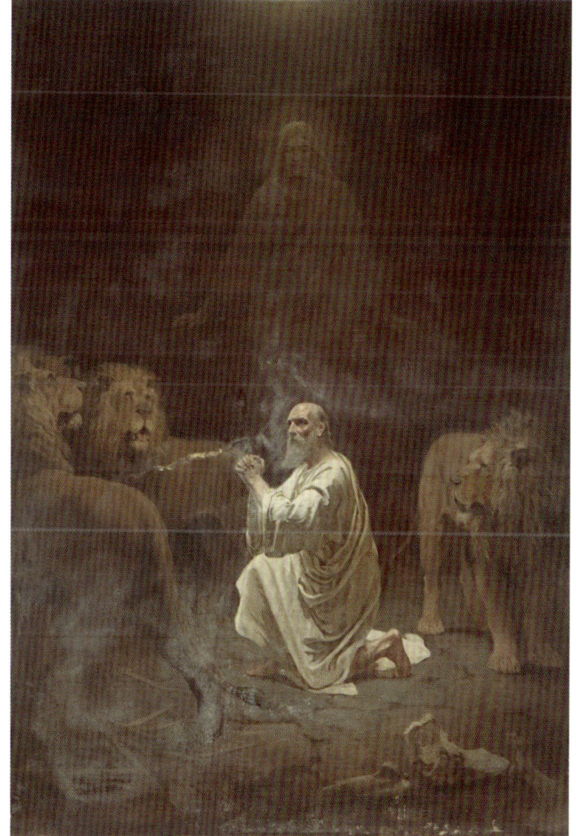

Robert Dowling
Daniel in the lions' den 1882
oil on canvas, 182.6 x 128.2 cm
Philadelphia Museum of Art

The aim of Dowling's visit to Cairo and the Holy Land in 1872–73 (and again in 1876 as indicated by the two water colours, *Cairo (camels)*; p 142) was two-fold: to gain authentic information and background for his biblical paintings; and to furnish himself with material for his new interest in exotic and picturesque Oriental subjects. He was among many European artists to do so, including Frederick Goodall, John Frederick Lewis, Jean-Léon Gérôme and Leopold Karl Müller.[36] (When Dowling lent his painting of the New Testament parable *Unequally yoked* to the National Gallery of Victoria in 1877 it was listed with the subsidiary title 'Ploughing in Egypt'.[37])

From the imperial experiments of Bonaparte in Egypt in 1798–1801 onwards, the 'mysterious East', in particular the shambling lands and cities of the decadent Ottoman Empire, opened the nineteenth-century European imagination to realms far beyond the confines of the traditional eighteenth-century Grand Tour. In the 1830s, Delacroix's voluptuous Algerian women raised the Orient to a major theme in Western high art. Exotic travel-art images of the 'Thousand and One Arabian Nights' cities—Damascus, Cairo and Baghdad—were also enormously popular. The opening of the Suez Canal in 1869 gave renewed impetus to these interests.

The precise dates of Dowling's visit to Egypt have not been established. The booklet, 'Mr Robert Dowling's Oriental Picture', that accompanied the exhibition in Launceston and Melbourne of his 1874 painting *A sheikh and his son entering Cairo, on their return from a pilgrimage to Mecca* (NGV) (pp 138–39), was presumably compiled from notes supplied by the artist. It states that 'he was resident in Cairo, chief of the Arabian cities' in 1872–73. This would be consistent with the number of Egyptian subjects—and Algerian, even though it is not certain he visited Algiers—exhibited from that time onwards at the Royal Academy and the Royal Society of British Artists. These include *The Upper Nile, Egypt* 1876, *A shady corner, Algiers* 1872 and *The Coptic market, Cairo* 1877, and the harem subjects, *The first advances* 1873 and *The slave dealer* 1880. Images of beautiful Oriental women include the oil paintings *The Egyptian* and *Evening on the housetop, Algiers* 1878 and the watercolour *Egyptian banana seller* 1878 (private collection) (p 141), each of which used the same female model, and display a heightened colour range resonant with the values of the Aesthetic Movement. Perhaps the Egyptian model inserted into an Algerian setting had been found in London.

Dowling's tour de force in this genre was *A sheikh and his son entering Cairo, on their return from a pilgrimage to Mecca*. He exhibited the painting at the Royal Academy in 1875, and subsequently consigned the large canvas to Australia. After a much-publicised Launceston exposition in January 1877 at Walch & Sons, the painting came to Melbourne, where it was given wide currency by its loan, and subsequent presentation 'by a committee of gentlemen', to the National Gallery of Victoria in 1878. As well as being Dowling's most ambitious Orientalist work, it is, along with Nicholas Chevalier's *Buddha's renunciation* 1884 (Ballarat), the most outstanding example of Orientalism in Australian art. The expensive, elaborate, Egyptianesque frame indicates how seriously Robert Dowling valued it.

The annual Muslim pilgrimage to Mecca—the distribution there of fragments of the previous year's black brocade 'Kisweh', woven in Cairo to cover the Kaaba stone at the centre of the Great Mosque at Mecca, the prescribed prayers and circuits around the Kaaba itself—were, and are, central to Muslim religious practice. The pilgrims' ceremonial return to their Ottoman cities constituted a popular public celebration. A correspondent to the London *Tim*es reported on such an event in Damascus:

> the street was one mass of moving colour lit up by sunshine … shops were filled with women and children … laughter filled the air … camels, horses and donkeys struggled through the crowds … bands played quaint Turkish music … crowds on the roof and ledge looked on … as does a pleased audience at a theatre.[38]

Dowling documents a similar homecoming, one he would have witnessed in Cairo.

The distinctive architecture of old Cairo, the houses with their latticed windows and other details of the crowded street scene are treated in a number of smaller related oil paintings, such as *Street scene, Cairo* c 1874 (NGA) (p 140). The exhibition booklet produced in Australia, and numerous press reviews,[39] make much of these elements: the procession of camels, horses and musicians, the sheikh's attendants, street children, harem women, Bedouins, Jews, an Italian monk, and shop-keepers and street vendors are described in detail. As the booklet states, it is 'a careful illustration of Oriental life, architecture and costume'. The painting also reaffirms Dowling's fondness for narrative, similar to his London *Breakfasting out* street scene of 1859. The Cairo painting, of some sixteen years later, differs from that work in scale, complexity, sophisticated handling of colour, and exotic appeal. As a contemporary tourist found in 1888:

> Cairo is so utterly different from anything in Europe[,] the outdoor life is so amusing, the streets, with their moving diorama of brilliant colour and marvellous costume, so picturesque that the most exacting traveller can hardly be disappointed, however highly he may have pitched his expectations.[40]

The most compelling aspect of *A sheikh and his son entering Cairo* is its demonstration of the artist as a colourist of some significance. Sensitive use of colour was a characteristic of earlier portraits and paintings such as the 1864 works, *Miriam* and *Grandfather's visit*. This large Cairo subject of ten years later gave Dowling the opportunity to use colour with symphonic richness. This palette is also found in Dowling's handsome watercolour *Egyptian banana seller* 1878 and the watercolours of 1882, *Shylock and Jessica* and *A merchant in Algiers* (QVMAG) (pp 144 and 145). They are of the highest quality, displaying the same virtuosity of colour, fondness for delineating the rich textures of silk and other fabrics, and illustrate his skilful command of the less-used watercolour medium.

Dowling said he sent the large Cairo oil painting to Australia 'for the gratification of his old friends and fellow Colonists … on the sole condition that the expense of conveyance to the colonies and transmission again to England shall not fall on him.'[41] When the work was on loan to the National Gallery of Victoria in February 1877, true to form, Robert Dowling's brother Henry pressed hard for its acquisition.[42] The painting had secured the endorsement of Eugene von Guérard, the gallery's curator: 'The best picture which I have seen from this artist … I consider this work to be well worth the consideration of the Honourable Trustees'.[43] It was eventually acquired by the trustees in August 1878, but by means of a subscription, again organised by Henry Dowling, with donations from relatives in Tasmania and Victoria, and from prominent Western District families. These included Sir Samuel Wilson and his brother John Wilson, Walter Manifold, Philip Russell and his cousin the Reverend Robert Russell, Thomas Shaw, the brothers John, William and Thomas Cumming, Sir William Clarke, the brothers John and Joseph Ware, and Charles Kernot's daughters.[44] Together they raised the £420 required, and the painting was given to the National Gallery of Victoria.

Before Robert Dowling's return to Australia in 1884, his brother Henry travelled to England in 1880 for celebrations marking the centenary of

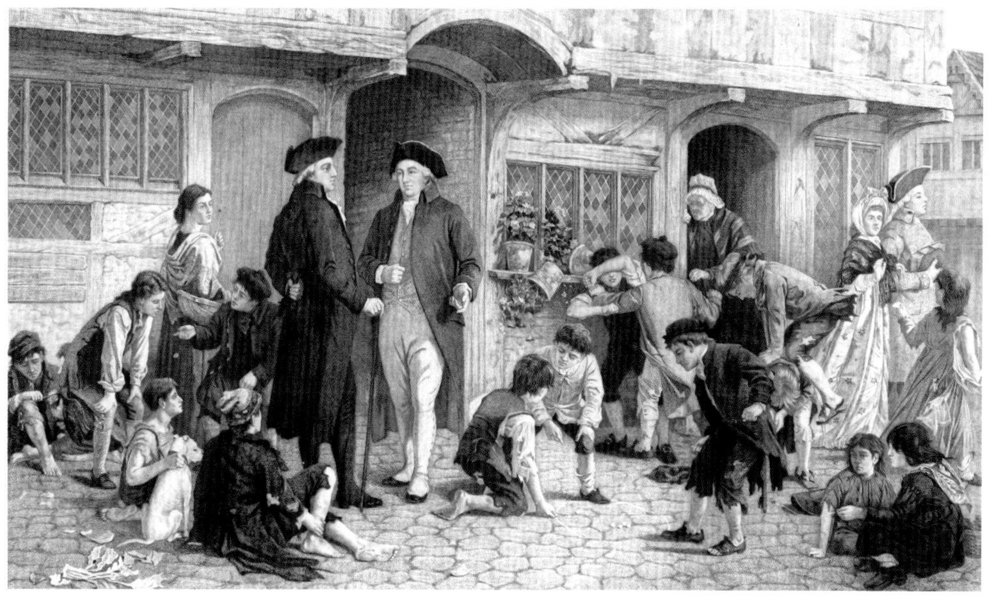

Robert Dowling (artist)
Leopold Lowenstam (engraver)
Origin of Sunday Schools, Hare Lane, Gloucester, 1780 1880
steel engraving on paper
Queen Victoria Museum and Art Gallery, Launceston

the founding, in Gloucester in July 1780, of the Sunday or Sabbath School movement by Robert Raikes (1735–1811). Henry Dowling, who in the 1830s had pioneered the Sunday School movement in Australia, was representing the Sunday School Union of Tasmania. He stayed some fifteen months in Britain, during 1880–81, spending time in London with Robert. The artist obligingly provided a commemorative oil painting for the centenary, *The meeting of Raikes and Revd T Stocks in regard to Sunday Schools* 1880, which he later brought to Melbourne and exhibited in his Collins Street studio. The painting is unlocated, but an engraving of it was made the same year and captioned *Origin of Sunday Schools Hare Lane, Gloucester, 1780 / Once by Severn's side / A little fountain rose / Now like the Severn's seaward tide / Round the world it flows* (QVMAG and other collections) (above). It was dedicated to the great Evangelical reformer, The Earl of Shaftsbury, engraved by Leopold Lowenstam, published by P E Reynolds and circulated widely throughout the British Empire.

Considering the massive art production of the British art world in the Victorian era, Robert Dowling's twenty-seven-year artistic sojourn in London can be seen as both critically and financially successful. His income through the 1860s and 70s was bolstered by a steady stream of sales in the Australian colonies, to which he returned in 1884.

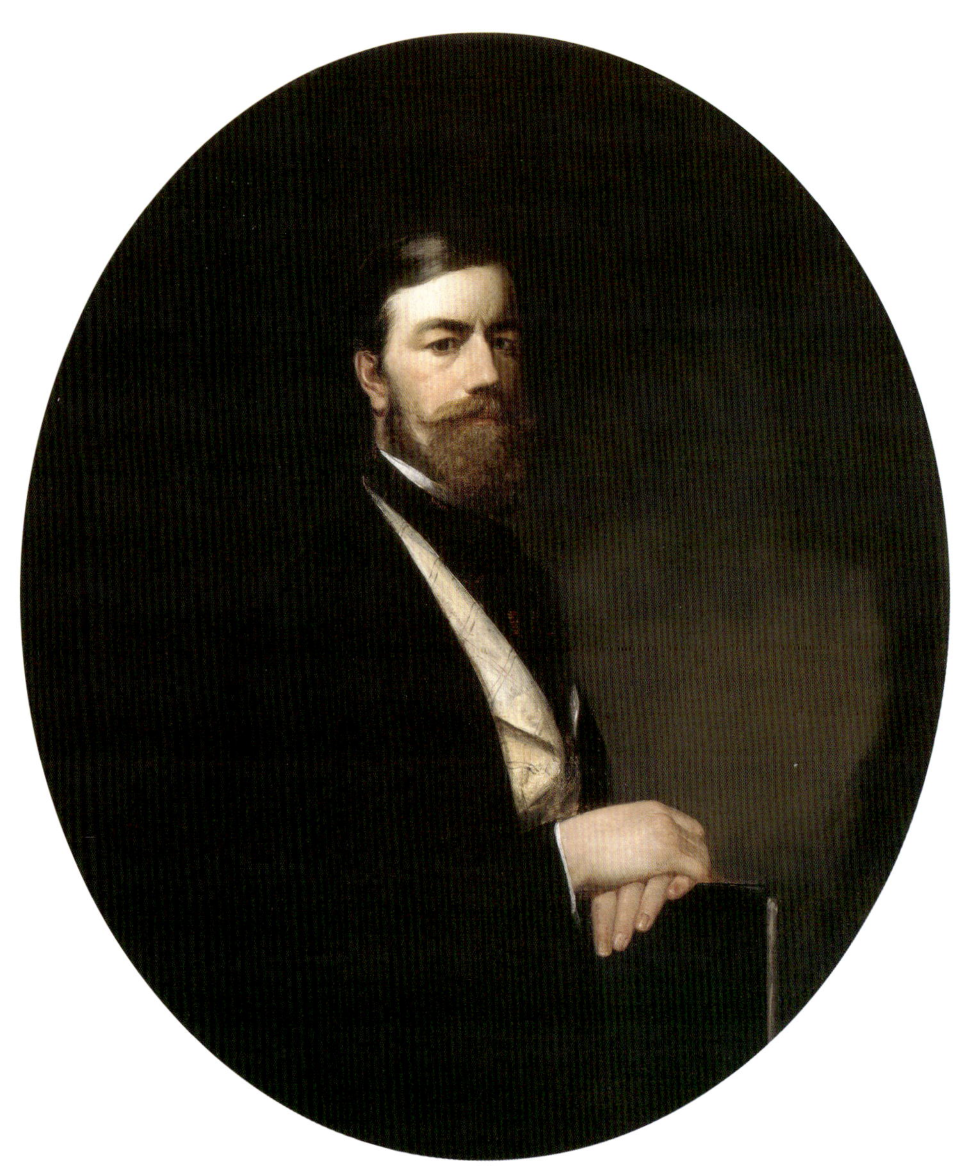

Self-portrait 1859
oil on canvas
Queen Victoria Museum
and Art Gallery, Launceston

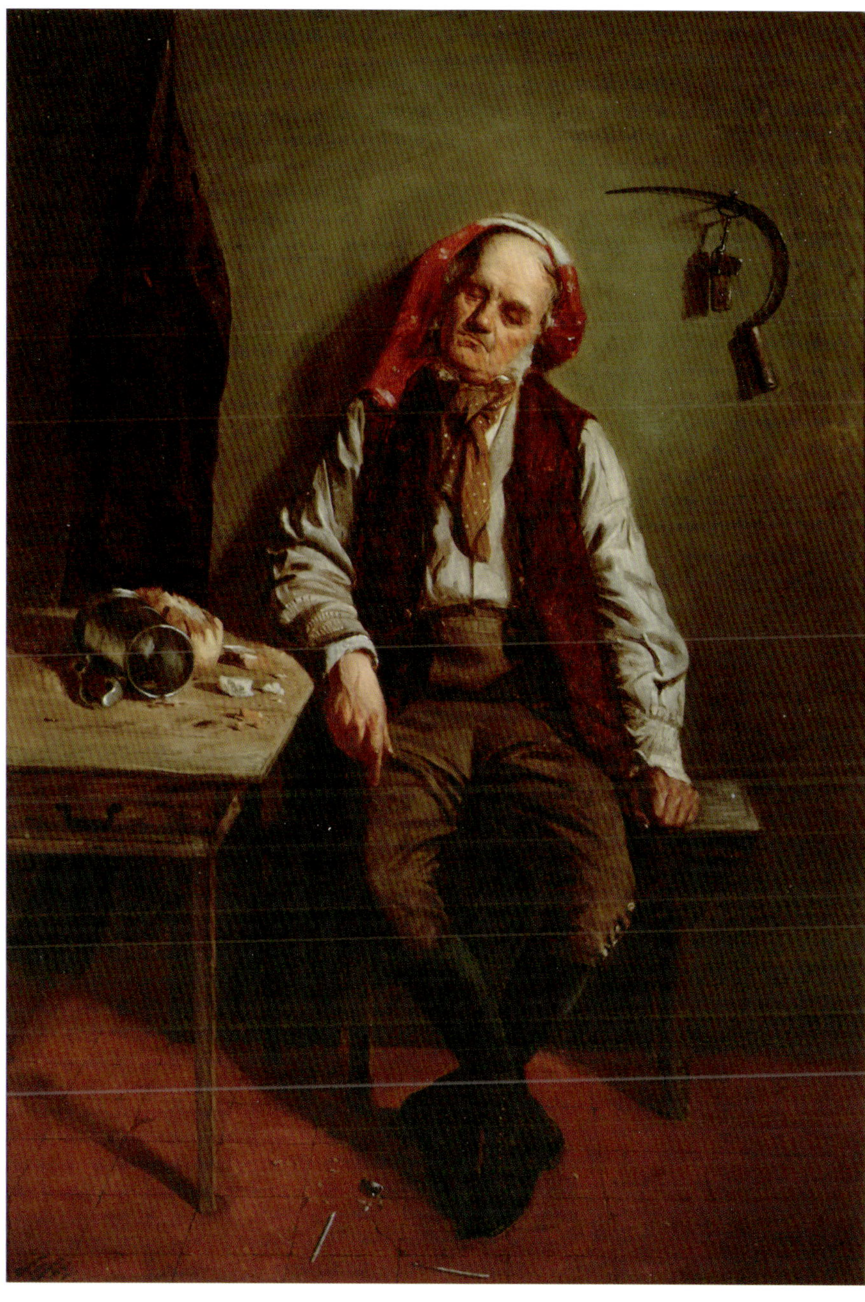

Sabbath in the country
1859
oil on canvas
private collection
Image courtesy of Menzies Art Brands, Melbourne and Sydney
Photographer: Andrew Murray

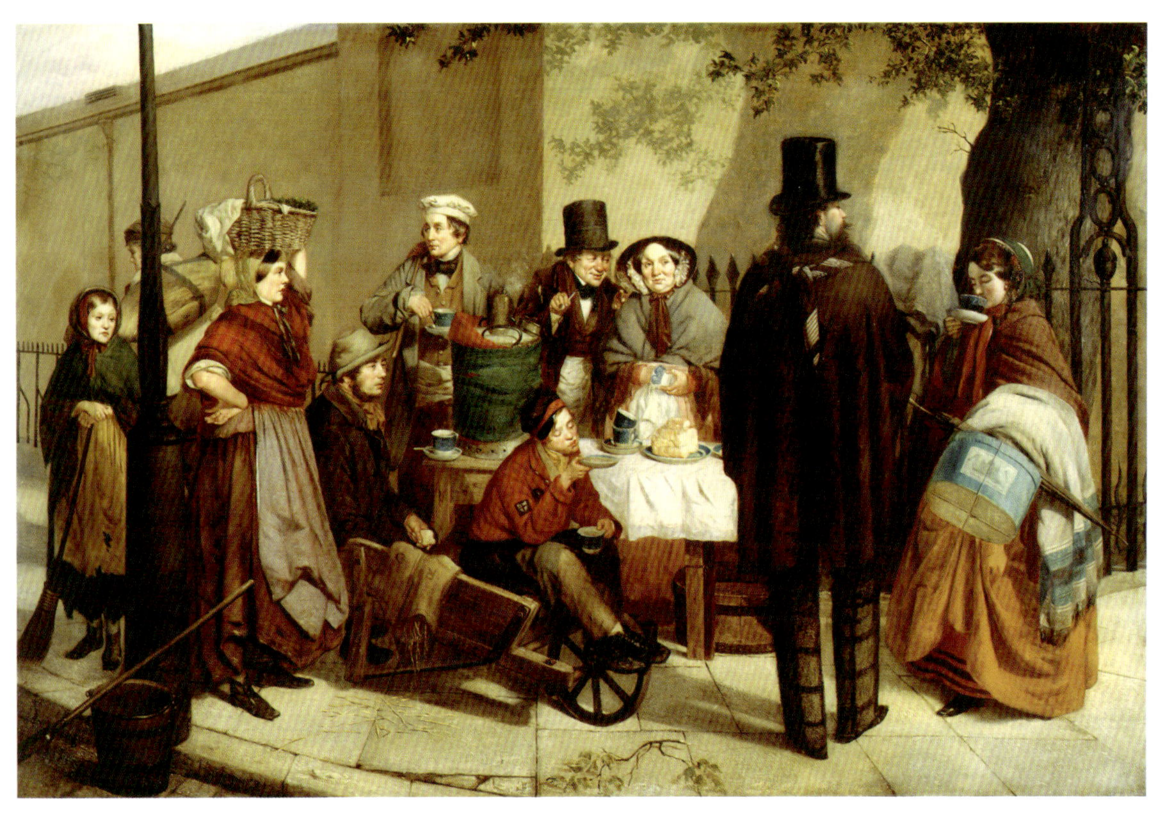

Breakfasting out 1859
oil on canvas
Museum of London, London

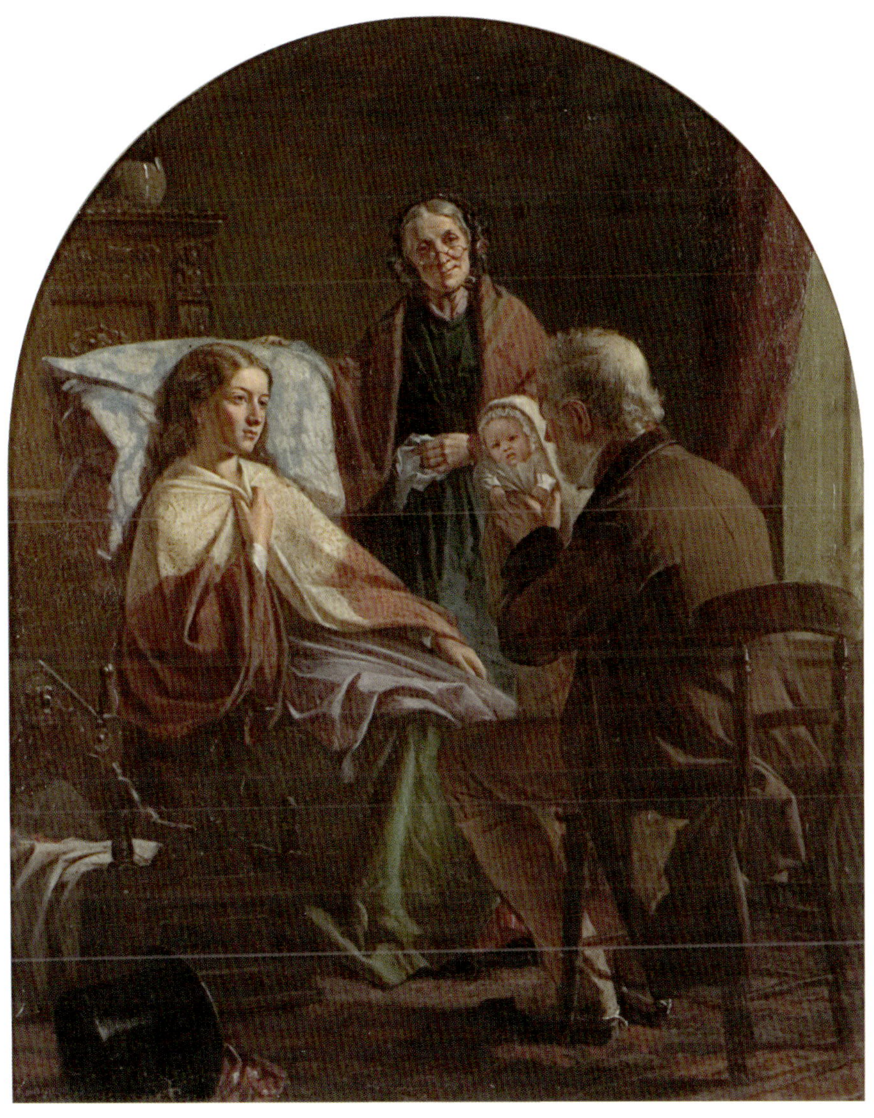

Grandfather's visit 1864
oil on canvas
Art Gallery of Ballarat, Victoria

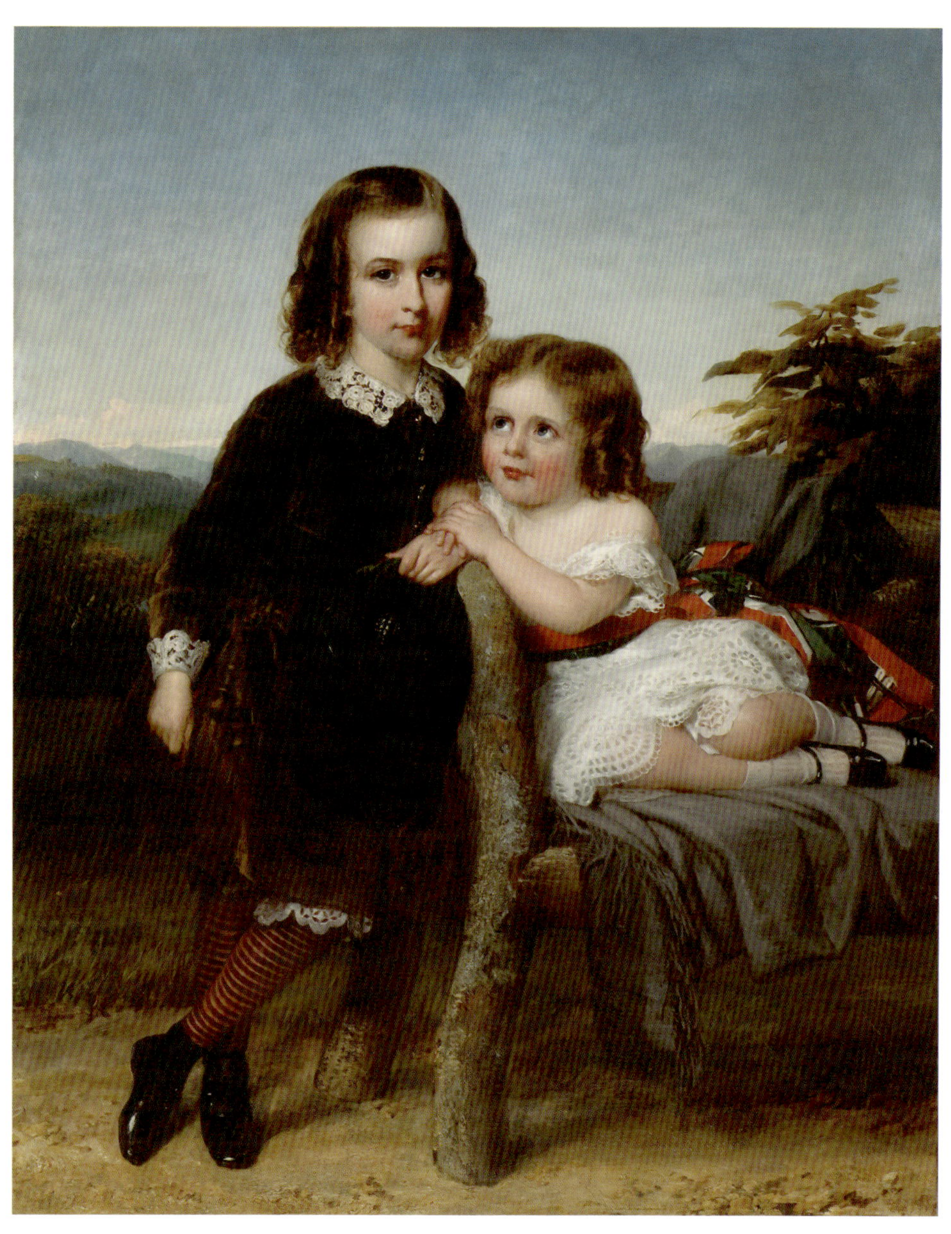

Masters Frederick and Arthur, sons of Henry Reed c 1862
oil on canvas
National Trust of Australia (Tasmania)

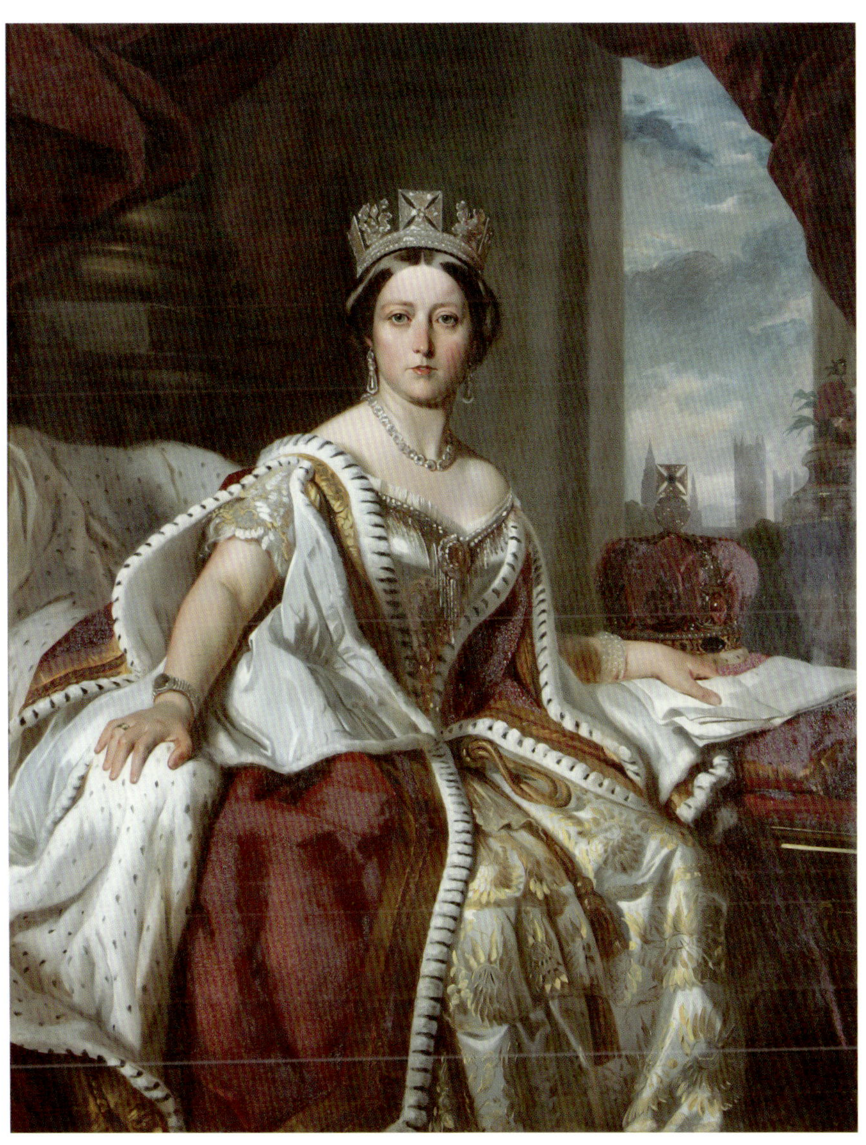

Robert Dowling after
Franz Xavier Winterhalter
(1806–1873)
Queen Victoria 1862
oil on canvas
Queen Victoria Museum
and Art Gallery, Launceston

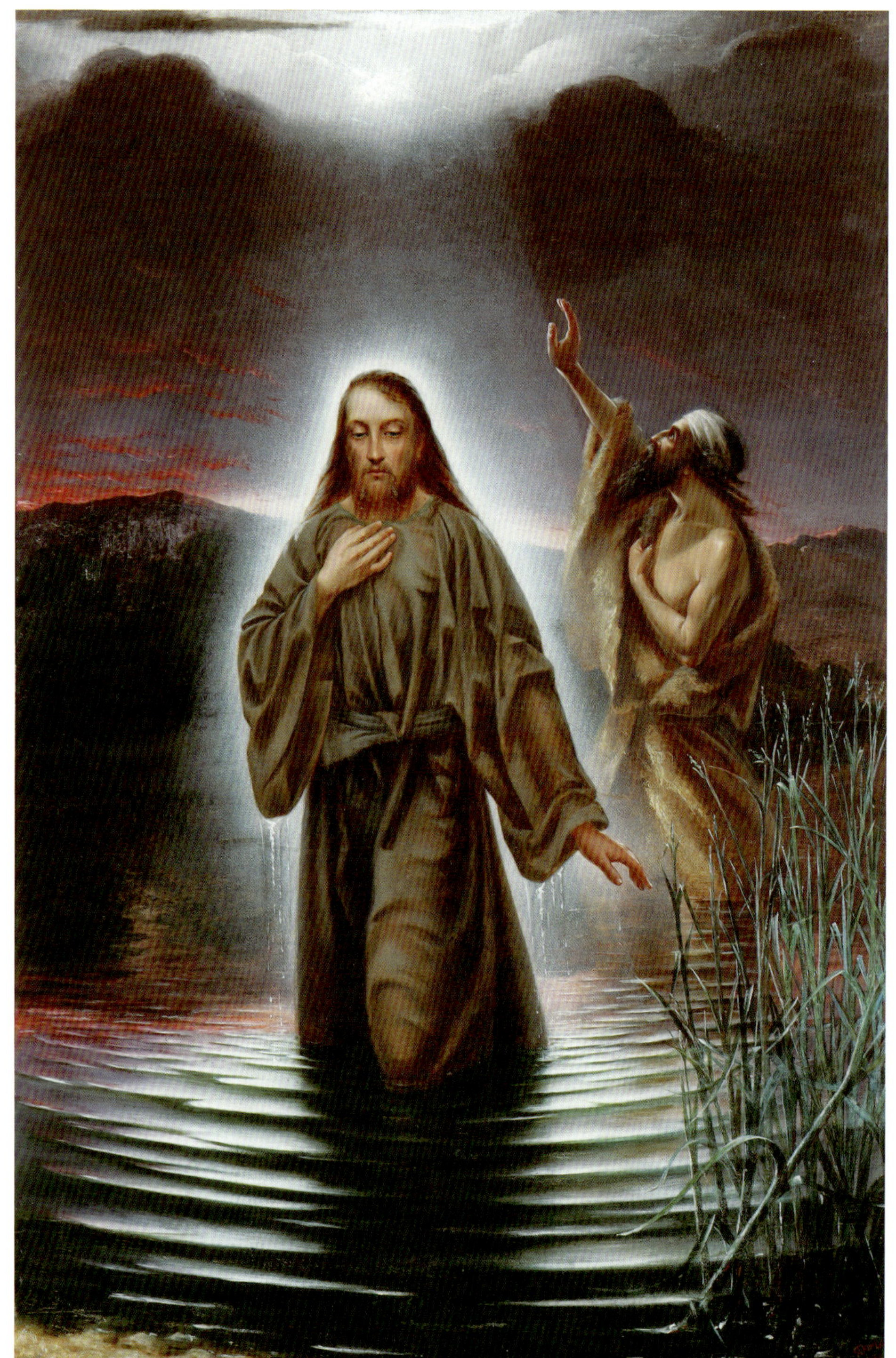

Sketch for 'The Baptism of Christ' 1863
oil on canvas
Queen Victoria Museum and Art Gallery, Launceston

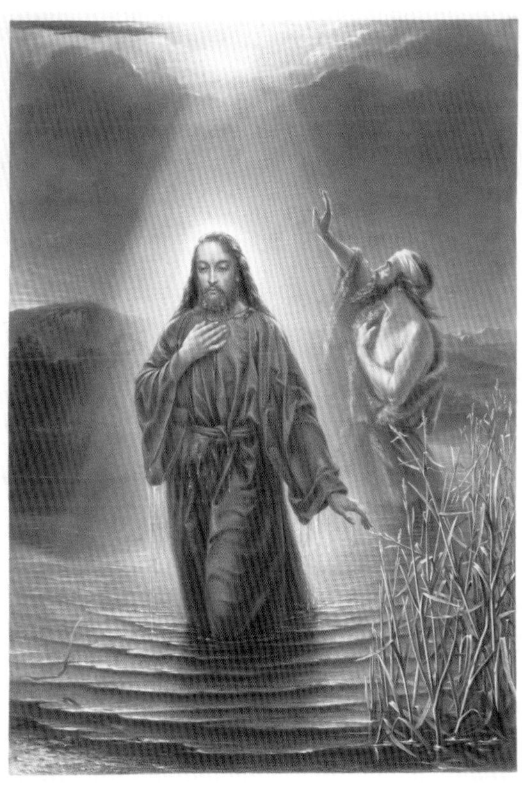

Robert Dowling
(artist)
James Stephenson
(engraver)
The Baptism of Our Lord 1865
steel engraving
on paper
Woolmers Estate,
Longford, Tasmania

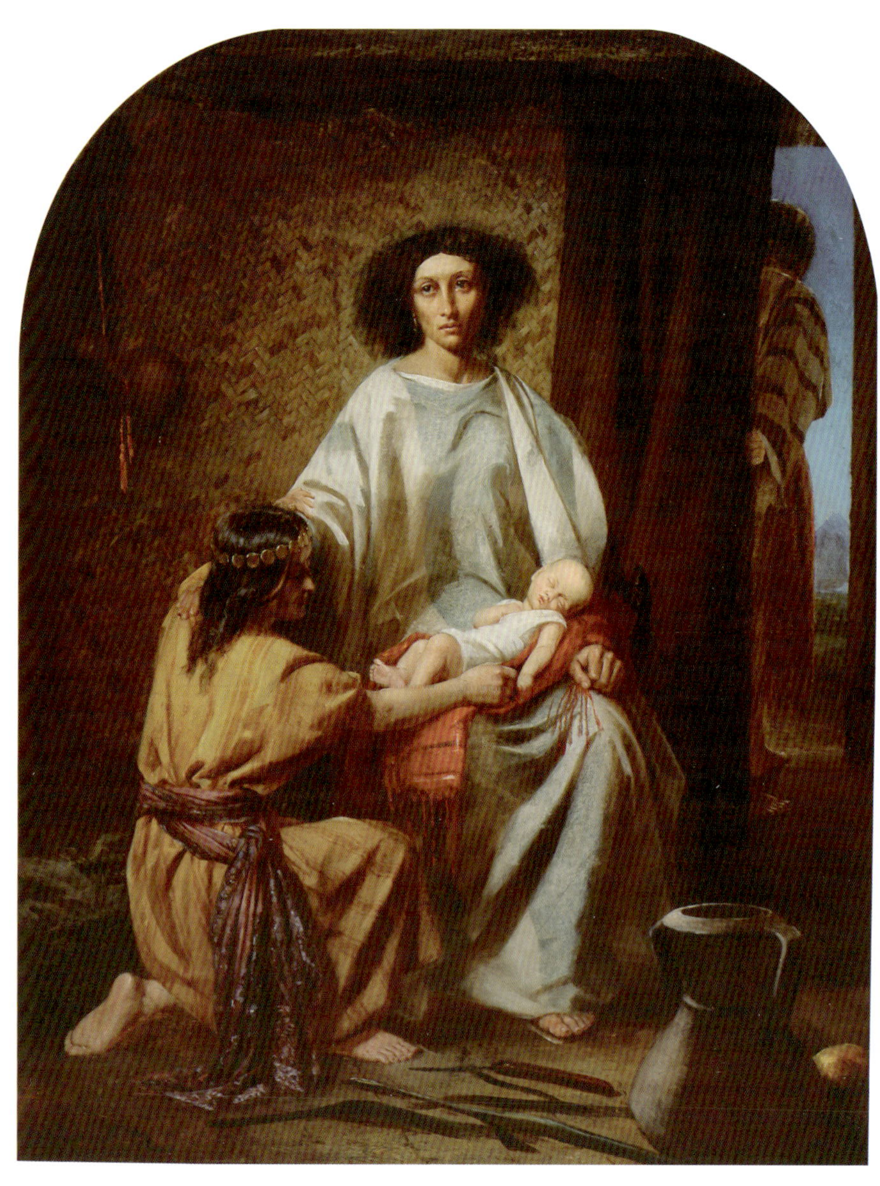

Miriam 1864
oil on canvas
Warrnambool Art Gallery,
Victoria

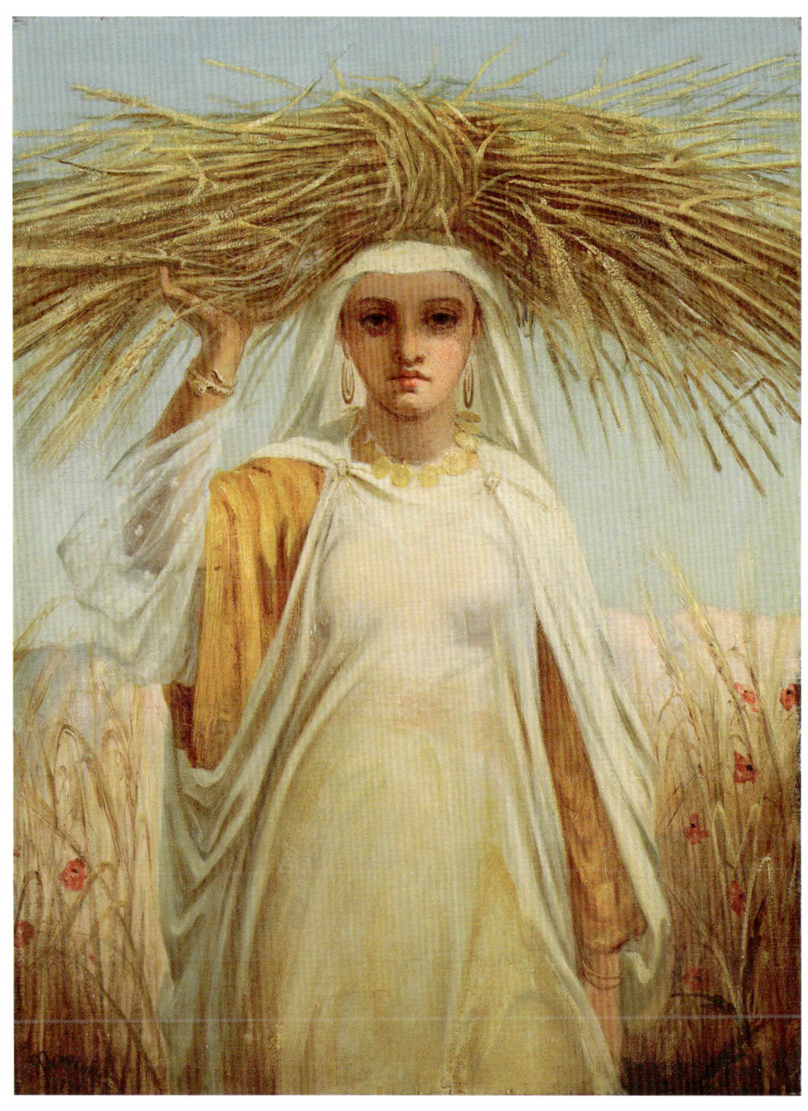

The gleaner (An Egyptian woman) 1873
oil on canvas
Tasmanian Museum
and Art Gallery, Hobart

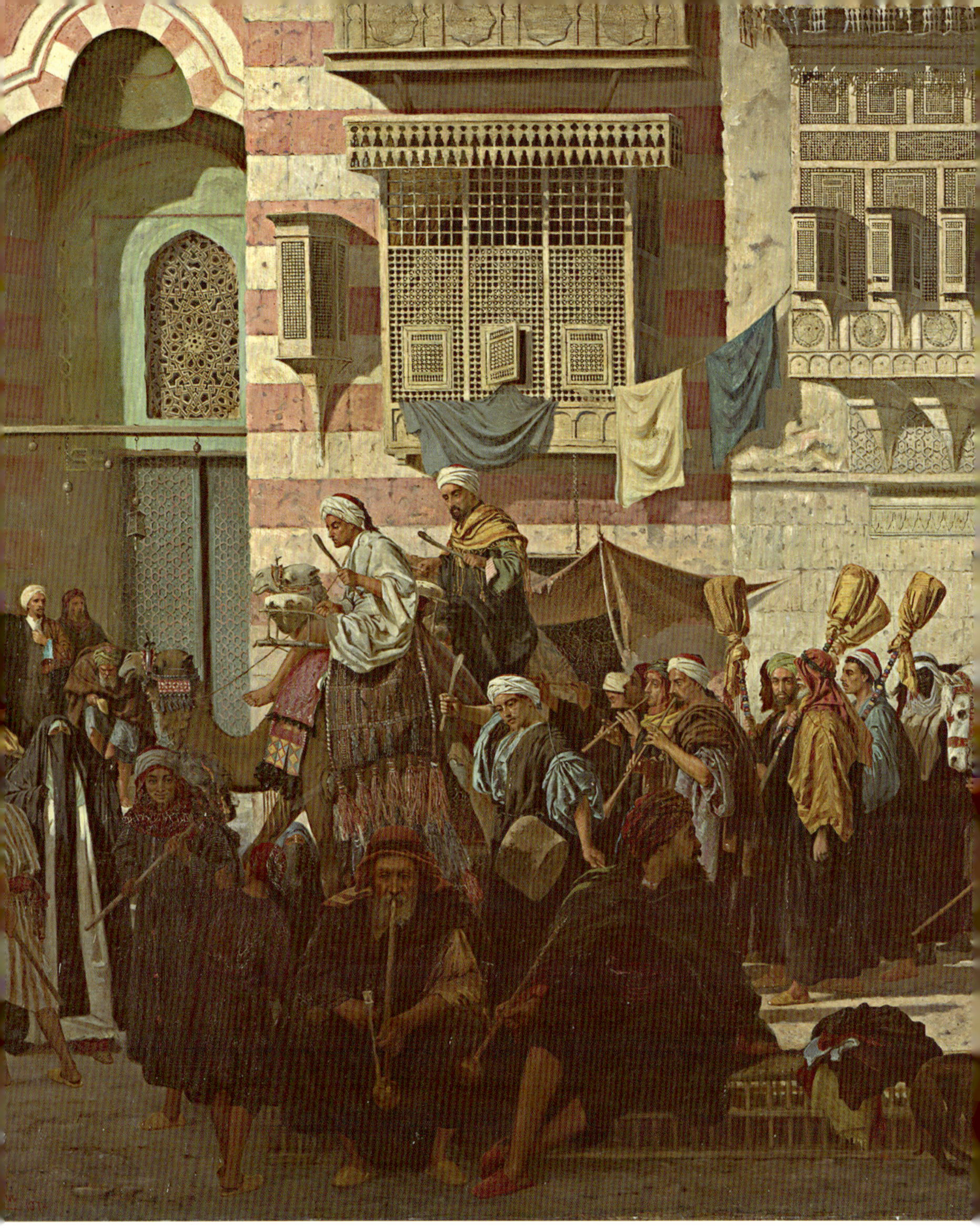

A sheikh and his son entering Cairo, on their return from a pilgrimage to Mecca 1874
oil on canvas
National Gallery of Victoria, Melbourne

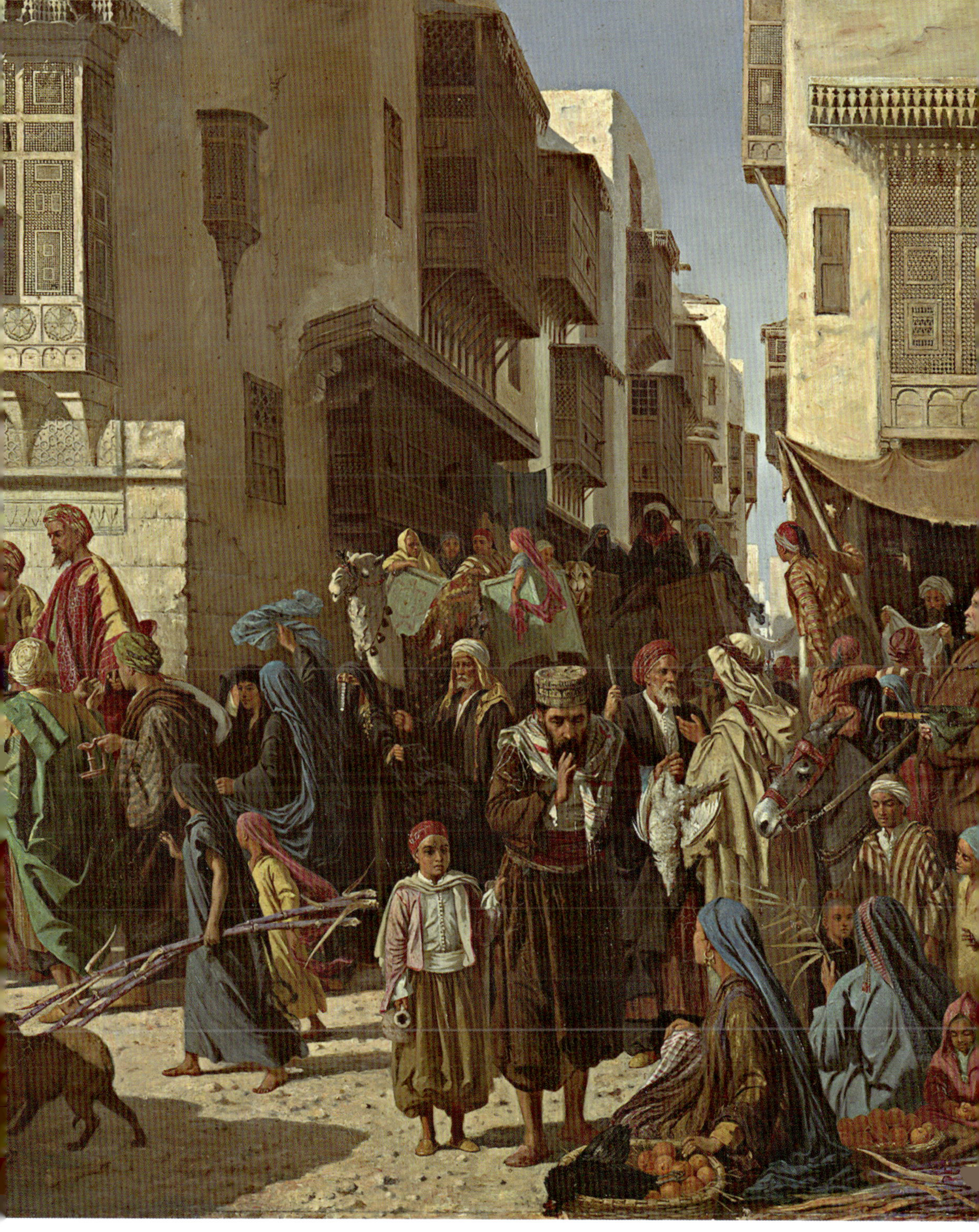

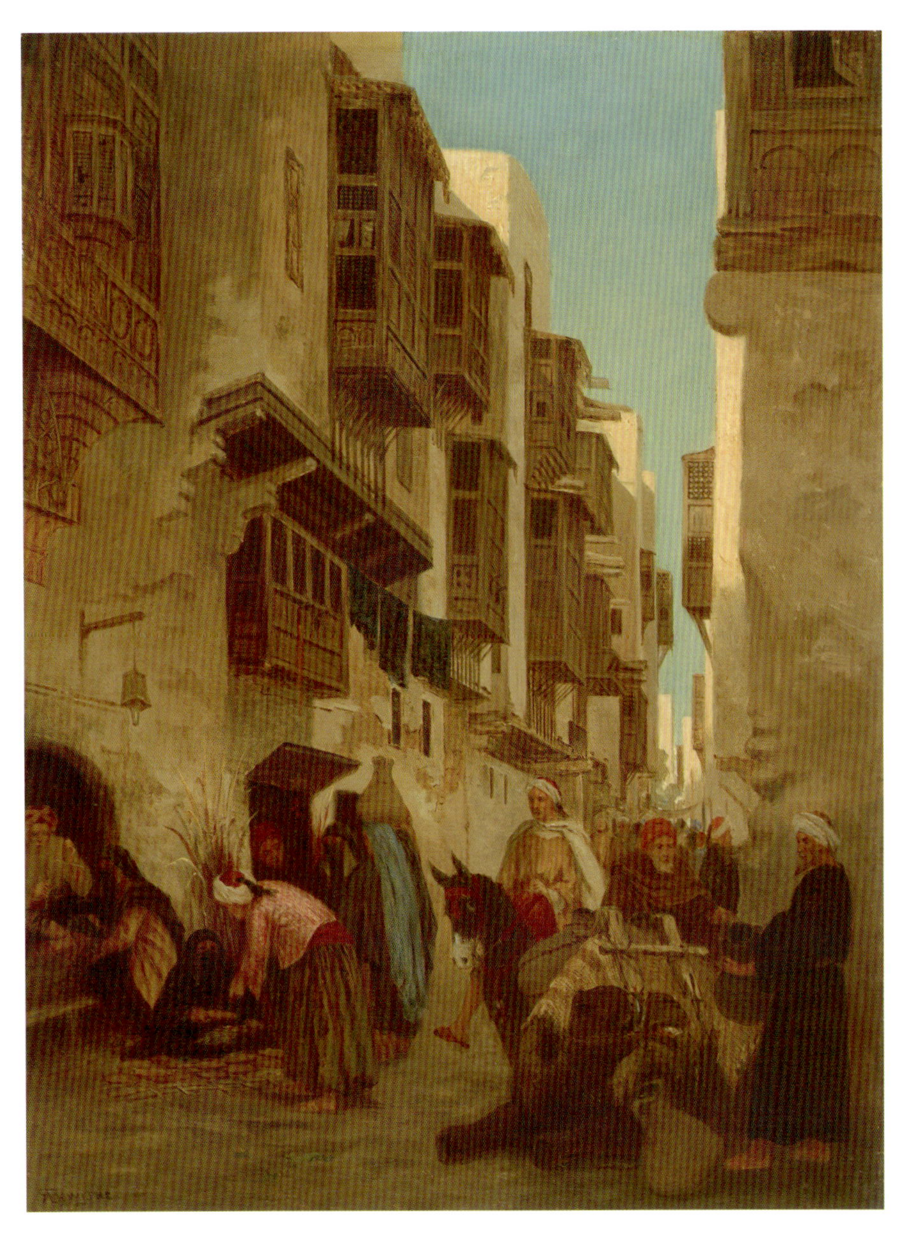

Street scene, Cairo c 1874
oil on canvas
National Gallery of Australia, Canberra

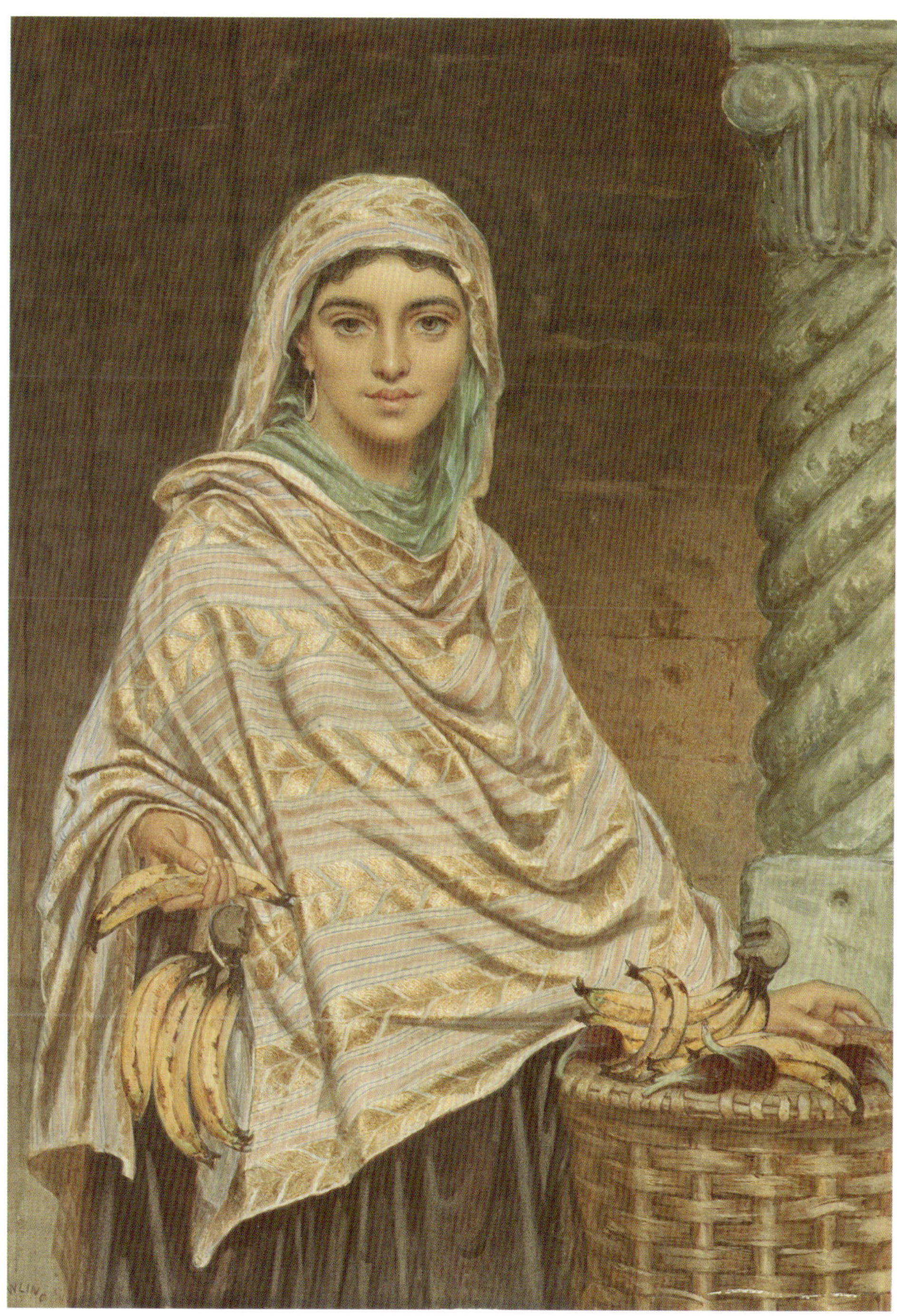

Egyptian banana seller 1878
watercolour with bodycolour over graphite on paper on board
private collection

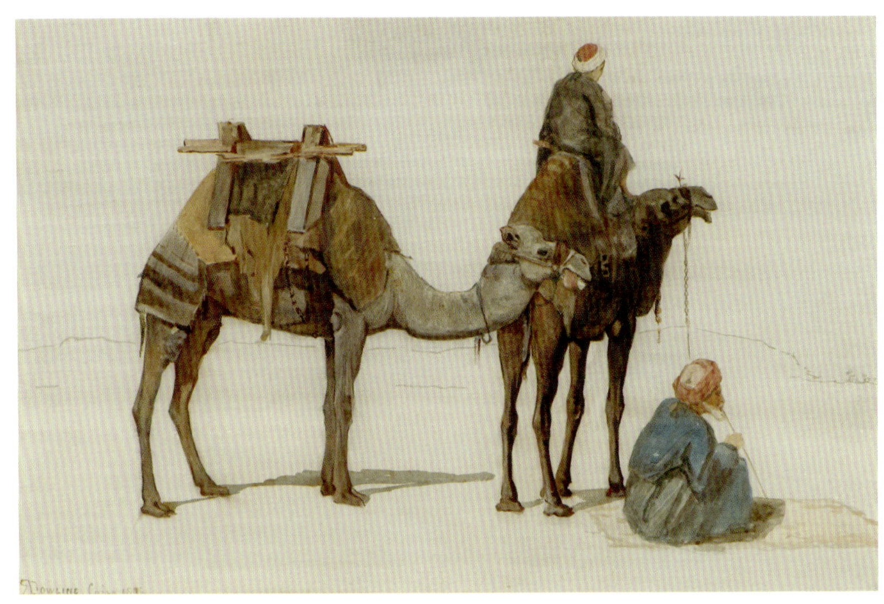

Cairo (camels) 1876
watercolour on paper
Warrnambool Art Gallery, Victoria

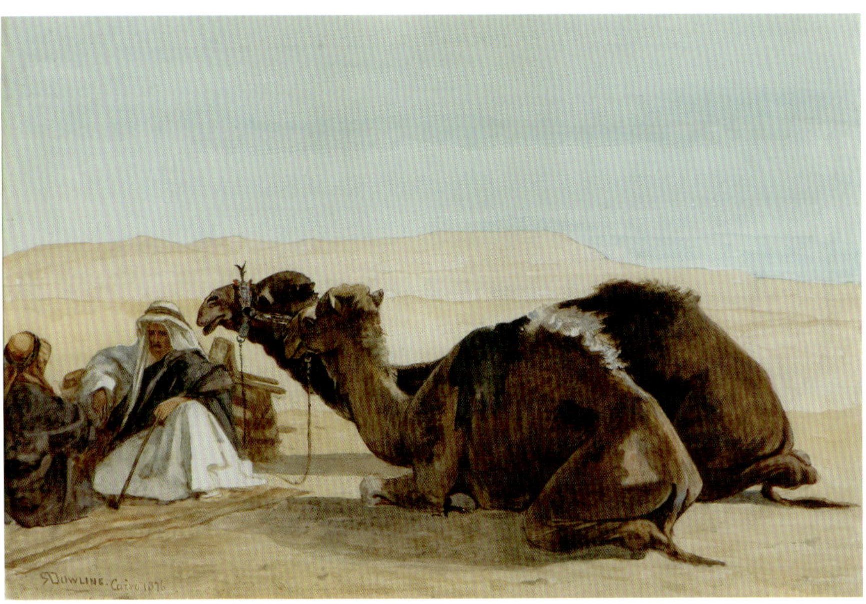

Cairo (camels) 1876
watercolour on paper
Warrnambool Art Gallery, Victoria

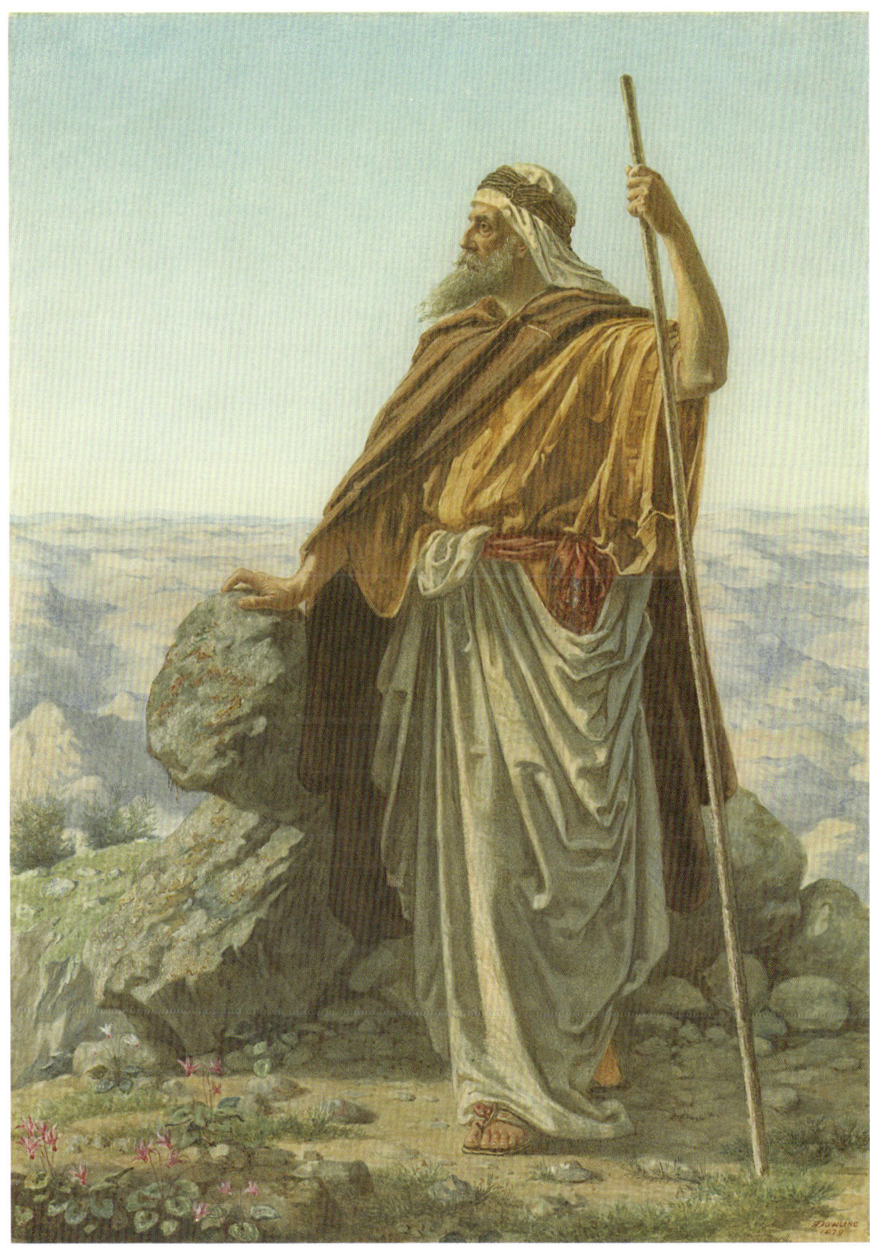

Moses viewing the Promised Land from Mount Nebo 1879
watercolour with bodycolour on paper
private collection

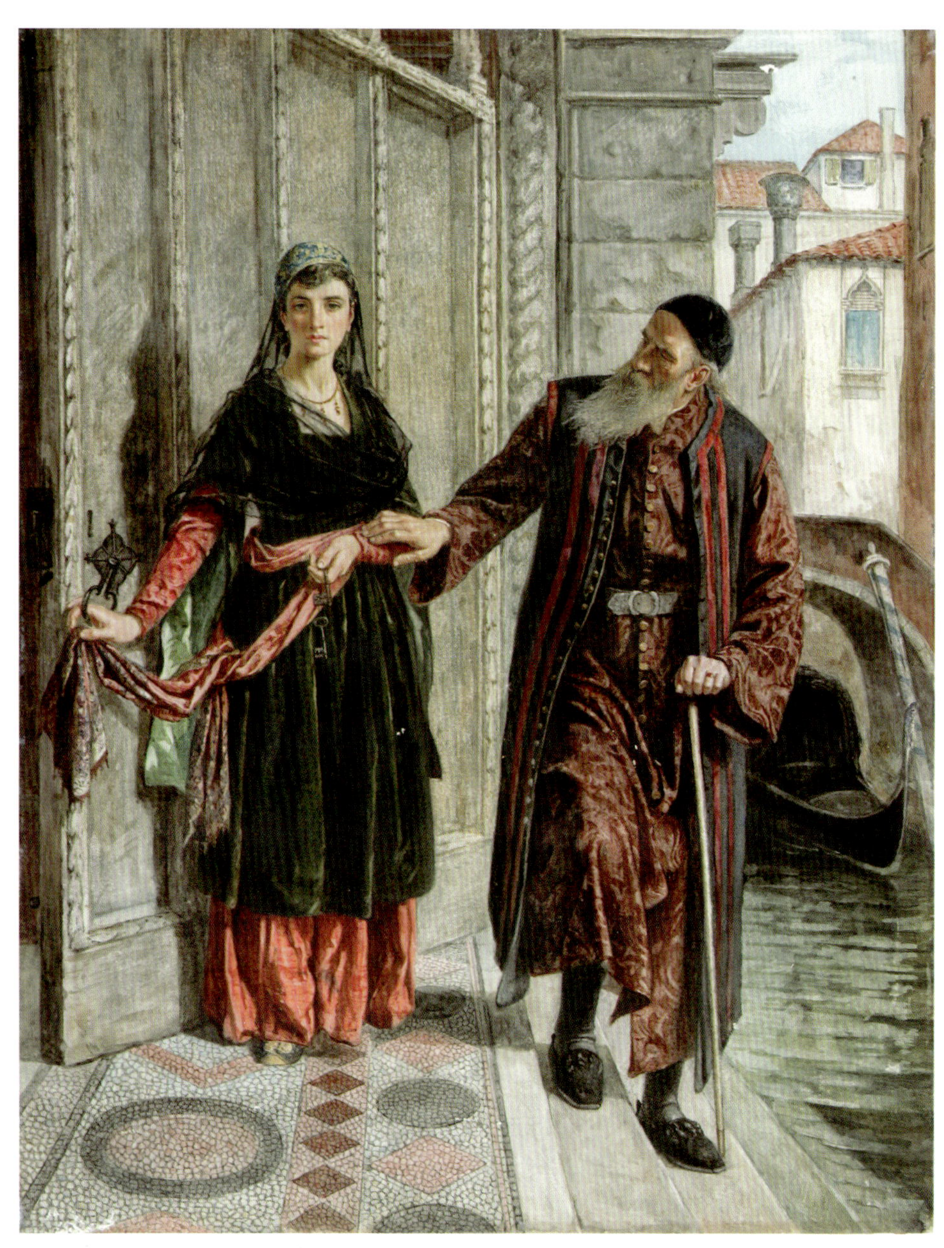

Shylock and Jessica 1882
watercolour and bodycolour
on paper on board
Queen Victoria Museum
and Art Gallery, Launceston

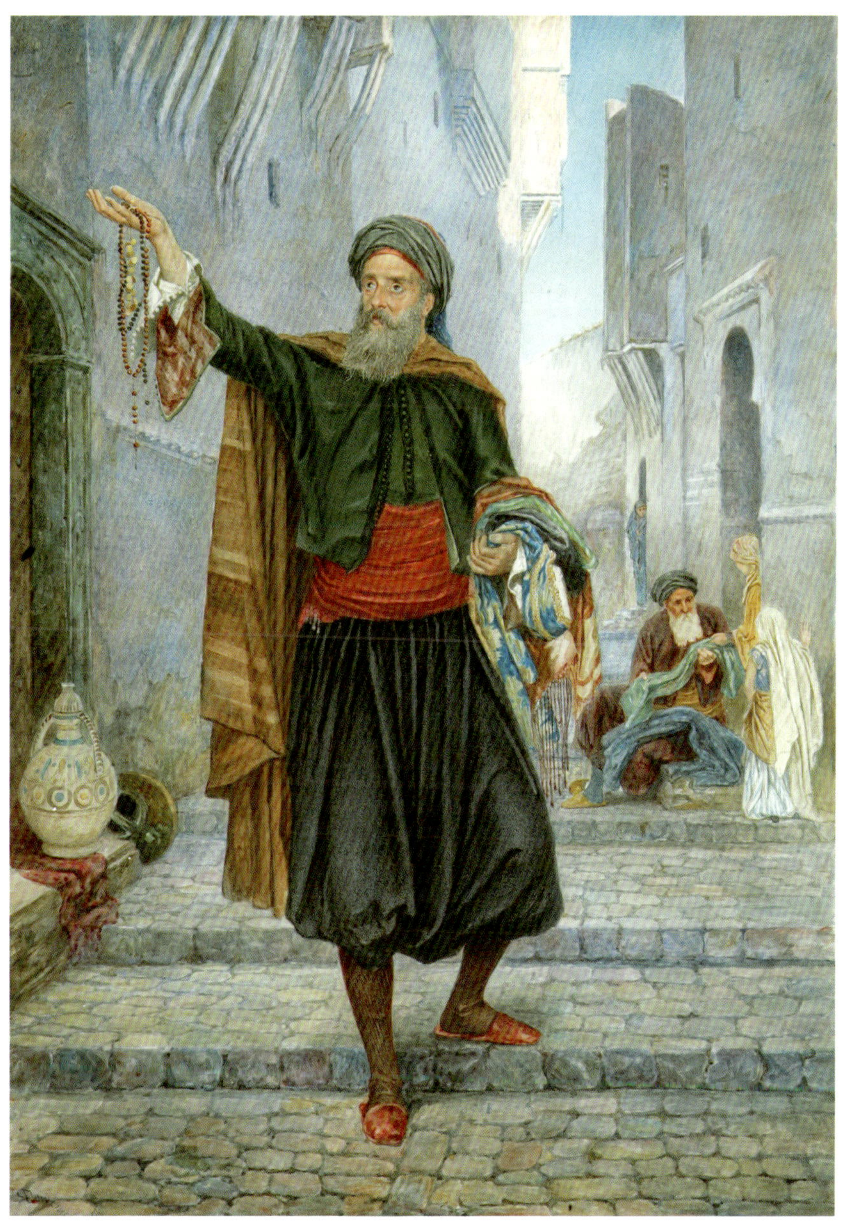

A merchant in Algiers 1882
watercolour and bodycolour
on paper on board
Queen Victoria Museum
and Art Gallery, Launceston

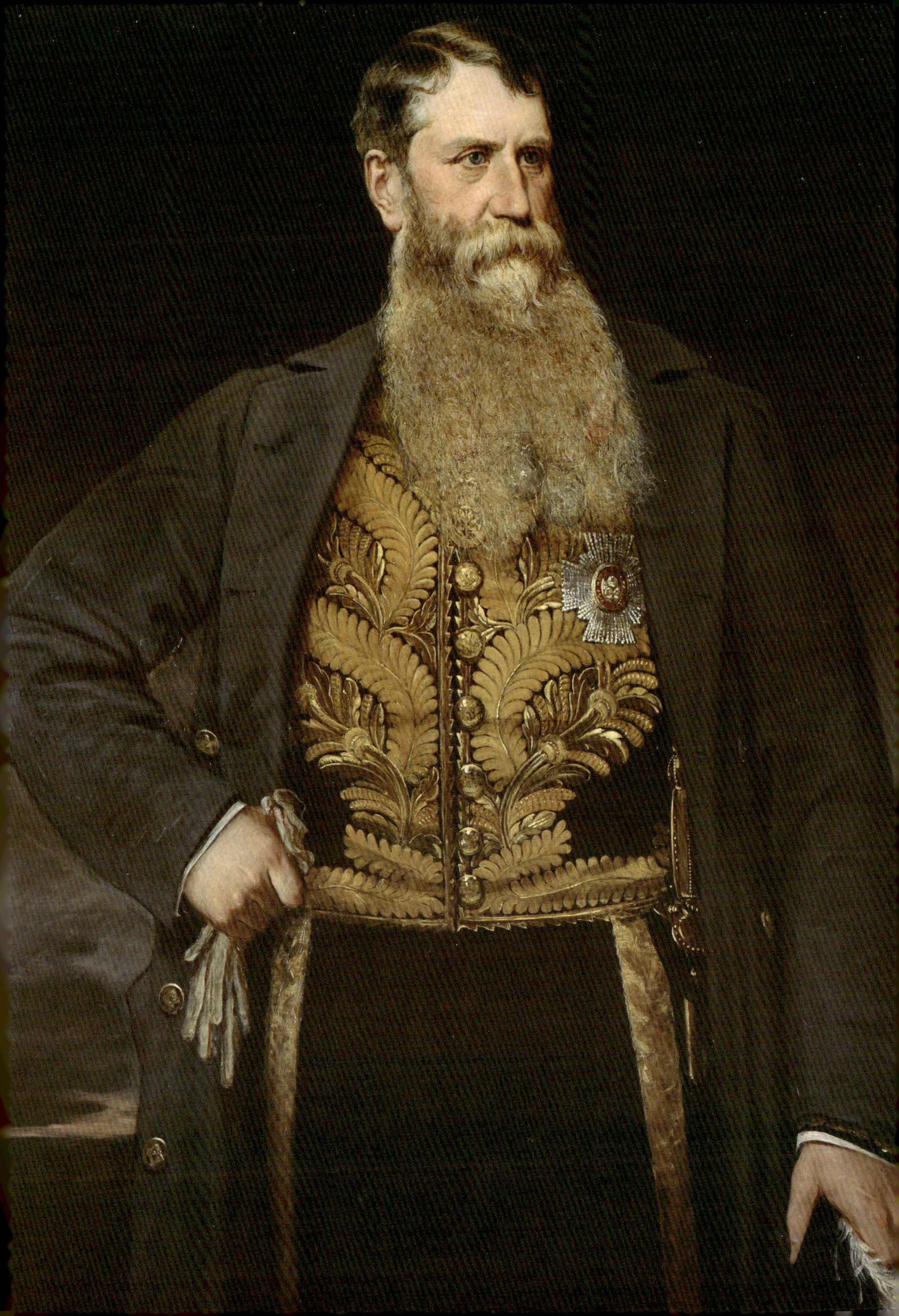

CHAPTER 5
Son of Empire: Melbourne 1884–86

Sir Henry Loch 1884
oil on canvas
State Library of Victoria, Melbourne

Visiting London in 1882 to be dubbed a baronet, the enormously wealthy Tasmanian-born Victorian pastoralist, politician and philanthropist Sir William Clarke commissioned Robert Dowling to paint a portrait of William Lamb, 2nd Viscount Melbourne (1779–1848) (NGV) (p 164). In 1837 the city of Melbourne had been named after the then prime minister of the United Kingdom. Dowling's portrait was based on an earlier painting by John Partridge, in the collection of the Earls of Carlisle, and later presented, in 1893, by the Howard family to the National Portrait Gallery, London. Clarke, in a patriotic gesture echoing Launceston's earlier Dowling commissions, had previously commissioned from Charles Summers four marble statues of Queen Victoria, her late husband Prince Albert, and the Prince and Princess of Wales. These he gave to the National Gallery of Victoria in 1878. Dowling's portrait of the Queen's mentor (and first prime minister) was given by Sir William to the National Gallery of Victoria in 1884, creating the setting for the artist's return to the colony that year and cementing his reputation as a portraitist to the Australian establishment.

Dowling underscored this reputation by bringing out with him and exhibiting his portrait of the current British prime minister, The Right Honourable W E Gladstone. With this reintroduction, twenty-seven years after leaving Australia, Robert Dowling came back to Victoria, where Melbourne, William Westgarth's 'modern Babel',[1] was the wonder city of Australia and the Empire. Even though other artists working in Australia could claim Royal Academy credentials, Dowling came back as the first Australia-formed artist to exhibit regularly at that venerable institution. It was an accolade Dowling had long used with Australian audiences, playing as the local colonial boy who had made good at 'Home'. In both Melbourne and Launceston, this was to a great degree orchestrated by his brother Henry. In July 1883, *The Argus* announced the artist's plan to return.[2] That notice was reiterated in January 1884, stating he had his passage booked on the *Sorata*,[3] which berthed in Melbourne on 22 March. Dowling opened a studio in Collins Street in early April 1884.[4]

While Dowling, in London in the 1870s, was trying to find Melbourne buyers for his work, *The Argus* claimed he had Victorian origins: 'Mr Dowling [is] an artist who commenced his career in Victoria twenty years ago [and] has now made his mark.'[5] Dowling's earlier presence in the colony in the mid 1850s was now reinforced by the artist himself, in heralding his return. He was thus tapping into the growing awareness of 'Marvellous' Melbourne's identity, its place in the Empire, its astonishing material progress, wealth and culture and pre-eminence among the colonial capitals worldwide. His claiming 'Victorian' instead of Tasmanian identity also coincided with a growing sense of Victoria's history, which was to culminate in the celebrations centred around the Victorians' Jubilee Exhibition of 1884. The Jubilee Exhibition was supervised by the entrepreneurial Alexander Fletcher, whose portrait Dowling painted in Melbourne. Dowling contributed to the exhibition his biblical painting *Daniel in the lions' den* (Philadelphia Museum of Art) and a portrait of the doyen of Melbourne's artistic community, the art critic James Smith. Dowling's 'Britishness', or successful British career, was a great advantage. All colonial public instrumentalities, the State, the Law and Education, sought to emulate those of the Mother

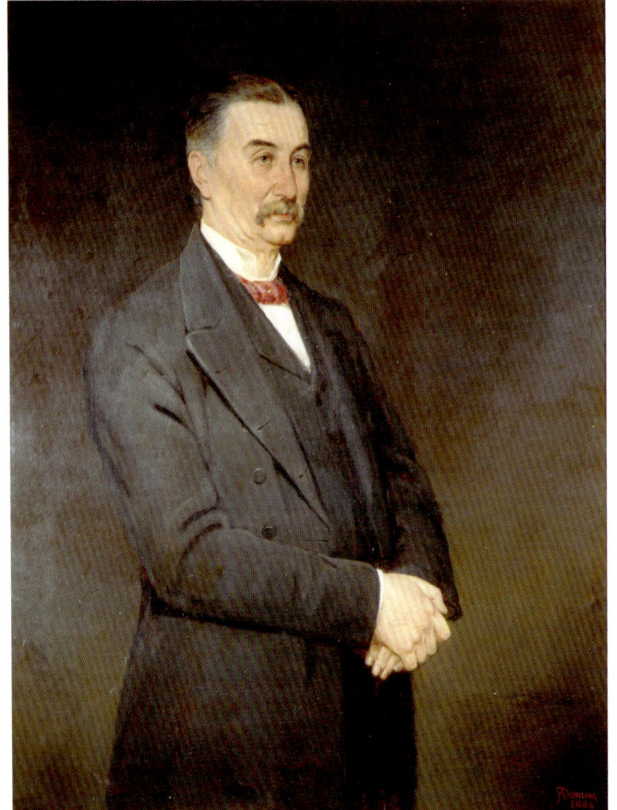

Robert Dowling
James Smith 1884
oil on canvas
110.5 x 86 cm
Pictures Collection,
State Library of Victoria

Country. Cultural institutions, in line with Ruskin's view that art is a tangible demonstration of progress and worth, also followed London models—with the founding in Melbourne of the Public Library and Museum in 1854, the National Gallery of Victoria in 1861, and the ambitiously titled Victorian Academy of Art in 1870. As has been noted previously, Dowling, unlike Thomas Woolner or Bertram Mackennal, was never elected to the Royal Academy, but his exhibiting credentials at that institution, then at the zenith of its power and influence, carried weight with the Melbourne establishment.

Victoria's artistic milieu during the 1860s and 70s had been dominated by Eugene von Guérard, Nicholas Chevalier, Thomas Clark and Louis Buvelot, all major interpreters of the Australian landscape. James Smith, reviewing the Fine Arts Gallery at the Inter-colonial Exhibition in Melbourne in 1866, noted the 'exclusive preference for landscape shown by the Colony's principal artists'.[6] Of these major players, von Guérard resigned in 1881 from his position as Curator at the National Gallery of Victoria and head of its School of Art and returned to Europe in early 1882; Buvelot had ceased productivity by 1882, and died in 1888; Thomas Clark produced little between 1876 and his death in 1883; and Chevalier had long left Australia for Britain, in 1868, in the visiting Duke of Edinburgh's retinue.

During the decades when Dowling was in London, subject painting and genre painting were minor aspects of art production in the colony of Victoria, the few exceptions being painted by Chester Earles, Louis Tannert and William Ford. This lack of interest by artists, however, was not reflected in the taste of collectors both public and private. The policy of the National Gallery of Victoria was to acquire original paintings by modern masters. Initially this was done with the advice of Sir Charles Eastlake, President of the Royal Academy and Director of the National Gallery in London, and a mixed bag of British and Continental genre paintings, among them works by George Folingsby, Charles West Cope, Guillaume Koller and Jehan-Georges Vibert, was acquired.[7] The tastes of a growing number of wealthy Melbourne private collectors ranged widely, from Old Master replicas to modern narrative or landscape paintings, particularly those by modern foreign artists. The former predilection was exemplified by the mass purchase of Old Master copies at Christie's in London in 1881, by Thomas Chirnside of Werribee Park. The taste for modern works was represented by the outstanding collection of contemporary British and European masters assembled with great discretion by Frederick Armytage of nearby Wooloomanata at Lara. Although purchasing locally, Armytage made his more important acquisitions in London. He was one of the few Australian nineteenth-century private collectors of international importance.[8]

These collectors were well informed about contemporary European, and particularly British, art. The colonial papers carried the reviews of each year's Royal Academy exhibitions. The most influential nineteenth-century London periodicals, *The Art Journal* (published 1829–1912) and *The Magazine of Art* (1879–1904), were readily available in the Australian colonies. Articles from these journals were sometimes reprinted in the colonial press. The year 1880 saw the opening of the Melbourne International Exhibition, in the new and spectacular Royal Exhibition Building in the Carlton Gardens. The lavish displays of contemporary British and Continental paintings reinforced the taste for foreign works of art in Melbourne. The notoriety of the star piece in the French Court, Jules-Joseph Lefebvre's seductively beautiful painting *Chloe* 1875—its purchase by Sir Thomas Fitzgerald, and the controversy it raised when he lent it to the National Gallery of Victoria in 1883—has overshadowed an assessment of the scope and depth of the other exhibits from Germany, Belgium, America and, particularly, the distinguished contents of the British Court. Some of the foremost names in modern British art were represented, including Frederic Leighton, G F Watts, Lawrence Alma-Tadema, Val Prinsep, Walter Crane, J W Buxton Knight and E A Waterlow. This eminent British group included Robert Dowling.[9]

The first exhibition of the Royal Anglo-Australian Society of Artists in Melbourne took place on 25 October 1885 at Alexander Fletcher's Gallery in Collins Street. It included works by modern British painters, among them Basil Bradley, T C Gotch, who had visited Australia in 1883, W Ayerst Ingram, the Adelaide-born Mortimer Menpes, and Augustus Weedon. It also included *A note in blue and green* by James McNeill Whistler, then the greatest celebrity of contemporary British art. This was further reinforcement of the popularity and availability of British art in Australia, as was the imported stock-in-trade of other Melbourne commercial galleries of the early 1880s.

If subject painting languished in art production in Victoria during the 1860s and 70s, so did portraiture, particularly when compared with the rich decade of the 1850s. Of the three best portrait painters in Victoria in the 50s, Robert Dowling left in 1857, Ludwig Becker died in 1861, and William Strutt returned to England in 1862. As James Smith lamented, reviewing the 1862 Exhibition of Fine Arts in Melbourne:

> there is no good portrait in the exhibition … since the departure of Mr Strutt this branch of the art seems to have fallen into a lamentable condition. No doubt the popularity of photographic portraits … operates to prejudice the more legitimate art of the painter on canvas … surely there is room for a first class portrait painter in this Colony.[10]

Smith's observation was correct. Portrait photography, or photographically based portraiture, was immensely popular with patrons and many competent artists were attracted to it, among them the gifted Victorian miniaturist and portrait painter John Botterill and the Tasmanian WP Dowling. A few colonists, like the Chirnside family, had their portraits painted when 'home' in Britain. And although Thomas Clark in Melbourne could provide the occasional vice-regal portrait in oils, on the whole, as a major genre it was, admirably, left to the sculptor Charles Summers (1825–1878) to fulfil the traditional role of portraitist. His noble, classically inspired marble images of eminent Australian men and women were produced in Melbourne, and then from 1867 in Rome, where he continued to work on major Australian commissions up to the time of his death in 1878. In Melbourne, James Smith was to wait some twenty years for the absence of a resident 'first class portrait painter' to be filled by Robert Dowling's return from London in early 1884.

Dowling came back to Melbourne with a secure reputation. He was well represented by religious and genre paintings in prominent private collections in the city and the Western District. More importantly, he was represented in the collection of the National Gallery of Victoria by his large and spectacular Oriental painting, *A sheikh and his son entering Cairo, on their return from a pilgrimage to Mecca* (pp 138–39). Despite his reputation for genre paintings, many of which he brought out from London with him for sale in Melbourne, portraits were the only product from his Collins Street studio. Even after the return from study in Europe, in April 1885, of the much younger and more modern Tom Roberts, Dowling was still the most sought-after portraitist in Melbourne. Apart from Roberts, he was working in competition with other artists attracted to the growing metropolis: the Munich-trained British painter George Folingsby was in Melbourne from 1879; the French-born painter and teacher Berthe Mouchette was active in Melbourne from 1881 to 1892; and the much publicised and lauded German painter Carl Kahler arrived in Melbourne in 1885. These artists occasionally exhibited portraits at the Victorian Academy of Art, the Australian Artists' Association or the National Gallery of Victoria's loan exhibitions during these years. None had the reputation or connections in the city, or with the old Western District squattocracy, that Dowling enjoyed.

Among the Melbourne celebrities and leaders to sit for Dowling in 1884 were the flamboyant Collins Street art entrepreneur Alexander Fletcher; the art critic of *The Argus* and a trustee of the National Gallery of Victoria, James Smith (SLV); Sir James MacBain, President of the Legislative Council and a trustee of the National Gallery of Victoria (Ormond College, University of Melbourne); and the Queen-Empress's representative in the Colony of Victoria, Sir Henry Loch (SLV) (p 165), 'an old and intimate friend'[11] of the artist.

During 1885 and 1886 other commissions followed, among them portraits of Buvelot's Western District patron, the late Hon John Cumming MLC of Terinallum, his brother William, and Miss Cumming. There was a family connection here: a third brother, Thomas Cumming, was married to Dowling's niece Selina. Another Western District figure to sit for Dowling was pastoralist and parliamentarian—and Melbourne lawyer—the Hon William Robertson MLA. Robertson also commissioned a posthumous portrait of his Tasmanian father, William (1798–1874). Revisiting his old Western District stamping ground of the 1850s and staying at Robertson's property, The Hill, near Colac, Dowling painted a portrait of the nineteen-year-old eldest daughter Elise, known as Dolly to her family (pp 166–67). In Melbourne in 1885 Dowling painted yet another posthumous portrait of the former Premier of Tasmania, Sir Richard Dry (QVMAG), to hang in the new wing of the Launceston Mechanics' Institute. Dowling visited Launceston for its presentation and exhibition, along with his portraits of the British prime minister and of Victoria's governor, Sir Henry Loch.[12] It was the artist's last meeting with his eldest brother, Henry, who since his youth had been the great supporter of his career. Henry died in Launceston on 18 September 1885, while Robert was in Sydney painting a portrait (for St Paul's College, University of Sydney), of another former Tasmanian, Sir Alfred Stephen, chief justice and lieutenant governor of New South Wales. Sir Alfred was a founder of the college and a trustee of the National Art Gallery of New South Wales, where a Dowling loan exhibition had recently been mounted. The National Gallery of Victoria had done so previously, in 1877, but this was the first showing of Dowling's work in Sydney.[13]

Among other Melbourne dignitaries to sit for Dowling were Dr Morrison, first headmaster of Scotch College (Ormond College); Francis Ormond, the philanthropic founder of Ormond College and the Royal Melbourne Institute of Technology (Ormond College); Dr James Moorehouse, second Church of England Bishop of Melbourne and patron of the Gothic Revival architect William Butterfield (Council Chamber, University of Melbourne); and Thomas Mowbray, businessman and former lord mayor of Melbourne. A portrait of Lady Ferguson was another commission, as was the Supreme Court of Victoria's request for a large portrait of the late Sir Redmond Barry, for the Supreme Court Library. Dowling painted some eighteen prominent figures from Church, State, Law and Academe, between April 1884 and his departure for London in April 1886. If he had thoughts of financial remuneration by returning to Australia, they were spectacularly realised during 1884–86.

Dowling's portrait style, like that of most of his contemporaries, was indebted to the later work of the most famous of all English Victorian portrait painters, John Everett Millais (1829–1896). Most of Dowling's Melbourne portraits are tonally restrained images, and essentially conservative, as befits their very sober, public-figure subjects. Destined often for institutions, they can be sometimes dull. There is none of the attractive, flashy 'swagger' characterisation, so marked a feature of British aristocratic and society portraits of the late nineteenth century, for example those by John Singer Sargent (1856–1925), Giovanni Boldini (1842–1931) or John Lavery (1856–1941).

For the handsome portrait of William Robertson (private collection), Dowling placed the pastoralist and lawyer against a rich, red background, a colour sometimes favoured by Tom Roberts in portraits like the latter's

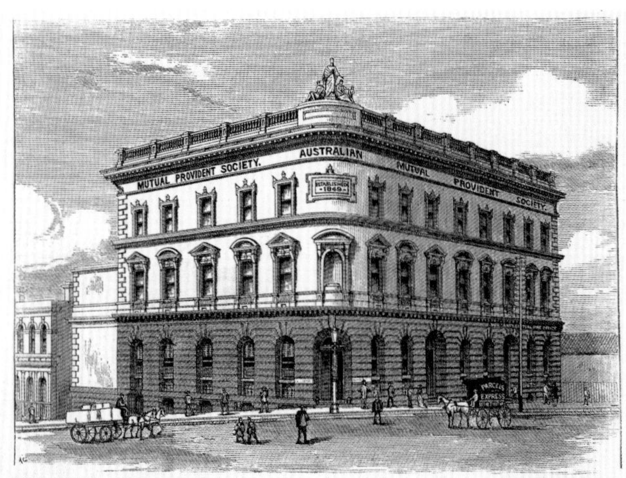

New offices of the Australian Mutual Provident Society, Collins Street West 1879
published in *The Illustrated Australian News* 22 January 1879
wood-engraving, 11.5 x 15 cm
Pictures Collection, State Library of Victoria, Melbourne

Annie Evans 1886 (Ballarat). Alternatively Dowling used a sombre Whistlerian grey, as in the restrained and colourless portrait of James Smith. Dowling's dignified portrait of the popular governor, Sir Henry Loch, is an impressive work by any criteria and the epitome of the High Victorian style for state portraits. Sir Henry, a Scottish soldier and veteran of the Crimean War and the Second Opium War, who escaped execution by minutes when imprisoned in Peking in 1860, took up office in Victoria only a few months after Dowling's arrival in 1884. He stands in this image as an Imperial colonial administrator, wearing a heavily embroidered dress uniform, orders, overcoat, and carrying gloves and hat. The Loch portrait, although dated 1886, must have been completed the previous year, for it was exhibited in Launceston in March 1885.

If these portraits resonated with Dowling's audience, so did his affability and personal style. Dowling was the first to introduce the notion of the studio/salon, in the London manner, to the Melbourne scene. He knew the importance of a fashionable address. He was also well aware of the importance of style and décor to impress prospective clients, provide attractive surroundings for taking portraits of wealthy sitters, entertain the press, and generally promote his work. (Tom Roberts was to emulate Dowling in this regard.) Dowling took studio rooms, suite number 6, in the Australian Mutual Providence Building, Collins Street West, erected in 1878 and one of a spate of handsome new structures to adorn that street. It was a commodious arrangement for, after Dowling's departure, the studio was occupied by two artists, Arthur Loureiro and Ugo Catani, and for a short time also by Girolamo Nerli, and was large enough to hold painting classes there on the European model.[14] Dowling's wife Arabella, who had accompanied him to Melbourne, furnished the studio. It was reported that Mrs Dowling, 'who had spent some years in the East', stylishly decorated the rooms in the 'eastern fashion with cushions and divans'. The artist held regular reception days, twice weekly, usually hosted by 'Miss Florrie Fuller, a niece[15] of the artist whom he was instructing in painting' and sister of the popular young concert singer and protégé of Lady Loch, Christie Fuller.[16] Florence Fuller later became a significant Australian painter.

In this fashionable setting Dowling exhibited his own works and those of others brought out from England. From November 1884, on view in his studio were the paintings *From Calvary to the Tomb*; *Going out with the tide*; *The meeting of Raikes and the Revd T Stocks in regard to Sunday Schools*; and the larger compositions *Moses viewing the Promised Land from Mount Nebo* and *Daniel in the lions' den*. Dowling also kept a stock of works by the younger British artist and specialist in Egyptian and Oriental scenes, John Varley junior (1850–1933). He also showed subject paintings by two of his London pupils, Miss Alice Grant (working 1879–1904) and Miss Ellen Connolly (working 1873–1885).[17] Dowling exhibited works by Varley, along with his own paintings, in the 1884 Victorians' Jubilee Exhibition and at the Victorian Academy of Art in 1884 and 1885. As in 1877, in July 1885 Dowling lent the subject and genre paintings *Sketch for 'The Baptism of Christ'* and *Going out with the tide* and the portraits of W E Gladstone and Sir Henry Loch to the National Gallery of Victoria. In June 1886, before his departure for London, he also submitted to the Victorian Academy of Art his *Daniel in the lions' den* and the now lost work, *From Calvary to the Tomb*.

Collins Street was an obvious choice for Dowling's Melbourne base. That beautiful boulevard, with The Block Arcade and its shops and cafes, was the smart social hub of the city. Then, as now, it was the most prestigious commercial centre. In the early 1880s it was already a mecca for Melbourne's artistic community. As Terence Lane has written, it became even more so towards the end of the decade, with the emergence of the movement known as Australian Impressionism.[18] Nevertheless, as Caroline Jordan has observed,[19] there has been little examination of the flowering of art dealership itself and private collecting activity in Melbourne in those earlier 1880s, apart from Gerard Vaughan's 1978 study.[20] As the artistic quarter, Collins Street abounded with 'picture galleries' servicing the rich with British and Continental paintings for their Italianate or Gothic Revival mansions then being erected along St Kilda Road or on the hills of nearby South Yarra, Toorak, Hawthorn and Kew. Among the galleries were the established firms of James W Hines and George Powis, Mr Freeman and Henry Gibbs. These were supplemented by the occasional presence of the Adelaide dealer EJ Wivell, who held sales at the Athenaeum, one of which, in 1883, included William Strutt's large painting *Black Thursday, February 6th 1851* 1864 (SLV). In 1884 the famous London art dealer, Henry Wallis, opened in Melbourne a branch of his French Gallery (purchased earlier from Ernest Gambart). The French Gallery was situated in the Imperial Chambers, 77 Collins Street and, despite its name, mainly traded German paintings, then very popular with Australian collectors. Collins Street was also the address of the art auctioneers Gemmell & Tuckett. Most important, at 87 Collins Street, were the premises and gallery of Alexander Fletcher.[21] The city's excellent picture framers were also based in Collins Street. They not only supplied frames, art materials and prints but were also exhibition venues. Isaac Whitehead, Melbourne's celebrated picture framer of the 1860s and 70s, had a 'Gallery of art' for his own paintings there. From 1878 the firm of J&T Thallon operated from Collins Street.[22]

The painter Eugene von Guérard and the sculptor Charles Summers, who cast his Burke and Wills Memorial statue there in 1864, had earlier worked in Collins Street from the 1850s. Robert Dowling was not alone in following their example. Other artists based there, on and off, included the sculptor JS Mackennal (father of the more famous Bertram Mackennal) and the painter Berthe Mouchette, before she moved to St Kilda in 1885 with her school for young women artists. The painters George Ashton, John Mather and Tom Roberts shared a studio at 95 Collins Street, well before the subsequent influx of other painters and the construction of purpose-built artist's studios such as Grosvenor Chambers in 1888 or the Austral Buildings in 1891.

James Smith found Robert Dowling a convivial man, who enjoyed the company of artists and involved himself in the vibrant Melbourne art scene.[23] Dowling joined Cyrus Mason's club, known as the Melbourne Fine Art Society or Buonarotti Club, founded in 1883 and meeting fortnightly in the city. Dowling would have participated, with his contemporaries, in the society's artistic, literary and musical programs.

He took up local causes. In 1885 the London firm of Arthur Tooth consigned to Fletcher's Gallery in Melbourne, Benjamin Leader's *A Worcestershire hamlet* and Millais's juvenile portrait *The love birds*, also known as *Une grande dame*. Over a period of two fruitless years these were offered for purchase consideration to the National Gallery of Victoria. Dowling joined the chorus of criticism of the trustees' inaction. In February 1886 he sent a cheque to an unsuccessful appeal conducted by *The Argus*, encouraging the National Gallery of Victoria to acquire these works, Dowling's stated concern being that 'art students had little to see in the way of high class figure and landscape painting'.[24]

The most serious issue facing Melbourne's artistic community in the early 1880s was the affairs of the faltering Victorian Academy of Art under its president, Chester Earles. The Victorian Academy of Art Exhibition of March 1885 was 'the worst yet held by that Society', according to the journal *Once a Month*.[25] *The Age* was equally scathing, and James Smith wrote in *The Argus*: 'excepting the works by Dowling, Mather and Carabain … it would be impossible to speak of this exhibition otherwise than in terms of either unqualified censure or absolute contempt'. As in his later, notorious review of the 9 by 5 Impression Exhibition in 1889, Smith could be savagely critical. He described Earles's painting *St John the Baptist* as 'hewn out of wood by a clumsy artificer ignorant of the form and proportions of the human frame'.[26] Concern for the general standard of the Academy had been mounting for some time. From 1882 George Folingsby refused to exhibit there and forbade his students at the National Gallery Art School to do so. The critic for *Once a Month* recommended that 'those interested in [its] future should seek the advice of Dowling, Loureiro, H. Hainsellin and J. Paterson … the whole management needs reforming'.[27] Nonetheless, these expressions of dissatisfaction by critics and artists alike did not preclude Dowling and others, including Tom Roberts, from exhibiting at the Academy in June 1886. Throughout 1885, moves to establish an alternative exhibiting venue were pursued by John Mather, Arthur Loureiro, John Ford Paterson, Ugo Catani and Robert Dowling. By September 1885 there was some resolve to the 'vexed question' of the standard of art in the colony. A group of 'some of our best artists', soon to be known as the Australian Artists' Association, held a meeting in Dowling's Collins Street rooms, 'hopefully settling the issue'.[28]

This eventually led, soon after Dowling's death in London, to the formal formation and First Annual Exhibition of the Association, at Buxton's Gallery in Swanston Street, in September 1886. This important exhibition marked the birth of Melbourne's plein-air and impressionistic school of painting. Among the numerous contributing artists were Frederick McCubbin, with the delightful oil sketch '*At the falling of the year'* (NGA), Walter Withers with *Near Kew* and *Near Alphington*, Tom Roberts with *Twenty minutes past three, The artists' camp* (NGV) and *A summer morning's tiff* (Ballarat). Others to exhibit paintings were Ugo Catani, J Llewelyn Jones, Arthur Loureiro, Julian Ashton, John Ford Paterson, Carl Kahler, John Mather and Charles Rolando. Florence Fuller contributed a tribute to her teacher, a *Portrait of the late Robert Dowling*, 'who took such a warm interest in the preliminaries of this exhibition'.[29]

Before departing Melbourne for London, Dowling consigned two paintings for the Victorian Court at the Colonial and India Exhibition, a great celebration of worldwide Imperial achievement that opened in London, the 'Heart of Empire', in May 1886. With that consignment he gave his Melbourne address, and exhibited as an Australian artist. Preoccupied with portrait commissions he contributed only the sentimental Cornish subject *Going out with the tide* and his grand portrait of Sir Henry Loch. For the other artists from Victoria, however, it was the most important exhibition of the decade. John Ford Paterson submitted five paintings, John Mather four and Tom Roberts the same number: *Coming south* (NGV); *Mary: a portrait*; *A quiet day on Darebin Creek* (NGA); and *Winter morning after rain, Gardiner's Creek* (AGSA).

In early 1886 Dowling had been working on his portraits of Francis Ormond, Sir Redmond Barry and Lady Loch. He must also have extensively reworked his 1885 portrait of Dolly Robertson (pp 166–67) then, as the painting bears the date 1886. In contrast to Dowling's portraits of dry and elderly worthies of the establishment, this image of a young Miss Robertson of Colac is a refreshing change. The artist must have enjoyed the experience of depicting someone youthful and engaging, after painting so many old and sometimes dead men. The work displays the same attractive naturalism of his three-quarter-length portraits, painted in London, of Annie Ware and Mary

Drysdale. Dolly Robertson's portrait is full-length and more casual. It was commenced in the late summer or early autumn of 1885 in the garden of her father's country property, The Hill, and was on view in Dowling's Melbourne studio in June.[30] Dolly was initially dressed in conventional summertime white, as a contemporary photograph of the artist at work on the painting shows. Apparently unhappy with the result, perhaps feeling it made her look too young, she asked Dowling to paint her in dark brown. The artist obliged, as well as altering and adding other elements to the composition, such as a garden tea-table and Dolly's cheerful pet spaniel. The portrait displays a new informality, a feature of Royal Academy portrait exhibits in the 1880s and seen in the work of Dowling's English contemporaries James Sant (1820–1916), John Dicksee (1817–1905) and James Hayllar (1829–1920). It recalls particularly the society and demi-monde portraits by the French artist James Tissot (1836–1902), who worked in London from 1871 to 1882.

Robert Dowling with the painting *Miss Robertson of Colac (Dolly)*. This photograph was taken at The Hill near Colac in 1855 and shows Dolly wearing a white summer dress which the artist changed to brown at her request.
private collection

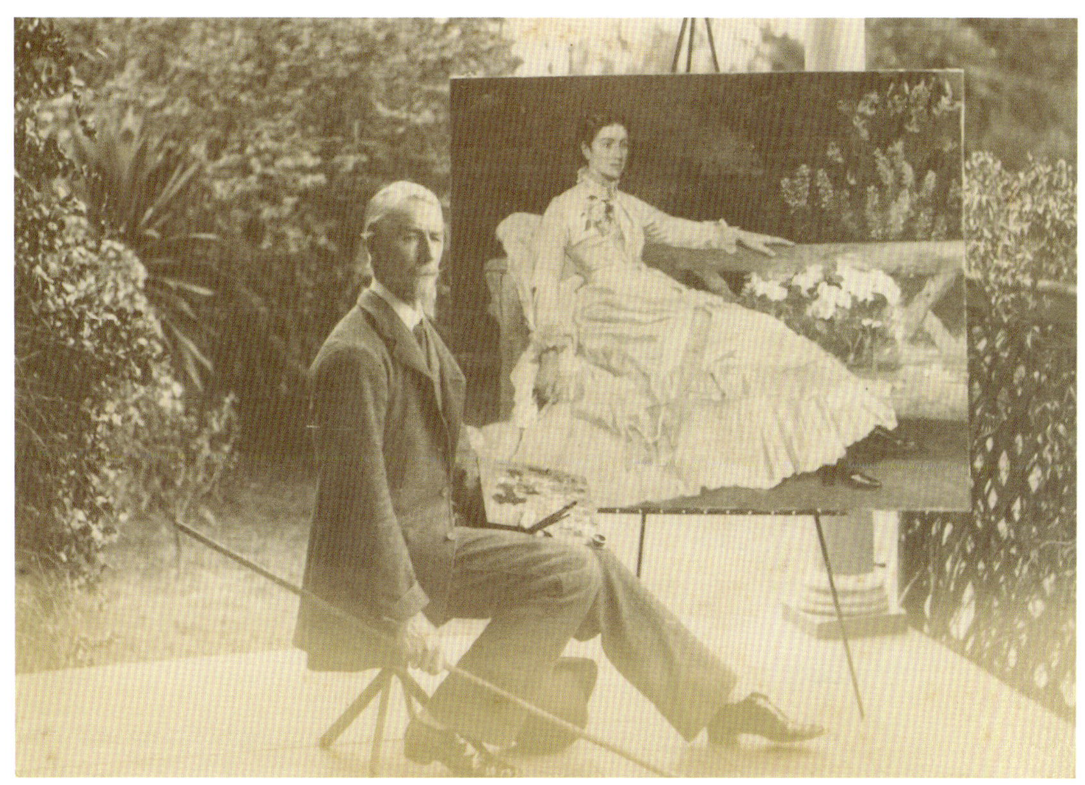

Dowling's painting shares Tissot's awareness of chic, with the inclusion of a Japanese cushion and tea service, then the height of fashion.[31] In Melbourne the casualness of the image would have seemed modern and unusual, striking a note not seen before in Australian portraits. This was about to change, especially with Tom Roberts's portraits.

Dowling left Melbourne on the *Liguria* in April 1886, sailing via the Suez Canal to Naples and then overland to London. He died there suddenly, at home at Coleherne Road, West Brompton, of a heart attack, on 8 July 1886. He left a great deal of work in Melbourne, including the unfinished and important portrait of Elizabeth Loch (née Villiers) the aristocratic wife of the popular governor of Victoria. (The portrait of Lady Loch was completed after Dowling's death by Florence Fuller.) These circumstances indicate that the artist intended to return to Melbourne, perhaps permanently, and that the fatal trip to London was undertaken to tidy up his affairs. James Smith confirms this in his obituary. So does a Launceston press report that 'Mr R. Dowling left Melbourne last week for London … but he purposes returning to Australia in a few months, and will probably make a longer stay'.[32]

Florence Fuller, after a year at the National Gallery of Victoria Art School in 1883, and while studying under Dowling from 1884 to 1886, herself painted Victorian Aborigines, as her relative and mentor had done in the Western District some thirty years previously. The Pictures Collection at the State Library of Victoria has a fine oil portrait, *Barak: last chief of the Yarra Yarra tribe of Aborigines*, painted by Fuller in 1885. She must have been eighteen or nineteen years old at the time—quite precocious and very talented.

Robert Dowling's death took Melbourne's artistic community by surprise. An obituary, written by James Smith, appeared in *The Argus* on Wednesday 14 July 1886.[33]

> THE LATE ROBERT DOWLING
> The numerous friends of the late Robert Dowling will receive with the utmost regret the unexpected tidings of his death, which must have occurred shortly after reaching England, on his return thither from these colonies. He left Melbourne by the Liguria on the 17th of April, and landed at Naples, where he expected to meet some members of his family, but the unhealthy conditions

of that city prevented them from carrying out that intention and he went on to Paris, in order to visit the Salon, and thence to London. The deceased artist was only 59 years old at the time of his death having been born in 1827. He was about seven years old when he accompanied his father, a minister of religion belonging to the Baptist denomination, to Tasmania, where the family settled in Launceston, we believe. Robert evinced a decided predilection for the arts of design at a very early age, and showed no little aptitude for portraiture, more especially. At the beginning of his career he was to a considerable extent self-taught; but in later years he was enabled to avail himself of the advantages of study in the Old World, by which he profited greatly. The subjects which exercised his pencil were sacred ones, but the branch of art in which he really excelled was portrait painting. He came out here on a visit about 18 months ago, opened a studio in Collins-Street West, and commissions soon began to flow upon him. Many of our leading citizens sat to him, His Excellency the Governor and the late Bishop of Melbourne among others; while in Sydney, Mr Dowling executed an admirable likeness of Sir Alfred Stephen. But apart from his talent as an artist, he was altogether estimable as a man. No one was more prompt to recognise ability, or more cordial to praise it, in a brother artist. He was absolutely free from envy or jealousy; and the writer has heard him say, 'If I could paint a picture like that' (in reference to something that had charmed him from the pencil of another painter), 'I would hasten back to Europe to-morrow and take my place in the first rank'. To help forward a struggling artist, to procure him commissions, to expend time and money on his behalf, to recommend him to wealthy patrons, and to befriend him by any means in his power, was an employment Robert Dowling delighted in. He loved his art, but he loved artists more, and it was a pleasure to hear him expatiating on the merits of a fine picture, or on what he regarded as most worthy of praise in the character, conduct or skill or genius of the executant. His own nature was breezy, genial and sympathetic. He took cheerful views of life, looked on the bright side of human nature, and was somewhat of a laughing philosopher. He had mixed a good deal with English artists, and was full of anecdotes concerning those [with] whom he was best acquainted; but his narratives and criticisms were always tinctured with kindness and good humour. He left Melbourne with the hope and intention of returning, and perhaps of settling here, as the climate possessed a great attraction for his sunny nature; and those who knew him best will feel deepest regret that this intention has been frustrated by death. He was a hard worker, and was engaged upon a portrait of the founder of Ormond College up to within half an hour of the

> time the Liguria was appointed to sail. It may be that he applied himself too closely to his easel, but if so he might expect that the rest of a six weeks' voyage would reinvigorate him. Certainly none of his friends were prepared for the melancholy news which has now reached them. Mr Dowling leaves behind him a wife and family to whom he was affectionately attached.

As for that family, Dowling's wife Arabella died twenty-three years later on 3 October 1909 at Barnes in Surrey. The unmarried daughter Marian predeceased her mother, dying in Kent in 1908. James Smith's comments that Dowling perhaps 'applied himself too closely to his easel', and needed a good rest, chime with a report at the beginning of 1885 after five or so weeks in Launceston and Hobart that 'the main object of his visit [to Australia], restored health, has been achieved'.[34] Approaching sixty, a permanent return to Australia from heavily polluted London would have been a wise intention.

Some of the paintings that Dowling brought out to Melbourne were sent back to London after his death. Some remained in Australia. Many are unaccounted for.

The Melbourne he planned to return to was the fastest-growing city, after London, in the British Empire. Its population was close to 500 000 by the end of the 1880s. In light of Dowling's success in Melbourne from 1884 to 1886, it is interesting to speculate how he would have fared had he returned. How would he have reacted to the 'national' school of painting he witnessed emerging in 1886 and the complexity of the Melbourne art scene of the 1890s? Dowling was a conservative artist, whose formation belonged to a much earlier age, but he was responsive to new developments in British art, as his *Miss Robertson of Colac (Dolly)* so admirably displays.

The economic crisis and depression that hit Melbourne in the early 1890s disrupted the local art scene and saw an eventual exodus of painters to Great Britain and France, some for very extended periods. In the context of Robert Dowling's twenty-seven year sojourn in London from 1857 to 1884, it is instructive to look at some of these. Arthur Streeton went to London in 1897 and stayed there (with intermittent visits to Australia) until 1923—some twenty-six years; in 1902 he painted, in homage to the great J M W Turner, a large atmospheric rendering of Trafalgar Square, titled

The centre of Empire. Tom Roberts, having spent some four years in London from 1881 to 1885, returned to England again in 1903. He finally settled back in Australia twenty years later, purchasing land at Kallista outside Melbourne in 1923. The most successful Australian artist of the period, the sculptor Bertram Mackennal, left Melbourne for London in 1883, a year before Dowling's own return. Mackennal carved out a career there, heaped with honours, until his death in 1931. The painter Rupert Bunny left Melbourne in 1884, living mainly in France for forty-nine years, before returning home in 1933. There were many others. These expatriate experiences, along with the cultural mores and emotional ties of the time, were shared by many other Australian artists until quite recently. For many of them, the distinctiveness of being Australian was not to deny being British.[35]

Over the thirty-six or so years of his productive artistic life, Robert Dowling's contribution to Australian art was multifaceted. He died, two years short of the centenary of white settlement of this country, having been from 1850 to 1886 a highly successful portrait painter of Australian settler society during the last third of those first hundred years of British colonisation. More importantly, he produced the largest body of mid-nineteenth-century images of Australian Aborigines from life in their shattered existence in the Western District of Victoria. He also composed, from another artist's studies, these images into elevated History Paintings, executed in Tasmania and, later, in London.

He lived in Great Britain for twenty-seven years, but was firmly focused on Australia. In London he was a gifted genre painter and the Australian Orientalist without peer. Finally, the profound religious works that Dowling painted in London are an Australian's response to the art of the Pre-Raphaelites. They reveal a moving familial resonance with the deep-seated roots of his Christian childhood in Tasmania.

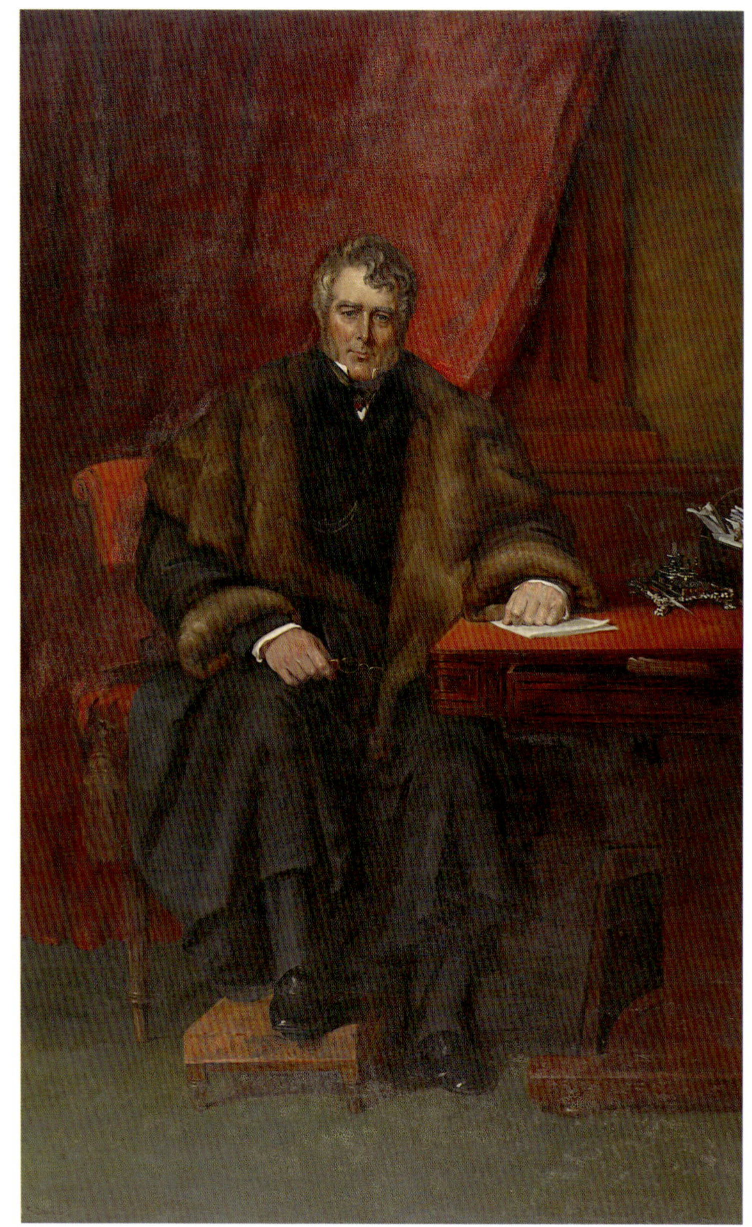

Robert Dowling
after John Partridge
(1789–1872)
Lord Melbourne
1884
oil on canvas
National Gallery of
Victoria, Melbourne

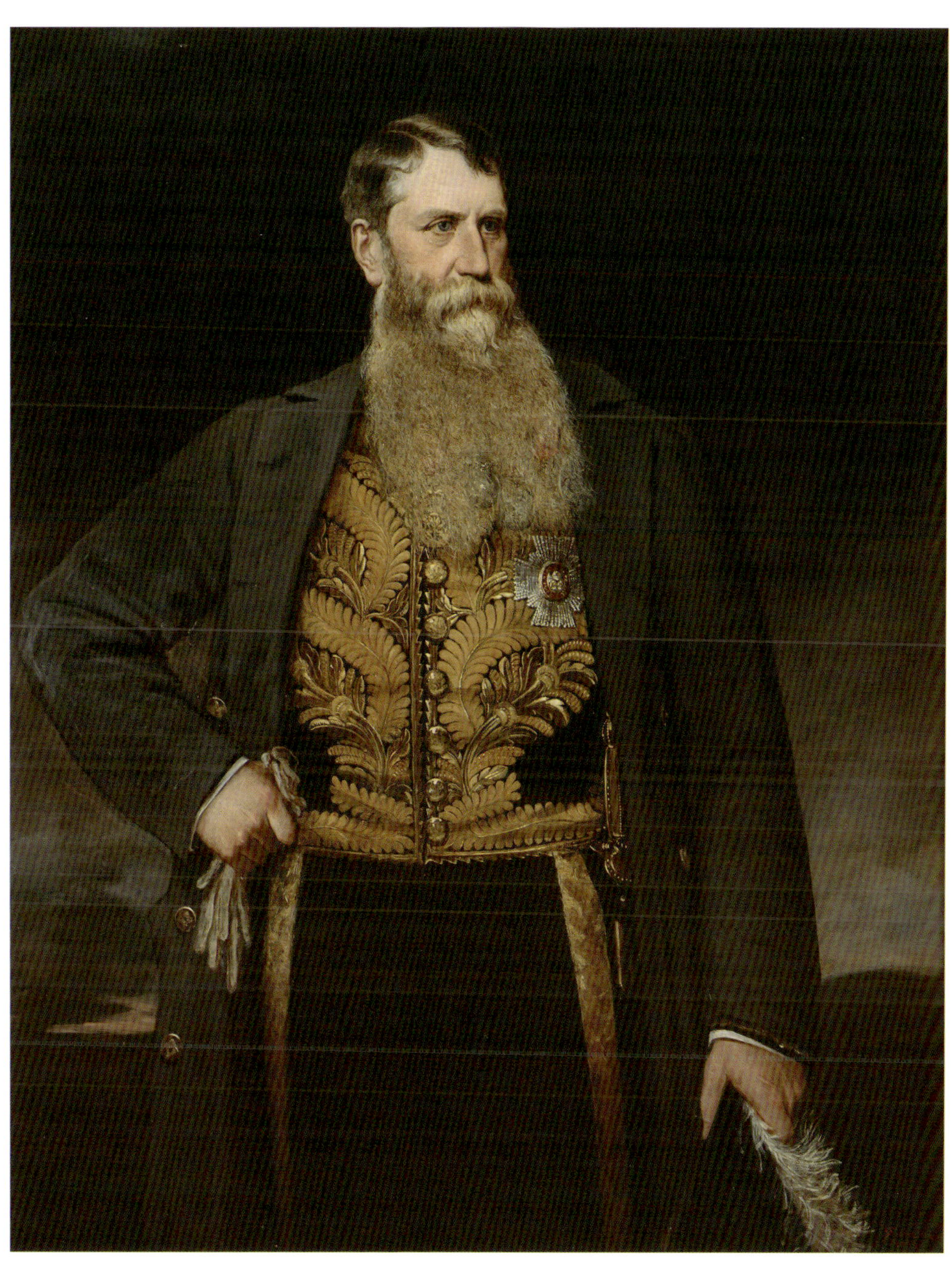

Sir Henry Loch 1884
oil on canvas
Pictures Collection, State Library of Victoria, Melbourne

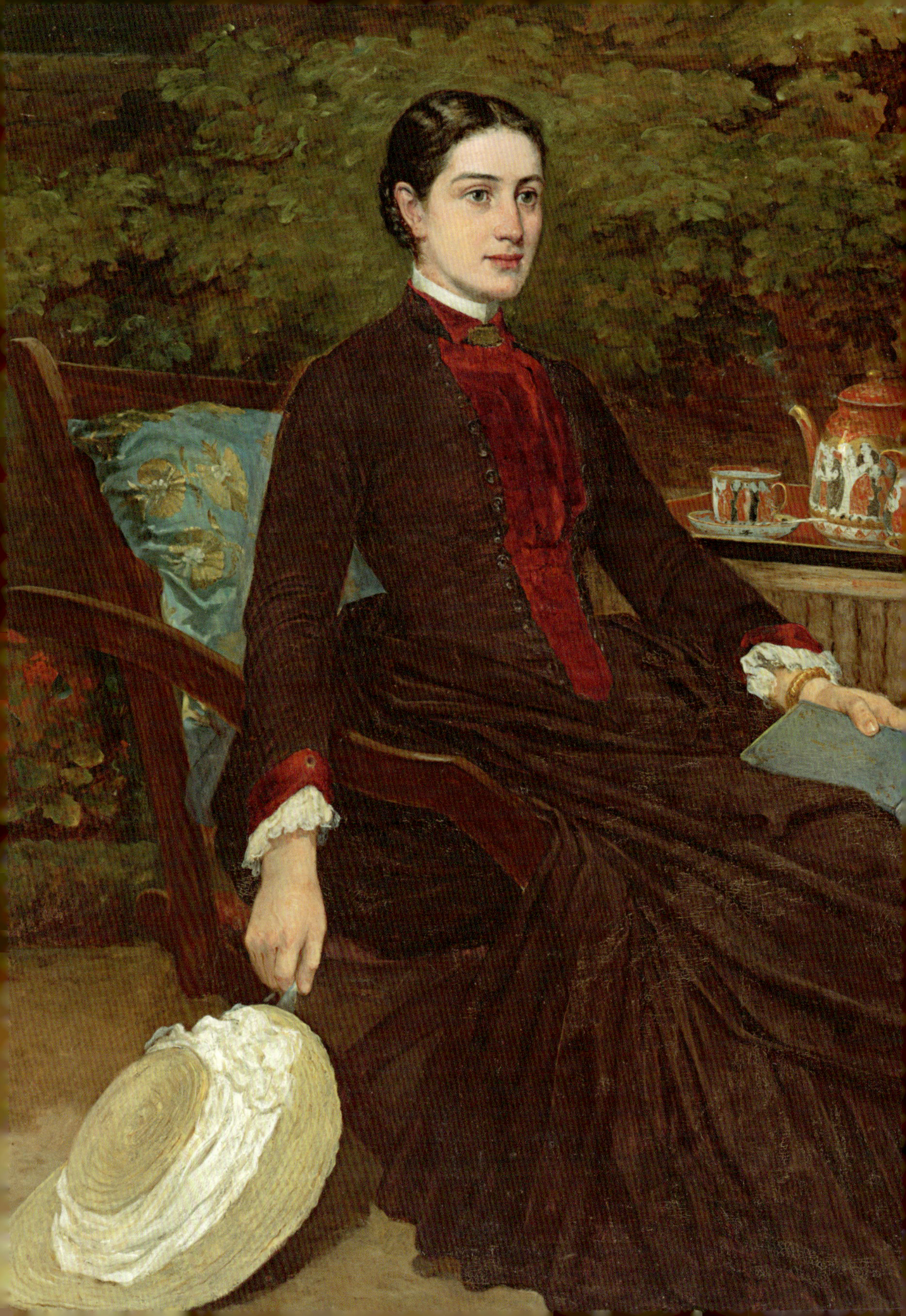

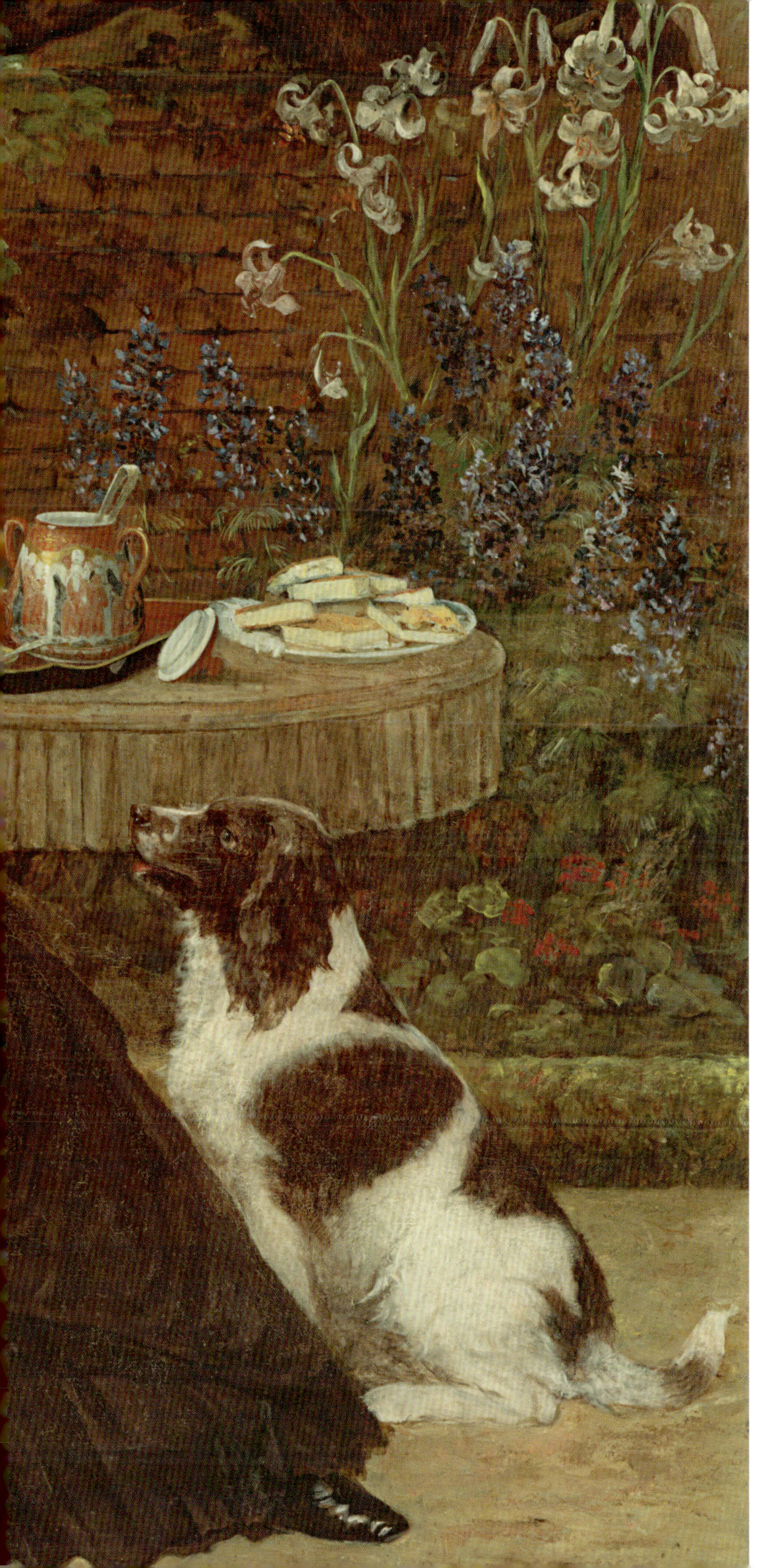

Miss Robertson of Colac (Dolly) 1885–86
oil on canvas
National Gallery of Australia, Canberra

Notes

Chapter 1

1 Samuel Cozens, *Incidents in the life of the Revd. Henry Dowling; formerly of Colchester, Essex and more recently of Launceston, Tasmania*, Fountain Barber, Melbourne, 1871, pp 73–75.

2 'Particular' Baptists held the theological view that Christ's Atonement for sin was made for particular individuals—the 'elect'—rather than for all men. 'Strict' refers to a closed position on membership and communion. Information from Laurence F Rowston.

3 Cozens, p 59.

4 Susan Patterson, 'Bridging the gap: my Dowling ancestors in colonial Launceston', MA Thesis, School of Historical Studies, University of Melbourne, 2008.

5 Laurence F Rowston, *Baptists in Van Diemen's Land: The story of Tasmania's first Baptist Church, the Hobart Particular Baptist Chapel, Harrington Street, 1835–1886*, The Baptist Union of Tasmania, Hobart, 1985, p 8.

6 The Chapel still exists, disfigured by a video rental shop and a surrounding car park.

7 Rowston, p 27.

8 Rowston, p 24.

9 Information from Anne Bartlett, Launceston, a descendant of John Tevelein, 26 Oct 2009.

10 Letter from Samuel Girle, 23 Feb 1893, Dowling Artist's File, QVMAG.

11 *The Cornwall Chronicle*, Launceston, 14 Aug 1850, p 535.

12 Clifford Craig & Isabella Mead, 'Frederick Strange—Artist c 1807–1873', *Papers and Proceedings of the Royal Society of Tasmania,* vol 97, Hobart, June 1965.

13 Suzanne Lester, *Spring Bay, Tasmania: a social history*, Artemis Publications, Hobart, 1994, p 221.

14 George Carr Clark's wife Hannah Maria (née Davice) at Ellinthorp has been said to be related to these Dowlings, but her connection came from a different Dowling family. Perhaps also there was a misinterpretation of the complicated facts that the assistant teacher she brought to Ellinthorp was a sister of Hannah Read née Purbrick, the niece of the Reverend Henry Dowling's second wife, and that Hannah Purbrick Read later immigrated as a widow to Tasmania and eventually married her widowed uncle to become the Reverend Henry Dowling's third wife. Information from Susan Patterson.

15 *The Examiner*, Launceston, 15 March 1851, p 178.

16 Patricia Fitzgerald Ratcliff, *The usefulness of John West: dissent and difference in the Australian colonies,* Albernian Press, Launceston, 2003.

17 Bernard Smith summarised West's lecture in his *Place, taste and tradition: a study of Australian art since 1788*, Ure Smith, Sydney, 1945, pp 93–95.

18 Ratcliff, pp 369–71.

19 *The Examiner*, 16 Nov 1850, p 742.

20 Letter from G C Clark to his son Charles, 21 June 1853, quoted in G T Stilwell, 'Mr and Mrs George Carr Clark of Ellinthorp Hall', *Tasmanian Historical Research Association*, vol 11, no 3, Sept 1963, pp 22–23.

21 These eventually passed to Robert Dowling's niece Leura. They had been identically framed in the 1870s to become a foursome with the National Gallery of Australia's pair of portraits of the Reverend Henry and Elizabeth Dowling.

22 *The Examiner*, 15 March 1851, p 178.

23 *The Examiner*, 19 March 1851, p 186.

24 'Notes by Alfred Bock to J.W Beattie', 1919, QVMAG files.

25 The shipping records from Launceston to Melbourne, 25 August 1849, list 'Mr & Mrs R. Dowling', *Index to Passenger Arrivals and Departures from early Launceston Newspapers, 1829–1865*, Launceston Branch of the Tasmanian Family History Society Inc.

26 *The Argus*, Melbourne, 20 Sept 1851, p 1.

27 *The Courier*, Hobart, 20 Oct 1852, p 4.

28 *The Colonial Times*, Hobart, 5 Nov 1852, p 3.

29 However, in 1859, as Mayor of Launceston, Robert Dowling's brother Henry could still have a fine photographic portrait taken of himself by W P & Matthew Dowling at their 'Portrait Gallery' in George Street.

30 *The Courier*, 23 Jan 1853, p 4.

31 The identity of the child is in question. The records at Narryna give the boy as Henry, who was not born until 1856. It may well be her first son Valentine, who was born in May 1853. Further study of these Narryna paintings would be helpful.

32 Robert Dowling's beloved mother Elizabeth died 24 March 1853. She had been an invalid for some years, nursed by her widowed niece, Hannah Read née Purbrick. After Elizabeth's death, the Reverend Henry Dowling married Hannah on 5 June 1854.

33 For W P Dowling, see Margaret Glover & Aif MacLochlainn, *Letters of an Irish patriot: William Raul Dowling in Tasmania*, Tasmanian Historical Research Association, Hobart, c 2005.

34 John McPhee, *The painted portrait photograph in Tasmania 1850–1900* (exhibition catalogue), QVMAG, Launceston, 2008.

35 *The Examiner*, 18 Aug 1852, p 558.

36 *The Colonial Times*, 24 Aug 1854, p 3.

Chapter 2

1 *The Examiner*, Launceston, 19 Sept 1854, p 2.

2 *The Argus*, Melbourne, 26 Sept 1854, p 8. Moubray, Lush & Co was a cloth and fabric merchant. Thomas Moubray came to Victoria from northern Tasmania in 1848 and would have known the Dowling family.

3 Burgess Roll, Cardinia Ward, Rate Payers of Geelong 1854–55/–56, p 5.

4 Henry Goulter was related to Robert Dowling's Aunt Elizabeth (née Goulter), wife of his uncle, John Dowling.

5 *The Geelong Advertiser*, 14 Dec 1854, p 1.

6 *Catalogue of works of art, exhibited in the Launceston Mechanics' Institute building on the occasion of its opening*, 9 April 1860, no 179.

7 Minute Book, York Street Baptist Chapel, 157, quoted in Susan Patterson, 'Bridging the gap: my Dowling ancestors in colonial Launceston', MA Thesis, University of Melbourne, 2008, p 35.

8 Gerard Hayes, 'A Portrait by Ludwig Becker', *Art & Australia*, vol 25, no 4, winter 1988, pp 514–15.

9 John Jones, 'Mrs Adolphus Sceales with Black Jimmie on Merrang Station 1856', in Anne Gray (ed), *Australian art in the National Gallery of Australia*, National Gallery of Australia, Canberra, 2002, p 55.

10 Conversation with Mrs John Crocker, a descendant of Harriet Ware, c 1984.

11 Burial Certificate 236/2, Warrnambool Cemetery Records.

12 Conversation with Ron Radford, 20 Nov 2009.

13 Ron Radford further suggests (conversation 23 Nov 2009) that these animals might have been painted with the use of photography despite no surviving evidence or matching photographic prints. Though popular in France in the mid 1850s, animal subject matter, because of the long exposure time required and the problem of animal movement, is rare in Australian photography before the 1860s. Gael Newton, Senior Curator of Photography at the National Gallery of Australia, confirms (email 23 Nov 2009) that a spaniel was photographed in Sydney in 1855 by Thomas Glaister 'in under a minute'; she believes photography of larger animals was possible at this time but estimates over a minute would be required for cows and horses, and in a confined environment not an open paddock.

14 John Jones, 'The Ware family of Koort-Koort-Nong, Minjah and Yalla-y-Poora in the Western District of Victoria and their patronage of the artists Robert Dowling and Eugene von Guérard', *artonview*, issue 12 summer 1997–98, National Gallery of Australia, Canberra, 2000, pp 17–22.

Chapter 3

1 James Boyce, *Van Diemen's Land*, Black Inc, Melbourne, 2009.

2 Henry Melville, *The history of Van Diemen's Land from the year 1824 to 1835 inclusive*, London, 1835, p 122.

3 Laurence F Rowlston, *Baptists in Van Diemen's Land*, Baptist Union of Tasmania, Hobart, 1985, ch 1, pp 4–5.

4 *Port Phillip Herald,* Melbourne, 22 Dec 1843, p 3.

5 *Catalogue of works of art, ornamental and decorative art*, Trustees of the Public Library & Museum, Melbourne, March–June 1869.

6 Mary Mackay, 'Early Tasmanian sculptures: a re-assessment', in *Bowyang: work on changing Australia*, no 5, April–May 1981, pp 6–12.

7 N J B Plomley, 'Thomas Bock's Portraits of the Tasmanian Aborigines', in Diane Dunbar, *Thomas Bock: convict engraver, society portraitist* (exhibition catalogue), QVMAG, Launceston, 1991, pp 32–49.

8 Henry Dowling's set was eventually sold by him to the Tasmanian Government and transferred to the Tasmanian Museum & Art Gallery in 1889.

9 'From my personal acquaintance with the subjects themselves, during the years 1831–33', *Mercury*, Hobart, 15 Aug 1884, p 3.

10 John West, reformist, newspaper editor and historian. See Patricia Fitzgerald Ratcliff, *The usefulness of John West: dissent and differences in the Australian colonies*, Albernian Press, Launceston, 2003.

11 John West, *History of Tasmania,* Henry Dowling, Launceston, 1852, vol 2, p 333.

12 John Jones, "Reclaimed from Barbarism': J M Crossland, *Nannultera, a young cricketer of the Natives' Training Institution, Poonindie*, 1854', in Daniel Thomas (ed), *Creating Australia: 200 years of art 1788–1988* (exhibition catalogue), ICCA and AGSA, Adelaide, for the Australian Bicentennial Authority, Sydney, 1988.

13 This was a misconception, due to the survivors being so few. Some full-blood Aborigines were alive in the mid 1850s and Truggernana (Trucannini) did not die until 1876.

14 Richard Broome, *Aboriginal Victorians: a history since 1800*, Allen & Unwin, Sydney, 2005; 'Reflections', p 22.

15 Ibid.

16 The signature and date, 'R Dowling / May / 1856', previously concealed by framing, was found by Michael Varcoe-Cocks.

17 For description and location see James Dawson, *Australian Aborigines: the language and customs of several tribes of Aborigines in the Western District of Victoria, Australia*, George Robertson, Melbourne, 1881, ch 1, p 2.

18 These were acquired, along with Dowling's oil-sketches after Bock, by Sir Leopold McClintock, whose portrait Dowling painted in 1880. They were later given by his family to the British Museum in 1924.

19 See the drawings: Black Johnny, *Eugene von Guérard sketching* 1855, collection Mitchell Library, SLNSW, and Eugene von Guérard, *Johnny Kangatong* 1855, collection Dixson Galleries, SLNSW, Sydney.

20 James Dawson's annotation, initialled and dated 1871 front and reverse of an 1860s carte-de-visite portrait of Weerat Kuyuut, by J Harvey, collection SLV, Melbourne.

21 Site identification by Bim Affleck, former owner of Minjah.

22 Letter from Henry Dowling to the Secretary of the Trustees, National Gallery of Victoria, item 43, packet no 8, Miscellaneous Correspondence.

23 *The Argus*, Melbourne, 17 March 1856, pp 4–5.

24 *The Examiner*, Launceston, 28 March 1857, p 5.

25 *The Geelong Advertiser*, 4 April 1857, p 4.

26 N J B Plomley has written extensively on Bock's and Dowling's Aboriginal studies: see his 'Pictures of Tasmanian Aborigines by Robert Dowling', *National Gallery of Victoria Art Bulletin*, no 3, 1961; *Thomas Bock's portraits of the Tasmanian Aborigines*, Launceston, QVMAG, 1965; and 'Thomas Bock's portraits of the Tasmanian Aborigines' in Diane Dunbar, *Thomas Bock: convict engraver, society portraitist* (exhibition catalogue), QVMAG, Launceston, 1991.

27 Terence Lane, *Nineteenth-century Australian art in the National Gallery of Victoria*, NGV, Melbourne, 2003, p 45.

28 Figures revealed by Michael Varcoe-Cocks in recent cleaning, National Gallery of Victoria, 2009.

29 *The Cornwall Chronicle,* Launceston, 18 May 1857, p 5.

30 *The Examiner*, 25 Aug 1860, p 3.

31 *The Examiner*, 24 April 1860, p 1.

32 *The Examiner*, 28 Aug 1860, p 2.

33 Five of these sketches are held by the National Library of Australia.

34 Reported in *The Cornwall Chronicle*, 14 April 1860, p 4.

35 *The Examiner*, 24 April 1860, p 1.

36 Without giving reasons: see William Moore, *The story of Australian art*, Angus & Robertson, Sydney, 1934, vol 1, p 36.

37 Unbelievably, removed and sold in the mid twentieth century. The present frame approximates it, a recreation from early photographs.

38 *The Cornwall Chronicle*, 30 Jan 1861, p 4.

39 Nicholas was painting with the aid of the London photograph for, unlike the QVMAG painting, Nicholas's copy has the same two boomerangs as the AGSA painting.

40 For a detailed study of this painting see Jane Hylton, 'Group of Natives of Tasmania 1860', in *Australian Colonial art 1800–1900*, AGSA, Adelaide, 1995, pp 75–78.

41 The misunderstanding was resolved in the early 1980s by Barbara Chapman, Curator at the QVMAG, after the Ethnographic Society's picture came out on long-term loan to the National Gallery of Australia and received some publicity.

42 The painting was found in London. It was acquired by the NGV in 1932, for £15, on recommendation from the Felton Bequest Advisor, Randall Davies.

43 Revealed in Michael Varcoe-Cocks's recent cleaning of the painting.

44 See, for one example, Humphrey Clegg & Stephen Gilchrist, 'Depictions of Aboriginal people in Colonial Australian art: settler and unsettling narratives in the work of Robert Dowling', in *Art Bulletin of Victoria* 48, NGV, Melbourne, 2008, pp 35–45.

45 In light of this it is hard to credit Tim Bonyhady's claim that between the canvases of Duterrau of c 1840 and Tom Roberts's eight head studies of Aborigines around 1900, 'no other Australian artist had ever produced such an extensive series of portrait paintings of either Aborigines or Colonists'.

See Tim Bonyhady, 'Introduction,' in Tim Bonyhady & Andrew Sayers (eds), *Heads of the people: a portrait of Colonial Australia* (exhibition catalogue), National Portrait Gallery, Canberra, 2000, p 11.

46 The painting recently known as *An afternoon siesta*, which is signed, inscribed and dated 'R Dowling / from / Tasmania / 1859' is now to be identified with *Sabbath in the country*, Dowling's first exhibit at the Royal Society of British Artists in 1859. *The London Illustrated News*, 8 Sept 1860, p 228, refers to Dowling as 'son of a minister in Australia' and states that he was 'entirely self taught'.

Chapter 4

1 G Gavin Casey, 'Commission to Mr Robert Dowling', printed appeal pamphlet, Tasmanian Archive & Heritage Office, Hobart.

2 *The Cornwall Chronicle*, Launceston, 21 Feb 1863, p 4.

3 *The Examiner*, Launceston, 19 Feb 1865, p 5.

4 'Works of Art Presented', file note QVMAG.

5 *Deed of Trust*, Launceston Mechanics' Institute 1879, in the State Library of Tasmania, Launceston, states in 'Schedule of paintings and plaster busts' that the donor of the portrait of Queen Victoria was Robert Dowling; the donor of the portrait of Prince Albert was Henry Dowling Jnr; the Prince of Wales was presented by public subscription; the Princess of Wales was given by Robert Dowling; the Duke of Edinburgh was given by Messrs Overend & Robb, contractors for the Launceston & Western Railway; the portrait of Sir Richard Dry given by Henry Dowling Jnr; the painting of Tasmanian Aborigines by Robert Dowling; and the pair of Benjamin Law busts by Henry Dowling Jnr. I am most grateful to Catherine Pearce, State Library of Tasmania, Launceston, for bringing this to my attention.

6 *The Hobart Town Mercury*, 20 Oct 1864, p 2.

7 *The Examiner*, 19 April 1860, p 2.

8 For this see, Lynda Nead, 'Seduction, prostitution, suicide: *On the brink* by Alfred Elmore', in *Art History*, vol 5, no 3, Sept 1982, pp 308–21.

9 *Walch's Literary Intelligencer*, Hobart & Launceston, Feb 1861, p 130.

10 *Art Journal*, London, June 1859, p 171.

11 Nothing is known of the painting's early history. Though often quoted in the colonial press and in the artist's obituaries of 1886, it was known in Australia only from a photograph. The work, currently bearing the signature of the English painter Charles Hunt (1803–1877) and the date 1881, was reproduced in Christopher Wood's book *Victorian panorama* (Faber, London, 1976, illus 16, p 153) and there recognised by the present author John Jones, who made contact with the Museum of London, in whose collection the painting has been since the mid twentieth century. The case was made for re-attribution. With further assistance from Michael Varcoe-Cocks, conservator at the National Gallery of Victoria, who identified its canvas as being no later than 1860, the painting has now been firmly given to Robert Dowling. The signature and date are a forgery.

12 *The Atlas*, London, 25 Aug 1860, p 688.

13 *London Illustrated News*, 28 Sept 1860, p 288.

14 For detailed description of this work, see Angus Trumble, *Love and death: art in the Age of Queen Victoria*, Art Gallery of South Australia, Adelaide, 2001, pp 114–15.

15 *Hobart Town Advertiser*, 12 Dec 1861, p 1.

16 *The Cornwall Chronicle*, 1 Aug 1866, p 4.

17 *The Argus*, Melbourne, 10 May 1877, p 5.

18 *The Argus*, loc cit.

19 Report of the Sectional Committee of the National Gallery, PP Victoria, 1878, vol 2t, no 7, p77, Schedule V.

20 *Catalogue of valuable oil paintings and water-colour drawings collected by the late William Lynch Esq*, Gemmel & Tuckett auction, 14–15 Oct 1903, State Library of Victoria.

21 *Exhibition of works of Victorian artists and a loan collection of pictures held under the auspices of the exhibition trustees and Victorian Artists Society*, 20 Dec 1890.

22 *The Argus*, 7 July 1883, p 4.

23 *Collection of the magnificent oil paintings and water-colour drawings collected by the late Sir Thomas Fitzgerald CB*, Gemmel & Tuckett auction, 24 Sept 1909, State Library of Victoria.

24 Peter Coats's brother, Sir Thomas, owned two paintings by Dowling, *Doubting Thomas* and *Moses on Mount Nebo*, now in the Paisley Museum & Art Gallery, Scotland.

25 The reviews were reprinted in *The Examiner*, 15 July & 29 July 1865.

26 *The Examiner*, 5 Dec 1864, p 4.

27 From Henry Dowling the painting passed to a Mr WT Bell and then to the Grubb family. Frederick William Grubb left it to the Paterson Street Wesleyan Church in Launceston in the early 1920s. It came thence, via the Pilgrim Uniting Church, Launceston, to the Queen Victoria Museum & Art Gallery in 1982.

28 *The Tasmanian Messenger*, Oct 1866, p 318. I am most grateful to Laurence F Rowlston for bringing this to my attention. 'Theresa Tasmania' is known also for *Our grandmama's stories* and *Among the black boys*.

29 By Joseph Lycett, WP Dowling, Adelaide Ironside, Alexander Schramm, and Marshall Claxton (in Sydney from 1850 to 1854 and exhibiting previous British work). William Strutt, perhaps closest in spirit to Dowling's work, sent religious paintings to Australia, but not until the 1880s. Arthur Loureiro, Dowling's contemporary in Melbourne from 1884, also painted religious subjects.

30 'Mr Dowling's Moses on Mount Nebo', *Art Journal*, 1879, p 142.

31 It is actually a ghostly figure of the pre-incarnate Saviour, not the Angel of the Bible text.

32 *Once a Month*, Melbourne, 15 July 1885, p 73.

33 *Once a Month*, 15 Jan 1885, p 76.

34 The painter Briton Rivière (1840–1920), famous for his animal subjects, particularly lions.

35 *Once a Month*, 1 June 1886, p 560.

36 Philippe Jullian, *The Orientalists: European painters of Eastern scenes*, Phaidon, Oxford, 1977, p 133.

37 Report of the Sectional Committee of the National Gallery of Victoria, PP Victoria 1878, vol 2t, no 7, p 77, Schedule V.

38 *The Times*, London, 1 May 1855, p 12.

39 For example 'A new picture by Mr Robert Dowling', *The Cornwall Chronicle*, Launceston, 29 Feb 1877, p 234.

40 The Revd Isaac Taylor, '1. Street-Life in Cairo', *Leaves from an Egyptian note-book*, Kegan Paul, Trench & Co, London, 1888.

41 *Mr Dowling's Oriental picture*, Messrs Walch Brothers & Birchall, Launceston, 1877.

42 Letter from Henry Dowling to the Secretary of the Trustees, 8 Feb 1877, National Gallery of Victoria, item 43, packet no 8, Miscellaneous Correspondence, Public Library, National Gallery & Museum, Public Records Office, Victoria.

43 Loc cit, letter from Eugene von Guérard to Mr Curtis, Secretary to the Trustees, 18 April 1877, pp 32–33. Von Guérard noted 'the defect in the drawing of some of the figures' but found 'The general effect of the picture is very good, the architecture is exceedingly well done, and the arrangement of the costumes, I believe to be perfectly correct and true to nature'.

44 Loc cit, p 27.

Chapter 5

1 William Westgarth, *Half a century of Australian progress: a personal retrospect*, London, 1889, pp 46–47.

2 *The Argus*, Melbourne, 10 July 1883, p 4.

3 *The Argus*, 25 Jan 1883, p 10.

4 *The Argus*, 3 April 1883, p 5.

5 *The Argus*, 19 May 1877, p 5.

6 *The Argus*, 25 October 1866, p 7.

7 Ann Galbally, Alison Inglis & Christine Downer, *The first collections: the Public Library and National Gallery of Victoria in the 1850s and 1860s*, University of Melbourne Art Museum, Melbourne, 1992.

8 Gerard Vaughan, 'The Armytage Collection: taste in Melbourne in the late nineteenth century', in Ann Galbally & Margaret Plant (eds), *Studies in Australian art*, Department of Fine Arts, University of Melbourne, 1978.

9 *Melbourne International Exhibition 1880: The official catalogue of exhibits*, Mason, Frith & McCutcheon, Melbourne, 1880, vol 2. Dowling was represented in the British Court with two paintings, *Morning in the market place, Cairo* and *Moses viewing the Promised Land from Mount Nebo*.

10 James Smith, *The Argus*, 29 Dec 1862, p 5.

11 *Once a Month*, Melbourne, 15 Nov 1884, p 395.

12 *Once a Month*, 1 June 1885, p 474.

13 *Once a Month*, 15 Sept 1885, p 230.

14 *Once a Month*, 1 June 1886, p 560.

15 Florence Fuller (1867–1946) was a distant relative of the artist. The term 'niece' was used in regard to propriety.

16 'Melbourne Tea Table Talk', *West Australian*, Perth, 19 Aug 1886, p 3.

17 *Once a Month*, 15 June 1885, p 474.

18 Terence Lane, 'Grosvenor Chambers: a phenomenon of Marvellous Melbourne', in his *Australian Impressionism* (exhibition catalogue), NGV, Melbourne, 2007, pp 146–51.

19 Caroline Jordan, 'Fletcher's of Collins Street: Melbourne's leading nineteenth-century art dealer', in *The LaTrobe Journal*, no 75, autumn 2005, SLV, Melbourne, pp 77–93.

20 Gerard Vaughan, op cit.

21 Caroline Jordan, op cit.

22 Hilary Maddocks, 'Picture framemakers in Melbourne c 1860 – 1930', and Claire Newhouse, 'John Thallon 1848–1918', in *Melbourne Journal of Technical Studies in Art*, vol 1 'Frames', University of Melbourne Conservation Service, 1999, p 2, pp 81–93.

23 *The Argus*, 14 July 1886, p 6.

24 *Once a Month*, 1 Feb 1885, p 167.

25 *Once a Month*, 15 April 1885, p 313.

26 *The Argus*, 28 March 1885, p 13.

27 *Once a Month*, 15 April 1885, p 313.

28 *Once a Month*, 15 Sept 1885, pp 230–31.

29 *The Argus*, 7 Sept 1886, p 7.

30 *Once a Month*, 15 June 1885, p 474.

31 There was a widespread interest in things Japanese. The Australian-born Mortimer Menpes painted there. Whistler and others were deeply influenced by the Japanese woodcuts of Hiroshige. A production of Gilbert & Sullivan's Japanese operetta *The Mikado* opened the new Royal Princess Theatre, Melbourne, in 1886.

32 *The Tasmanian*, Launceston, 24 April 1886, p 24.

33 *The Argus*, 14 July 1886, p 6.

34 *The Examiner*, 16 Feb 1885, p 2.

35 As discussed in regard to Tom Roberts, see Virginia Spate, 'Where the sun never set: Tom Roberts and the British Empire', in Ron Radford (ed), *Tom Roberts* (exhibition catalogue), AGSA, Adelaide, 1996, pp 62–65.

A sheikh and his son entering Cairo, on their return from a pilgrimage to Mecca
1874 (detail)
oil on canvas
National Gallery of Victoria, Melbourne

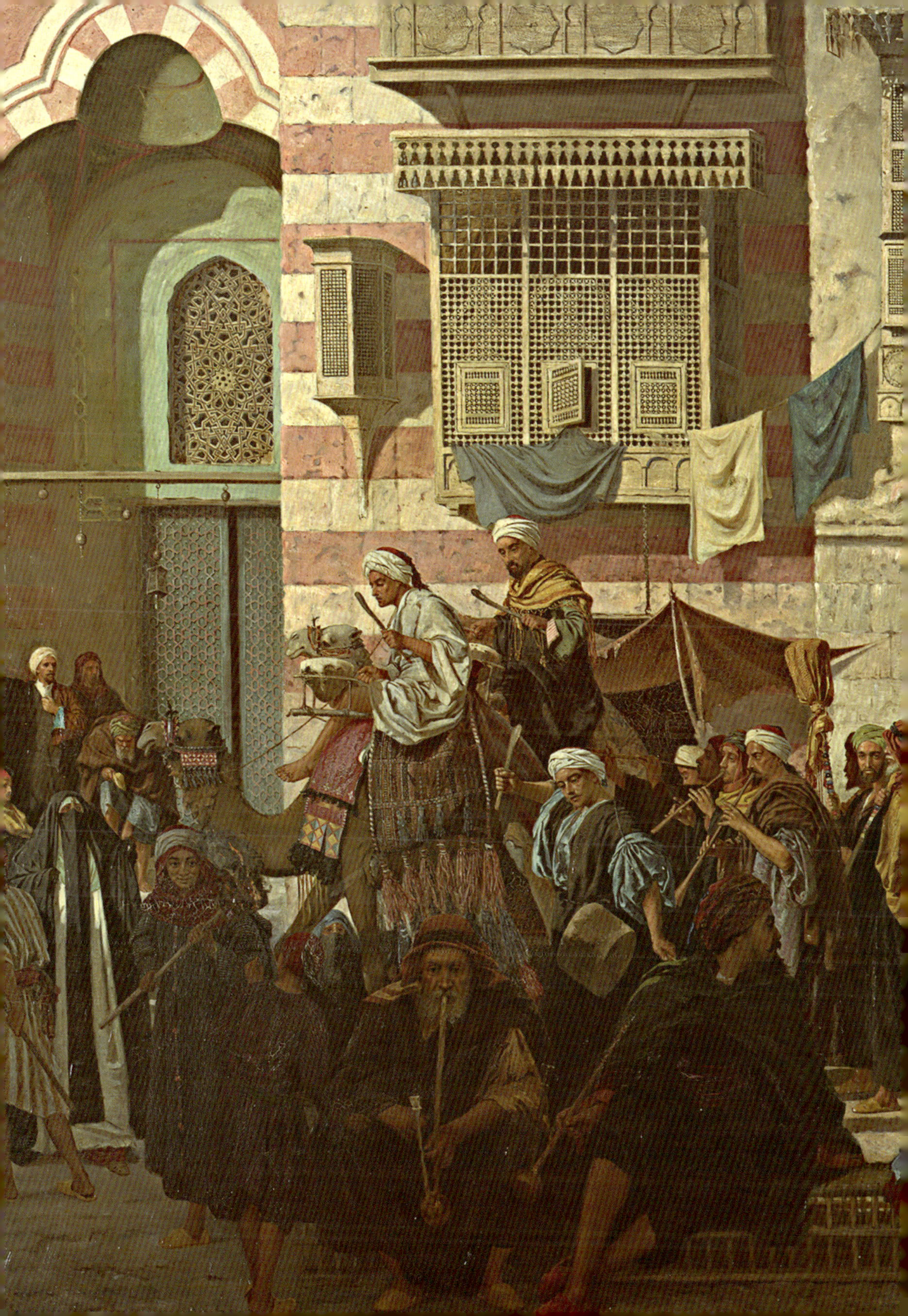

Bibliography

Books

Bonyhady, Tim and Sayers, Andrew (eds), *Heads of the people: a portrait of Colonial Australia*, National Portrait Gallery, Canberra, 2000.

Boyce, James, *Van Diemen's Land*, Black Inc, Melbourne, 2009.

Broome, Richard, *Aboriginal Victorians: a history since 1800*, LaTrobe University and the Australian Academy of Humanities, Allen & Unwin, Sydney, 2005.

Cozens, Samuel, *Incidents in the life of the Revd. Henry Dowling: formerly of Colchester, Essex and more recently of Launceston, Tasmania*, Fountain Barber, Melbourne, 1871.

Davies, Alan and Stanbury, Peter, *The mechanical eye in Australia: photography 1841–1990*, Oxford University Press, Melbourne, 1985.

Dawson, James, *Australian Aborigines: the language and customs of several tribes of Aborigines in the Western District of Victoria,* George Robertson, Melbourne, 1881.

Hylton, Jane, 'Group of Natives of Tasmania 1860', in *Australian Colonial art 1800–1900*, Art Gallery of South Australia, Adelaide, 1995.

Jones, John, 'Mrs Adolphous Sceales with Black Jimmie on Merrang Station 1856', in *Australian art in the National Gallery of Australia,* Anne Gray (ed), National Gallery of Australia, Canberra, 2002.

Jullian, Philippe, *The Orientalists: European painters of Eastern scenes*, Phaidon, Oxford, 1977.

Lane, Terence, *Nineteenth century Australian art in the National Gallery of Victoria*, National Gallery of Victoria, Melbourne, 2003.

Lester, Suzanne, *Spring Bay, Tasmania: a social history*, Artemis Publications, Hobart, 1994.

Melville, Henry, *The history of Van Diemen's Land from the year 1824 to 1835 inclusive*, London, 1835; reprint George Mackanass (ed), Review Publications, Dubbo, NSW, 1978.

Moore, William, *The story of Australian art*, Angus & Robertson, Sydney, 1934.

Plomley, N J B, *Thomas Bock's portraits of the Tasmanian Aborigines*, Queen Victoria Museum and Art Gallery, Launceston, 1965.

Ratcliff, Patricia Fitzgerald, *The usefulness of John West: dissent and difference in the Australian Colonies,* The Albernian Press, Launceston, 2003.

Rowston, Laurence F, *Baptists in Van Diemen's Land: the story of Tasmania's first Baptist Church, the Hobart Town Particular Baptist Chapel, Harrington Street 1835–1886*, The Baptist Union of Tasmania, Hobart, 1985.

Smith, Bernard, *Place, taste and tradition: a study of Australian art since 1788*, Ure Smith, Sydney, 1945.

West, John, *History of Tasmania*, Henry Dowling, Launceston, 1852, vol 2.

Westgarth, William, *Half a century of Australian progress: a personal retrospect*, Sampson Low, Marsten, Searle & Rivington, London, 1889.

Journals

Clegg, Humphrey and Gilchrist, Stephen, 'Depictions of Aboriginal people in Colonial Australian art: settler and unsettling narratives in the work of Robert Dowling', *Art Bulletin of Victoria 48*, National Gallery of Victoria, Melbourne, 2008.

Craig, Clifford and Meade, Isabella, 'Frederick Strange— Artist c 1807 – 1873', *Papers and Proceedings of the Royal Society of Tasmania,* vol 97, Hobart, June 1965.

Glover, Margaret and MacLochlainn, Aif, 'Letters of an Irish Patriot: William Paul Dowling in Tasmania', *Tasmanian Historical Research Association*, Hobart, c 2005.

Hayes, Gerard, 'A Portrait by Ludwig Becker', *Art &Australia,* vol 25, no 4, Winter 1988.

Jones, John, 'The Ware family of Koort-Koort-Nong, Minjah and Yalla-y-Poora in the Western District of Victoria and their patronage of the artists Robert Dowling and Eugene von Guérard', *artonview*, issue 12 summer 1997–98, National Gallery of Australia, Canberra, 2000.

Jordan, Caroline, 'Fletcher's of Collins Street: Melbourne's leading nineteenth-century art dealer', *The LaTrobe Journal*, no 75 Autumn 2005.

Mackay, Mary, 'Early Tasmanian sculptures: a re-assessment', in *Bowyang: work on changing Australia,* no 5, April/May 1981.

Maddocks, Hilary, 'Picture framemakers in Melbourne c 1860–1930', *Melbourne Journal of Technical Studies in Art*, vol 1, Frames, The University of Melbourne Conservation Service, 1999.

Nead, Lynda, 'Seduction, prostitution, suicide: *On the brink* by Alfred Elmore', *Art History*, vol 5 no 3, September 1982.

Newhouse, Claire, 'John Thallon 1848–1918', *Melbourne Journal of Technical Studies in Art*, vol 1, Frames, The University of Melbourne Conservation Service, 1999.

Plomley, N J B, 'Pictures of Tasmanian Aborigines by Robert Dowling', *National Gallery of Victoria Art Bulletin,* no 3, Melbourne, 1961.

Stilwell, Geoffrey, 'Mr and Mrs George Carr Clark of Ellinthorp Hall', *Tasmanian Historical Research Association*, vol 2, no 3, Hobart, September 1963.

Vaughan, Gerard, 'The Armytage Collection: taste in Melbourne in the late nineteenth century', *Studies in Australian art*, Ann Galbally and Margaret Plant (eds), Department of Fine Arts, The University of Melbourne, 1978.

Thesis

Patterson, Susan Elizabeth Acteson, 'Bridging the gap: my Dowling ancestors in Colonial Launceston', MA thesis, School of Historical Studies, Faculty of Arts, The University of Melbourne, 2008.

Manuscripts

Beattie, JW, 'Notes by Alfred Bock to J W Beattie', Artist's File, 1919, Queen Victoria Museum & Art Gallery.

Burgess Role, Cardinia Ward, Rate Payers of Geelong, 1854–55.

Burial Ccrificate 236/2, Warrnambool Cemetery Records.

Casey, G, Gavin 'Commission to Mr Robert Dowling', printed appeal pamphlet, Tasmanian Archive and Heritage Office.

'Deed of Trust', Launceston Mechanics' Institute, 1879, State Library of Tasmania, Launceston.

Girle, Samuel, letter, 23 February 1893, Artist's File, Queen Victoria Museum & Art Gallery.

Letter from Henry Dowling to the Secretary of the Trustees, National Gallery of Victoria, item 43, packet no 8, Miscellaneous Correspondence.

'Report of the Sectional Committee of the National Gallery of Victoria', PP Victoria 1878, vol 2t, State Library of Victoria.

'Works of Art Presented', File note, Queen Victoria Museum & Art Gallery.

Catalogues

Catalogue of valuable oil paintings and water-colour drawings collected by the late William Lynch Esq, Gemmel & Tuckett auction, 14–15 Oct 1903, State Library of Victoria.

Catalogue of works of art, ornamental and decorative, Melbourne, Trustees of the Public Library and Museum March–June 1869, State Library of Victoria.

Catalogue of works of art, exhibited in the Launceston Mechanics' Institute Building on the occasion of its opening, 9 April 1860.

Collection of the magnificent oil paintings and water-colour drawings collected by the late Sir Thomas Fitzgerald CB, Gemmel & Tuckett auction, 24 Sept 1909, State Library of Victoria.

Exhibition of works of Victorian artists and a loan collection of pictures held under the auspices of the Exhibition Trustees and the Victorian Artists' Society, 20 December 1890, State Library of Victoria.

Galbally, Anne, Inglis, Alison and Downer, Christine, *The first collections: the Public Library and National Gallery of Victoria in the 1850s and 1860s* (exhibition catalogue), The University of Melbourne Art Museum, Melbourne, 1992.

'Grosvenor Chambers, A phenomenon of Marvellous Melbourne', in *Australian Impressionism* (exhibition catalogue), National Gallery of Victoria, Melbourne, 2007.

McPhee, John, *The painted portrait photograph in Tasmania 1850–1900* (exhibition catalogue), Queen Victoria Museum and Art Gallery, Launceston, 2008.

Melbourne International Exhibition 1880, the official catalogue of exhibits, Melbourne, Mason, Frith and McCutcheon, 1880 vol 2, State Library of Victoria.

Mr Dowling's Oriental picture, Launceston, Messrs Walch Brothers & Birchall, 1877, State Library of Victoria.

'"Reclaimed from Barbarism": J M Crossland, Nannultera, a young cricketer of the Natives' Training Institution, Poonindee', in *Creating Australia: 200 years of art 1788 –1988* (exhibition catalogue), ICCA and Art Gallery of South Australia, Adelaide, for the Australian Bicentenary Authority, Sydney, 1988.

Spate, Virgina, 'Where the sun never set, Tom Roberts and the British Empire', in *Tom Roberts* (exhibition catalogue), Ron Radford (ed), Art Gallery of South Australia, Adelaide, 1996.

Taylor, the Rev, Isaac, *Leaves from an Egyptian note-book*, Kegan Paul Trench & Co, London, 1877.

'Thomas Bock's Portraits of the Tasmanian Aborigines', in Dianne Dunbar, *Thomas Bock: convict engraver, society portraitist* (exhibition catalogue), Queen Victoria Museum and Art Gallery, Launceston, 1991.

Trumble, Angus, *Love and death: art in the age of Queen Victoria* (exhibition catalogue), Art Gallery of South Australia, Adelaide, 2001.

Acknowledgments

Author

My initial interest in the work of Robert Dowling was encouraged by Dr Anne Galbally, who suggested I treat the artist as subject for an MA thesis in the Department of Fine Arts at the University of Melbourne. That was many years ago, the MA fell into abeyance but my involvement endured in the context of an increasing number of scholarly studies on complementary material in Australian Colonial art.

Two years ago, Ron Radford, who has contributed significantly to that scholarship, asked if I would curate a Robert Dowling exhibition for the National Gallery of Australia. I agreed, and this publication, I hope, will finally bring Dowling's career into focus, distinguishing him from his peers and charting his rather complex place in the annals of Australian art.

I am very grateful to Ron Radford, for without his keen interest this project would have come to nought. He has helpfully read the text and contributed pertinent insights. I also owe a debt of gratitude to his staff at the National Gallery of Australia, particularly Dr Anne Gray, Head of Australian Art. They have been most helpful in overcoming the problems which distance posed for this project, as I am based afar in rural Victoria.

The staff of the Queen Victoria Museum and Art Gallery, Launceston, have been equally helpful. I am particularly indebted to Yvonne Adkins, Curator, Nineteenth-Century Australian Art and Ross Smith, Research Officer, Family History Branch, for their patient answers to constant enquiries.

Daniel Thomas, my former revered Senior Curator and colleague at the National Gallery of Australia has, from rural Tasmania, kindly read and edited the text. His insightful knowledge and meticulous attention to detail has enhanced it enormously. I am deeply grateful to him. Daniel also, together with my friends Alison Inglis and Terence Lane wrote letters of support for a Visions Grant for the tour of this exhibition.

The opportunity to work on the artist has involved others, and their encouragement has been unqualified. Susan Patterson, also from rural Victoria, is a great-great-great granddaughter of Reverend Henry Dowling, and a great-great niece of the artist; she must 'carry the palm' for her unstinting support, her reading and correcting of the chapters, and her role as oracle on the intricacies of Dowling family relationships. Megan Pannu has been so helpful in patiently correcting my somewhat ponderous grammar.

Michael Varcoe-Cocks, Conservator of Paintings 1850–1950 at the National Gallery of Victoria has revealed new aspects of Dowling's paintings in his care, as well of information on the artist's career. Michael's technical knowledge was of enormous importance in convincing the Museum of London to reattribute the painting *Breakfasting out* from Charles Hunt, back to Robert Dowling.

Laurence F Rowlston, the authority on Baptist Church history in Tasmania, has been equally generous with his research and knowledge. Other friends in Tasmania also have contributed with thoughtful advice, information and checking, particularly Catherine Pearce and the staff at the State Library of Tasmania, Launceston; Ian Morrison at the Tasmanian Archives and Heritage Office, Hobart; Sue Backhouse, Tasmanian Museum and Art Gallery; Barbara Valentine; Anne Bartlett; Joan Green; Dr EVR Ratcliff; Margaret Glover; Dr David de Little; Dr Tony Brown and Rosanna Cameron.

Christine Downer kindly read the two Victorian Chapters and Terence Lane has been very supportive of this project. Others have also been helpful: John McPhee, Barbara Chapman and Mary Eagle (for old research notes from the State Library of Victoria). So have Rebecca Andrews at the Art Gallery of South Australia and Humphrey Clegg and Elena Taylor at the National Gallery of Victoria. Malcolm Robertson, Bill Robertson and Sadie Robertson have supplied useful information about the family and the portrait, *Miss Robertson of Colac (Dolly)*.

I am very grateful to the staff of the Pictures Collection, State Library of Victoria: Madeleine Say, Mary Lewis and particularly Gerard Hayes. Bishop James Grant has been very helpful with information on Charles Perry, first Bishop of Melbourne. Among the National Gallery of Australia staff, Gael Newton, Miriam Kelly and Roger Butler have been forthcoming with useful information, as has Harry Persaud, Curator, Library Collections, British Museum and Francis Marshall, Senior Curator of Paintings, the Museum of London.

Finally my sincere gratitude goes to Douglas Neale for his constant support, forbearance and cheerful goodwill over the last twelve months.

National Gallery of Australia

The National Gallery of Australia gratefully acknowledges the private lenders and the following institutions for loaning works for the exhibition:

Queen Victoria Museum and Art Gallery, Launceston

Warrnambool Art Gallery, Victoria

Art Gallery of South Australia, Adelaide

Geelong Gallery, Victoria

National Gallery of Victoria, Melbourne

National Library of Australia, Canberra

The University of Queensland Art Museum, Brisbane

National Trust of Tasmania

Art Gallery of Ballarat, Victoria

Woolmers Estate, Longford, Tasmania

Tasmanian Museum and Art Gallery, Hobart

Pictures Collection, State Library of Victoria, Melbourne

The British Museum, London

Museum of London, London

Many National Gallery of Australia staff have been involved in the development and the production of the exhibition and the book, including Dominique Nagy, Manager of Travelling Exhibitions; Bronwyn Campbell, Assistant Manager of Travelling Exhibitions; Anna Gray, Head of Australian Art; Gael Newton, Senior Curator of Photography; Melanie Beggs-Murray, Executive Assistant; David Wise, Senior Paintings Conservator; Kate Buckingham, Assistant Registrar; Hester Gascoigne, Executive Advisor to the Director; Julie Donaldson, Head of Publishing; Paul Cliff, Senior Editor; Kirsty Morrison, Senior Designer; Kirsten Downie, Head of Marketing and Communications; as well as the Gallery's Publishing, Photography and Marketing teams.

The Gallery acknowledges the generous contribution of the American Friends of the National Gallery of Australia Inc, New York, with the support of Dr Lee MacCormick Edwards, toward the production of this publication.

List of works

Works are listed broadly chronologically. Measurements are in centimetres (cm), height x width

Adye Douglas c 1850
Launceston, Tasmania
watercolour on ivory
7.7 x 5.9 cm
Queen Victoria Museum and Art Gallery, Launceston
purchased through the Launceston Museum and Art Gallery Foundation 1989

Mrs Eleanor Douglas c 1850
Launceston, Tasmania
watercolour on glass
7.7 x 5.7 cm
Queen Victoria Museum and Art Gallery, Launceston
purchased through the Launceston Museum and Art Gallery Foundation 1989

Master Archibald Douglas c 1850
Launceston, Tasmania
watercolour on glass
7.7 x 5.8 cm
Queen Victoria Museum and Art Gallery, Launceston
purchased through the Launceston Museum and Art Gallery Foundation 1989

Miss Ada Douglas c 1850
Launceston, Tasmania
watercolour on ivory
7.5 x 5.9 cm
Queen Victoria Museum and Art Gallery, Launceston
purchased through the Launceston Museum and Art Gallery Foundation 1989

The Reverend Henry Dowling 1851–52
Launceston, Tasmania
oil on board
30.5 x 25.5 cm
National Gallery of Australia, Canberra
purchased 2009

Mrs Elizabeth Dowling 1851–52
Launceston, Tasmania
oil on board
30.5 x 25.5 cm
National Gallery of Australia, Canberra
purchased 2009

Self-portrait c 1852
Launceston, Tasmania
oil on board
30 x 25 cm
private collection

Mrs Arabella Dowling c 1852
Launceston, Tasmania
oil on board
30 x 25 cm
private collection

Self-portrait miniature for brooch c 1852
Launceston, Tasmania
oil on ivory
3 x 2.5 x 0.4 cm
private collection

Self-portrait c 1852
Launceston, Tasmania
oil on ivory
10.4 x 13.2 cm
National Gallery of Australia, Canberra
purchased 2009

Mr W P Weston c 1852
Launceston, Tasmania
oil on canvas
76.2 x 63.6 cm
Queen Victoria Museum and Art Gallery, Launceston
gift of E D Weston 1948

Robert Dowling (artist)
Campbell & Ferguson (lithographer)
The Reverend John West 1852
Melbourne, Victoria
lithograph, printed in colour and hand-coloured with oil paint, on paper
39 x 23.2 cm
private collection

Jeremiah Ware Snr c 1852–53
Hobart, Tasmania
oil on board
27.5 x 21.8 cm
Warrnambool Art Gallery, Victoria
purchased 1980

Mrs Mary Ware c 1852–53
Hobart, Tasmania
oil on board
28 x 21.5 cm
Warrnambool Art Gallery, Victoria
purchased 1980

Skelton Buckley Emmett c 1852–53
Hobart, Tasmania
oil on cardboard
10.2 x 7.9 cm
private collection

Francis Butler c 1853
Hobart, Tasmania
oil on board
30.2 x 23.3 cm
Art Gallery of South Australia, Adelaide
M J M Carter AO Collection 2006

Master Harry Downing 1853
Hobart, Tasmania
oil on cardboard
30.6 x 25 cm
Queen Victoria Museum and Art Gallery, Launceston
gift of Laura Downing 1942

Miss Emily Downing 1853
Hobart, Tasmania
oil on cardboard
30.4 x 25 cm
Queen Victoria Museum and Art Gallery, Launceston
gift of Laura Downing 1942

Master Ernest Downing 1853
Hobart, Tasmania
oil on cardboard
25.2 x 19.3 cm
Queen Victoria Museum and Art Gallery, Launceston
gift of Laura Downing 1942

Master Albert Downing 1853
Hobart, Tasmania
oil on cardboard
30.5 x 24.9 cm
Queen Victoria Museum and Art Gallery, Launceston
gift of Laura Downing 1942

The Hon Thomas Dowling 1855
Geelong, Victoria
oil on canvas
93 x 74 cm
National Library of Australia, Canberra
purchased 1980

Mrs Maria Dowling 1855
Geelong, Victoria
oil on canvas
94 x 74 cm
National Library of Australia, Canberra
purchased 1980

Robert Dowling after Thomas Bock (1790–1855)

Larratong, of Cape Grim, Van Diemen's Land 1853–54
Launceston, Tasmania
or 1854–56 Geelong, Victoria

Truggernana (Trucannini), of Recherche Bay, Van Diemen's Land 1853–54
Launceston, Tasmania
or 1854–56 Geelong, Victoria

oil on board
30.3 x 25.2 cm each
The British Museum, London
gift of Admiral Sir Leopold McClintock's family 1924

Dowling's oil portraits of Tasmanian Aboriginal people differ from the watercolours by Thomas Bock in some colour aspects, and by the addition of atmospheric or landscape backgrounds. This suggests that Dowling planned to use them as part of a full figure group in an extensive landscape—as he did.

Robert Dowling after Thomas Bock (1790–1855)

Jinny, profile 1853–54
Launceston, Tasmania
or 1854–56 Geelong, Victoria

Woureddy, of Bruny Island 1853–54
Launceston, Tasmania or 1854–56 Geelong, Victoria

Jimmy, profile 1853–54
Launceston, Tasmania
or 1854–56 Geelong, Victoria

oil on board
30.5 x 25.4 cm each
The British Museum, London
gift of Admiral Sir Leopold McClintock's family 1924

Robert Dowling after Thomas Bock (1790–1855)

Jimmy, of Hampshire Hills, Van Diemen's Land 1853–54
Launceston, Tasmania
or 1854–56 Geelong, Victoria

Jack, of Cape Grim, Van Diemen's Land 1853–54
Launceston, Tasmania
or 1854–56 Geelong, Victoria

oil on canvas on board
17.4 x 13.3 cm each
The British Museum, London
gift of Admiral Sir Leopold McClintock's family 1924

Mrs Margaret McArthur of Meningoort 1856
Geelong, Victoria
oil on canvas
98.5 x 74 cm
Geelong Gallery, Victoria
purchased with the generous assistance of the Trustees of the Howard Hitchcock Bequest, and with additional support from the Friends of the Geelong Gallery, 2001

Mrs Adolphus Sceales with Black Jimmie on Merrang Station 1856
Merrang Station and Geelong, Victoria
oil on canvas mounted on plywood
76 x 101.5 cm
National Gallery of Australia, Canberra
purchased from the Founding Donors Fund 1984

Masters George, William and Miss Harriet Ware with the Aborigine Jamie Ware 1856
Minjah Station and Geelong, Victoria
oil on canvas
63.7 x 76.4 cm
National Gallery of Victoria, Melbourne
Eleanor M Borrow Bequest 2007

Jeremiah Ware's stock on Minjah Station 1856
Minjah Station and Geelong, Victoria
oil on canvas
74.5 x 100.5 cm
Art Gallery of South Australia, Adelaide
Mrs Mary Overton Gift Fund 1997

King Tom and the Mount Elephant tribe 1856
Meningoort, Camperdown, Victoria
oil on board
25.5 x 30.4 cm
National Library of Australia, Canberra
Rex Nan Kivell Collection

Man from Maria River 1856
Minjah Station, Victoria

Woman from Maria River 1856
Minjah Station, Victoria

oil on canvas on board
14.3 x 12 cm each
The British Museum, London
gift of Admiral Sir Leopold McClintock's family 1924

Queen Laratong, Spring Creek, Port Fairy, Victoria 1856
Minjah Station, Victoria

King Laratong, Spring Creek, Port Fairy, Victoria 1856
Minjah Station, Victoria

oil on canvas on board
13.9 x 11.3 and 13.8 x 11.3 cm
The British Museum, London
gift of Admiral Sir Leopold McClintock's family 1924

King Marpoura, Spring Creek, near Port Fairy, Victoria 1856
Minjah Station, Victoria

Queen Marpoura, Spring Creek, near Port Fairy, Victoria 1856
Minjah Station, Victoria

oil on canvas on board
14.3 x 11.9 and 14.3 x 11.7 cm
The British Museum, London

Minjah in the Old Time (Weerat Kuyuut and the Mopor people at Minjah Station) 1856
Minjah Station, Victoria
oil on canvas
76.4 x 101.7 cm
Warrnambool Art Gallery, Victoria
presented by Joseph Ware 1886

Weerat Kuyuut and the Mopor people, Spring Creek, Victoria 1856
Minjah Station, Victoria
oil on canvas
52 x 108.5 cm
The University of Queensland Art Museum, Brisbane
gift of Miss Marjorie Dowling 1952

Tasmanian Aborigines 1856–57
Launceston, Tasmania
oil on canvas
63.6 x 118.6 cm
National Gallery of Victoria, Melbourne
purchased 1949

Self-portrait 1859
London
oil on canvas
63.5 x 52.5 cm
Queen Victoria Museum and Art Gallery, Launceston
gift of W Dowling 1930

Aborigines of Tasmania 1859
London
oil on canvas
152.7 x 304.3 cm
Queen Victoria Museum and Art Gallery, Launceston
gift of the artist to the people of Launceston, to hang in the Mechanics' Institute 1860, transferred to QVMAG 1891

Key to *Aborigines of Tasmania* 1859
London
ink on paper
45.8 x 91.5 cm
Queen Victoria Museum and Art Gallery, Launceston
gift of the artist to the Mechanics' Institute 1860, transferred to QVMAG 1891

Sabbath in the country 1859
London
oil on canvas
50.8 x 35.6 cm
private collection
Image courtesy of Menzies Art Brands, Melbourne and Sydney, photographer: Andrew Murray

Breakfasting out 1859
London
oil on canvas
61 x 91.5 cm
Museum of London, London
purchased in 1953

H J Betjemann & Son
Breakfasting out 1859
photograph
19.1 x 28.6 cm
Queen Victoria Museum and Art Gallery, Launceston

Early effort—art in Australia 1860
London
oil on canvas on board
76.6 x 122.3 cm
National Gallery of Victoria, Melbourne
Felton Bequest 1934

Group of natives of Tasmania 1860
London
oil on canvas
45.6 x 91.4 cm
Art Gallery of South Australia, Adelaide
gift of the Art Gallery of South Australia Foundation and the M J M Carter AO Collection 1988

Masters Frederick and Arthur, sons of Henry Reed c 1862
Tunbridge Wells and London
oil on canvas
102 x 126.5 cm
National Trust of Australia (Tasmania)
bequest of Eric Lyndon Reed 1971

Robert Dowling after Franz Xavier Winterhalter (1806–1873)
Queen Victoria 1862
London
oil on canvas
142.5 x 112 cm
Queen Victoria Museum and Art Gallery, Launceston
commissioned by local subscribers to the Mechanics' Institute 1860, received 1863, transferred to QVMAG 1891

Sketch for 'The Baptism of Christ' 1863
London
oil on canvas
122.3 x 81.7 cm
Queen Victoria Museum and Art Gallery, Launceston
gift of the Pilgrim Uniting Church 1982

Grandfather's visit 1864
London
oil on canvas
74 x 64 cm
Art Gallery of Ballarat, Victoria
purchased 1975

Miriam 1864
London
oil on canvas
91 x 70.5 cm
Warrnambool Art Gallery, Victoria
gift of Joseph Ware 1892

Robert Dowling (artist)
James Stephenson (engraver)
The Baptism of Our Lord 1865
London
steel engraving on paper
68 x 47 cm
Woolmers Estate, Longford, Tasmania

The gleaner (*An Egyptian woman*) 1873
London
oil on canvas
73 x 55 cm
Tasmanian Museum and Art Gallery, Hobart
purchased 1976

Street scene, Cairo c 1874
London
oil on canvas
61 x 45.6 cm
National Gallery of Australia, Canberra
purchased 1976

A sheikh and his son entering Cairo, on their return from a pilgrimage to Mecca 1874
London
oil on canvas
139.3 x 244.5 cm
National Gallery of Victoria, Melbourne
presented by a committee of gentlemen 1878

Cairo (*camels*) 1876
Cairo
watercolour on paper
33.8 x 51 cm
Warrnambool Art Gallery, Victoria
gift of the Estate of Mrs Joan Dowling Rogers 2006

Cairo (*camels*) 1876
Cairo
watercolour on paper
33.8 x 50.8 cm
Warrnambool Art Gallery, Victoria
gift of the Estate of Mrs Joan Dowling Rogers 2006

A sheikh and his son entering Cairo, on their return from a pilgrimage to Mecca
printed pamphlet
12.5 x 9 cm
Walch Brothers & Birchall, Launceston, 1877
State Library of Victoria , Melbourne

Egyptian banana seller 1878
London
watercolour with bodycolour over graphite on paper on board
71.7 x 50.7 cm
private collection

Moses viewing the Promised Land from Mount Nebo 1879
London
watercolour with bodycolour on paper
73.5 x 53.5 cm
private collection

Robert Dowling (artist)
Leopold Lowenstam (engraver)
Origin of Sunday schools, Hare Lane, Gloucester, 1780 1880
London
steel engraving on paper
53 x 78.5 cm (plate)
Queen Victoria Museum and Art Gallery, Launceston 1983

Shylock and Jessica 1882
London
watercolour and bodycolour on paper on board
75 x 54.7 cm
Queen Victoria Museum and Art Gallery, Launceston
gift of A G Taylor

A merchant in Algiers 1882
London
watercolour and bodycolour on paper on board
75.2 x 54.4 cm
Queen Victoria Museum and Art Gallery, Launceston
gift of A G Taylor

Robert Dowling after John Partridge (1789–1872)
Lord Melbourne 1884
London
oil on canvas
241.4 x 147.2 cm
National Gallery of Victoria, Melbourne
gift of the Hon Sir William Clarke 1884

Sir Henry Loch 1884
Melbourne, Victoria
oil on canvas
127 x 89 cm
Pictures Collection, State Library of Victoria, Melbourne

Miss Robertson of Colac (Dolly) 1885–86
Colac and Melbourne, Victoria
oil on canvas
91 x 120 cm
National Gallery of Australia, Canberra
purchased with the assistance of the Masterpieces for the Nation Fund 2010

Index

Page numbers in italics indicate illustrations.

About the author

John Jones is a curator and art historian with a research focus in Australian art and British and European art post 1800. A former curator of Australian Painting and Sculpture at the National Gallery of Australia, he contributed to the *Dictionary of Australian artists: painters, sketchers, photographers and engravers to 1870* (ed. Joan Kerr; OUP, Melbourne, 1992) and was an adviser and contributor to the Australian Bi-Centenary celebration art exhibition and its publication *Creating Australia, 200 years of art 1788–1988* (ICCA, Adelaide and Art Gallery of South Australia, 1988). He co-authored with Mary Eagle *A story of Australian painting* (Macmillan, 1994) and currently advises the National Gallery of Australia on its frame restoration and re-creation program.

nga.gov.au

The National Gallery of Australia is an Australian Government Agency

Produced by the Publishing Department of the National Gallery of Australia
Text editor: Paul Cliff*
Designer: Kirsty Morrison*
Rights and permissions: Nick Nicholson*
Indexer: Sherrey Quinn
Publishing manager: Julie Donaldson*
Pre-press and printing: Lindsay Yates Group
*National Gallery of Australia

National Library of Australia Cataloguing-in-Publication entry
Author: Jones, John James, 1941–
Title: Robert Dowling: Tasmanian son of Empire / John Jones
Edition: 1st ed
ISBN: 9780642334107 (pbk)
Subjects: Dowling, Robert, 1827–1886.
Painters–Australia–Biography
Art, Australian–History
Art, Colonial–Australia.
Portrait painting, Australian–19th century
Aboriginal Australians in art
Other authors/contributors: National Gallery of Australia.
Dewey Number: 759.994

Distributed in Australia by
Thames and Hudson
11 Central Boulevard Business Park
Port Melbourne, Victoria, 3207

Distributed in the United Kingdom by
Thanes and Hudson181A High Holborn
London WC1V 7QX, UK

Distributed in the United States of America by
University of Washington Press
1326 Fifth Avenue, Ste 555
Seattle, WA 98101-2604

Published in conjunction with the National Gallery of Australia's travelling exhibition *Robert Dowling: Tasmanian son of Empire*

Queen Victoria Museum & Art Gallery,
Launceston, Tasmania
6 March 2010 – 25 April 2010

Geelong Gallery, Geelong, Victoria
8 May – 11 July 2010

National Gallery of Australia, Canberra
24 July – 3 October 2010

Robert Dowling: Tasmanian son of Empire
is supported by the
National Gallery of Australia Council
Exhibitions Fund

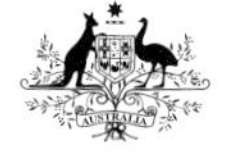

Australian Government
National Collecting Institutions
Touring and Outreach Program

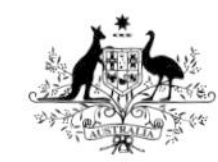

Australian Government
Visions of Australia

This exhibition is supported by the National Collecting Institutions Touring and Outreach Program and Visions of Australia—Australian Government programs aiming to improve access to and support touring of Australian cultural material

Media partner

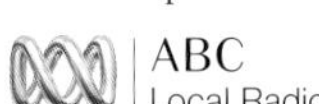